IMAGES
of America

AFRICAN AMERICANS IN EL PASO

ON THE COVER: Douglass School, pictured around 1909, was named after former slave and leader of the abolitionist movement Frederick Douglass. Founded in 1883, the school was created out of necessity. Wanting a safe place to educate their children, the black community in El Paso created a private school for black children that provided more than just an education. Douglass was considered a refuge and haven where the children of African American El Pasoans, who were barred from attending schools with white children (often their neighbors), could thrive in a community that was fully supportive and committed to their success and academic achievement. The school was eventually desegregated in 1955 after *Brown v. Board of Education*. (Courtesy of El Paso Public Library.)

IMAGES
of America

African Americans in El Paso

Maceo Crenshaw Dailey Jr.,
Kathryn Smith-McGlynn,
and Cecilia Gutierrez Venable

ARCADIA
PUBLISHING

ISBN 978-1-4671-3177-3

Published by Arcadia Publishing
Charleston, South Carolina

Printed in the United States of America

Library of Congress Control Number: 2014933132

For all general information, please contact Arcadia Publishing:
Telephone 843-853-2070
Fax 843-853-0044
E-mail sales@arcadiapublishing.com
For customer service and orders:
Toll-Free 1-888-313-2665

Visit us on the Internet at www.arcadiapublishing.com

To the black community in El Paso,
and to the memory of Imani Achebe Wsandisi,
philosopher, teacher, and best friend. Thanks!
—Dr. Maceo Crenshaw Dailey Jr.

Contents

Acknowledgments		6
Introduction		7
1.	Establishing a Community: 1528–1899	11
2.	The Enduring Community: 1900–1927	23
3.	A Poised Community: 1928–1955	45
4.	A Civil Rights Community: 1956–1976	65
5.	The Conclusion of the 20th Century: 1977–Present	75
Bibliography		127

ACKNOWLEDGMENTS

This project depended heavily on the contributions of both public and private institutions that serve the city of El Paso. We wish to especially thank Frances Grundy Hills, who invited us to her home and shared her knowledge of the community, and her son Jethro Hills Jr., who allowed Kathryn Smith-McGlynn to scan some of their pictures for this book. We are also indebted for the kindness of Dr. William McIver and Edna Nixon McIver, who not only allowed Dr. Maceo Crenshaw Dailey Jr. and Cecilia Gutierrez Venable to scan pictures at their Albuquerque home but also prepared a fabulous brunch. They warmly shared their home and knowledge of El Paso. The staff at the Department of Special Collections and Archives, University of Texas at El Paso Library, extended their expertise, and we are indebted to Laura Hollingsed for her help in finding images, Yvette Delgado for scanning these pictures, and Claudia A. Rivers for making some suggestions on where to look. We would also like to thank *El Paso Times* librarian Trish Long for her help in locating and scanning pictures we needed. Barbara J. Angus of El Paso History Museum also spent several hours talking about the community and advising us where we might find some information. El Paso Public Library staff provided us with their vertical file, which helped with writing our captions. We also greatly appreciate Jennifer Nielsen, acting director and curator at Fort Bliss, who provided us with several images and the use of the fort's vertical file. El Paso County Historical Society and the Burges House made available their facilities for research. We would also like to thank Ron Dawson for sharing his train photographs as well as his knowledge of the railroads in El Paso. The staff at the Prints and Photographs Division at the Library of Congress also helped in locating images. The McCall Neighborhood Center and the efforts of Leona Washington (deceased) contributed much to this project. Finally, a thank-you goes to Maria Michel, administrative assistant in the University of Texas at El Paso African American Studies Program, for scanning images from Dr. Maceo Crenshaw Dailey Jr.'s personal collection.

INTRODUCTION

Paso del Norte (Pass of the North) has undergone many permutations to become the modern city of El Paso, with its current population of 672,538. In 1539, Spanish friars founded the small village and agricultural enclave in what is today's Ciudad Juarez, Mexico. As conquest ruled and boundary lines were redrawn, the settlement known as Paso del Norte evolved into a Texan, and later an American, township with individuals of diverse backgrounds. This diversification continued until the American Civil War. The economy that emerged to sustain the township, and later city, was built on farming, oil, the railroad, and military.

A defining moment in the early era of colonization was the crossing of the Rio Grande (now the border of the United States and the city of El Paso) by Conquistador Juan de Oñate in 1598. In his party were Africans, some of whom were characterized as slaves and others as servants. During Black History Month in El Paso, distinguished historian Quintard Taylor gave a presentation titled "When Africans were Spaniards" that chronicled this expedition. Taylor identified José Antonio, who was born in the Congo, brought to El Paso in 1752 as a slave, and, after living in the area for eight years, married an Apache woman named Marcela. These Africans and their descendants constituted the early El Paso black community and are indicative of the rich cultural past of Africans as they evolved into African Americans.

Communities spring from covenants—written, spoken, or silently observed. The following is El Paso's African American Second Baptist Church's covenant, which encompasses the essential ethos and sustenance of the city's black community as it began to take shape and form from the 1880s to the present:

> In case of difference . . . we will strive to avoid a contentious spirit, and if we cannot unanimously agree, we will cheerfully recognize the right of the majority to govern . . . We further agree to watch over, to pray for, to exhort and stir up each other unto every good word and work; to guard each other's reputation, nor needlessly exposing the infirmities of others; to participate in each other's joy, and with tender sympathy bear one another's burdens and sorrows.

On the southwest border of Texas and the hinterlands of the United States in a largely arid region, El Paso's black community maintained a solemn commitment to many of the ideas expressed in this covenant, which morphed into the brotherhood and sisterhood of success as leadership emerged, institutions were established, organizations formed, and relationships were forged.

The border struggle between Mexico and the United States left the African American El Paso community in a state of flux as Indians, Spaniards, Mexicans, Anglos, and Asians settled in the area and vied for power. The number of blacks living in El Paso prior to the Civil War was miniscule—approximately 30. About half of them were slaves, and the others were free persons of color. In the immediate aftermath of this conflict and the abolishment of slavery, the black population increased significantly as the railroads and the military took hold of the area in the 1880s. Working as Pullman porters and cooks, serving as famed Buffalo Soldiers, and establishing small businesses, African Americans began developing a foothold in El Paso. Significantly, churches, a single school from kindergarten to secondary, social clubs, and a chapter of the National Association for the Advancement of Colored People (NAACP) all came into being by 1914 in the city's Second Ward neighborhood, which became home to the majority of black El Pasoans. Among the prominent African Americans residing in El Paso were minister Andrew Morelock, businessman H.J. Daniels, military officer Lt. Henry O. Flipper, Florida "Lady Flo" Wolfe (consort to the Irish Lord Delaval James Beresford), physician Dr. Lawrence A. Nixon, and poet Bernice Love Wiggins.

In the latter portion of the 19th century and first half of the 20th century, El Paso witnessed an expanding, enterprising, and enduring black community with the establishment of the Sunset Lodge No. 76, the Oro Temple No. 9, and the Phillis Wheatley Club. The formation of clubs, fraternities, and sororities continued to grow with the addition of Delta Sigma Theta, Omega Psi Phi, Alpha Kappa Alpha, Zeta Phi Beta, Kappa Alpha Psi, Star of the West, Golden Circle, Prince Hall Freemasonry, the Elks, Walker Art Club, and the Jolly Wives. The community attracted nationally known blacks to the city during the segregation era, including Booker T. Washington, Langston Hughes, Marian Anderson, Gen. Benjamin O. Davis, and Philippa Duke Schuyler. Later, the city was graced with the presence of such luminaries as Benjamin Hooks, Jesse Jackson, Colin Powell, and Pres. Barack Obama.

The African American El Paso community continued to grow and build from the 1930s to the 1960s. A glance at the *Negro Business Directory of 1947*, published by the El Paso Black Chamber of Commerce, reveals the expanding entrepreneurship in the black community at that time, with such businesses as Curley's Taxi Cab, Little Harlem Restaurant, Berry's Beauty Salon, White Star Barbershop, Ralph Smith's Confectionery, Hotel Daniel, and Golden Moon Hotel Bar and Café, the last of which advertised "Always a Delightful Atmosphere" and "Hot and Cold Baths." The Murray Theatre also opened that same year, and featured films such as *Harlem on Parade*, *That Man of Mine*, *Paradise in Harlem*, *Ragtime Cowboy Joe*, and *Tarzan's New York Adventure*.

In 1955, Thelma White, a graduate of Douglass High School (the lone secondary school for blacks in El Paso), won a lawsuit to desegregate Texas Western College, allowing for the first 12 black students to enter the city's institute of higher learning. The black community, along with the help of several notable whites, secured passage of one of the nation's first equal housing statutes in 1961.

Practically all basketball fans have seen the 2006 movie *Glory Road*, the true story of Texas Western College starting five black players, coached by Don Haskins, who bested the powerhouse Adolph Rupp–coached Kentucky team in 1966. This upset contributed to the recruitment in both college and professional sports of more African American athletes. Also in 1966, Texas Western College (now the University of Texas at El Paso) hired its first black faculty member, Margarie Lawson.

Since the 1960s, black Americans in El Paso have been a significant presence in all aspects of life in the city, frequently rising to rarefied heights. A native son of the city, Maj. Gen. Dana Pittard, completed a stint as the base commander of Fort Bliss, an encampment larger than the state of Rhode Island. Chief Greg Allen leads the police force. An African American served as the head of the city branch of the Federal Bureau of Investigation. The executive director of the nation's larger chapter of the Young Women's Christian Association is Dr. Sandra Braham. Famed basketball coach Nolan Richardson was born in El Paso and became bilingual, as many black El Pasoans are, because of his interactions with the Mexican American community. Alvin and Louise Johnson and Bob and Paulette Wingo represent two of the most enterprising business families. Both families have made their marks, locally and nationally, as entrepreneurs. The Black El Paso Democrats, led by former judge Donald William, and the present-day El Paso Branch of the NAACP, guided by its branch president Harold Howell, are both significant entities for progress in the black community and betterment in race relations.

The community has remained true to its credo of betterment for African Americans and sanguine ties with other groups in El Paso. Among the many icons of El Paso, Leona Ford Washington, a retired schoolteacher, stood supreme in her concern for development in the African American community. She established and maintained the McCall Neighborhood Center, which became the bedrock for community gatherings, discourse, and just plain fun. The Inter-Club Council (the distinguished array of organizations, fraternities, and sororities) meets monthly in the McCall Neighborhood Center for fellowship and focuses on the activities important to the African American community, including Juneteenth, Kwanzaa, Martin Luther King Jr. Day Celebration, Black History Month, the Miss Black El Paso Pageant, scholarship fundraising, health fairs, political dialogue, and educational classes. More recently in the realm of politics, three African Americans have been elected to El Paso City Council and contributed to the governance and growth of the city.

The Inter-Denominational Ministerial Alliance is an organization of the city's religious leaders impacting the direction of the city. Each Sunday morning, Betty Robinson has a four-hour radio program on KTEP (an NPR affiliate) known as *The Best of Gospel*, and practically the whole black community tunes in for spiritual uplift provided by music, notices, and news pertaining to sacred and secular activities in the city. El Paso's black community has made contributions on a cultural level with music and literature. Jazzmen Gerald Art Lewis and Billy Townes kept this music at the forefront in the city, and the poet Bernice Love Wiggins published *Tuneful Tales*, a wonderful volume of poetry, in the 1920s. The book was republished in 2002 as testimonial to its importance.

Given all the dynamics of El Paso's black community, one can safely conclude that there has been little room for the "halfway saved" or "lonesome sinner," though some have managed to venture into the realm of questionable ethical and legal conduct. "If they can't be taught to be good, however," as black educator Benjamin Brawley observed, "they are at least taught to behave." Herein lies the story of the success of El Paso's black community.

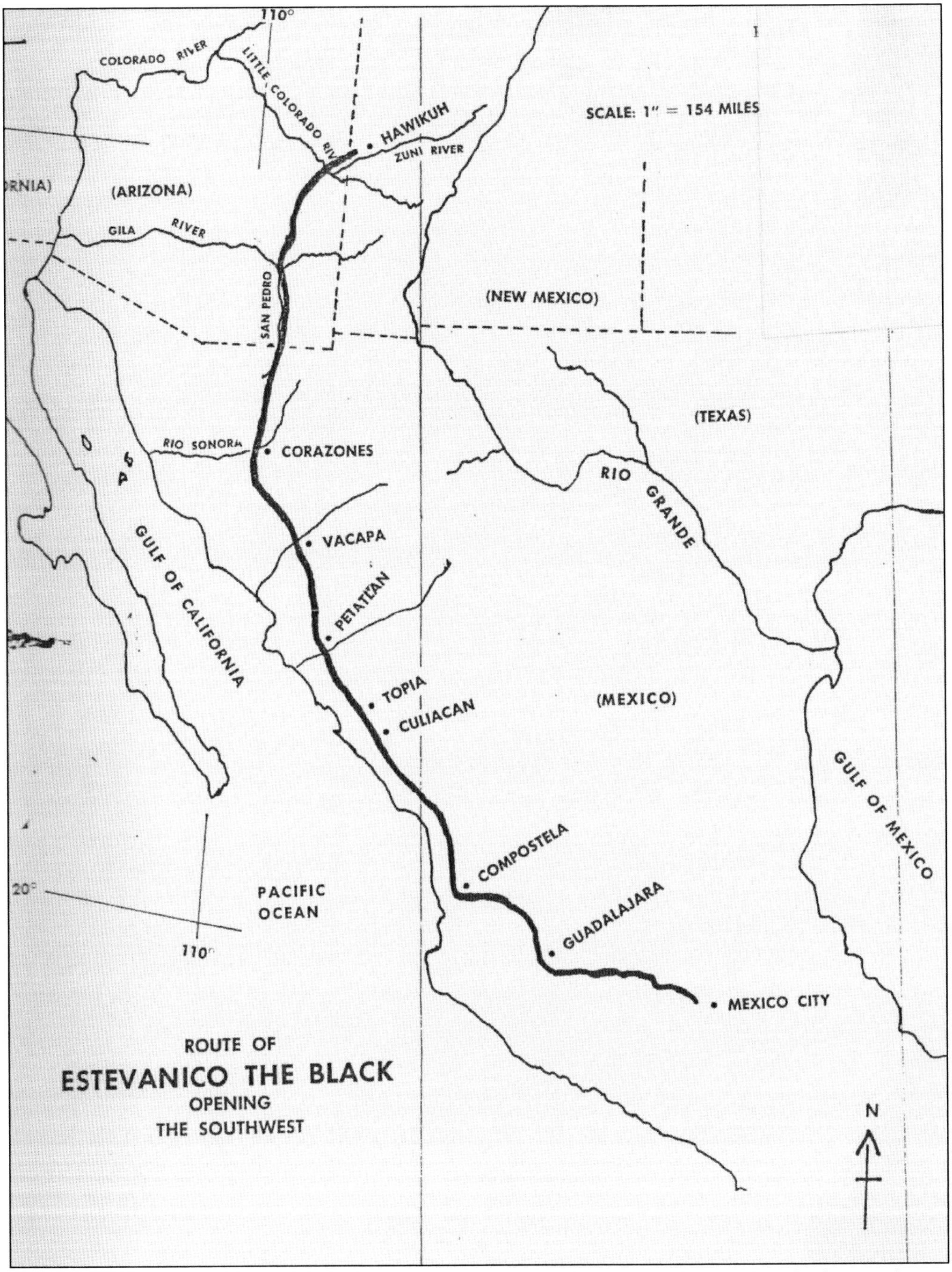

This map traces the path of Estevanico, a black Moroccan slave who traveled through the Southwest region, exploring parts of what are now Texas, Arizona, and New Mexico. While Estevanico never reached El Paso, his journey marks the opening of this area to people of African ancestry. His stories of the Seven Cities of Cibola enticed other explorers who brought their slaves, who later intermarried and settled the El Paso area. (Courtesy of Dr. Maceo Crenshaw Dailey Jr.)

One

Establishing a Community 1528–1899

The West and Southwest offered African Americans new opportunities to carve out spaces and build communities. Many succeeded in the region. The allure and freedom of the West in American history remains sacred in the nation's mindset, owing to historian Frederick Jackson Turner. Over time, Turner's version of history transitioned into myth since it largely overlooked the struggle of blacks and other minority groups moving and seeking better opportunities in the West. There were, however, blacks who succeeded in the region. Some were posted in the region as they took up their roles as soldiers. Lt. Henry Flipper, West Point's first black graduate, found himself assigned to the West and, subsequently, drummed out of the military to take up residency in El Paso in the 1880s. Florida "Lady Flo" Kennedy left her imprimatur on the city as the common-law wife to Lord Delaval James Beresford, a wealthy landowner and cotton grower. Drawing on Beresford's wealth, she contributed to El Paso's fire department and police department.

William Alexander Henderson, an Army scout, was discharged in the city and became a brick maker. He purchased property that he later bequeathed to the city. Former slaves John and Mary Woods emerged as prosperous entrepreneurs, owning a saloon, boardinghouse, and blacksmith shop. John was killed in 1898 in what seems to have been a bushwhacking by a marshal. Dan Daniels, another businessman, owned a hotel, Chinese restaurant, and taxicab service. Flipper, Lady Flo, the Woodses, and Daniels are some of the stellar personalities of El Paso, but the solid story of community building involves those who established institutions and organizations that became the foundation of community growth and development.

In 1883, Andrew Morelock established Franklin School, which eventually became Douglass School. It enjoyed stunning success in the training of leaders and solid citizens. Rev. E.M. Griggs organized the Second Baptist Church, and the Visitors Chapel African Methodist Episcopal Church ministered to the black community in 1884. The formation of the El Paso Clark Club Black Republicans pointed to serious political activities, and the organization of the Sunset Lodge No. 76, Prince Hall Freemasonry, indicated a significant self-help focus.

A sense of entitlement to democracy came with the encampment of black soldiers at Fort Bliss in 1867, and later when Buffalo Soldiers at Fort Stockton were deployed in the "Salt Wars" of 1877—a dispute between the Mexican and American governments over salt deposits 100 miles east of El Paso. The clearest sense that a solid black community was present in El Paso in this era of segregation was the employment of the first African American US postal carrier, James William Shanklin, assigned to distribute mail in the city's Second Ward, home to the majority of black El Pasoans.

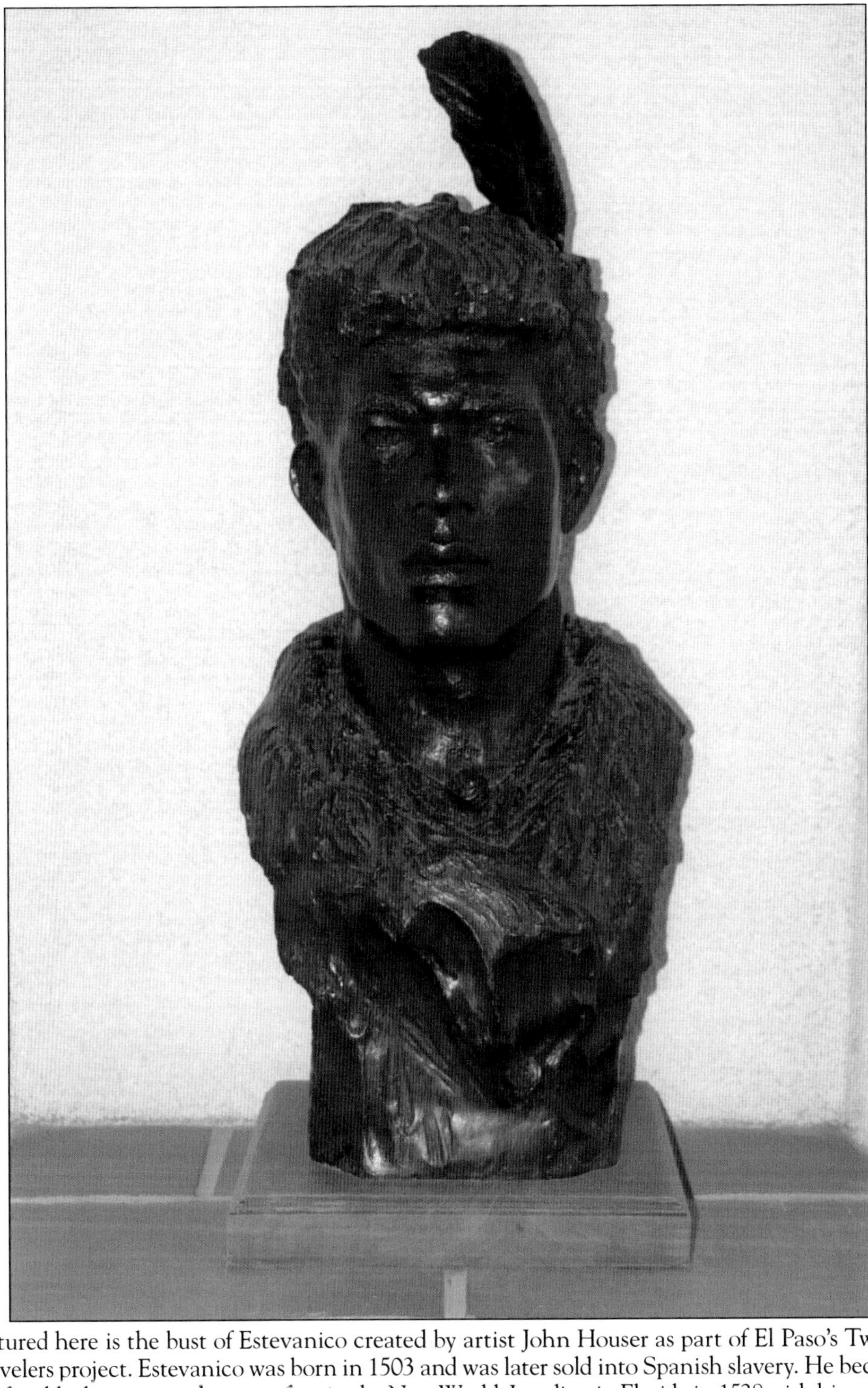

Pictured here is the bust of Estevanico created by artist John Houser as part of El Paso's Twelve Travelers project. Estevanico was born in 1503 and was later sold into Spanish slavery. He became the first black conquistador to set foot in the New World. Landing in Florida in 1528 with his master Andres de Dorantes, he eventually traveled to Sinaloa, Mexico. Leading a party into New Mexico, he was killed in 1539 by the Zuni Indians. (Courtesy of Dr. Maceo Crenshaw Dailey Jr.)

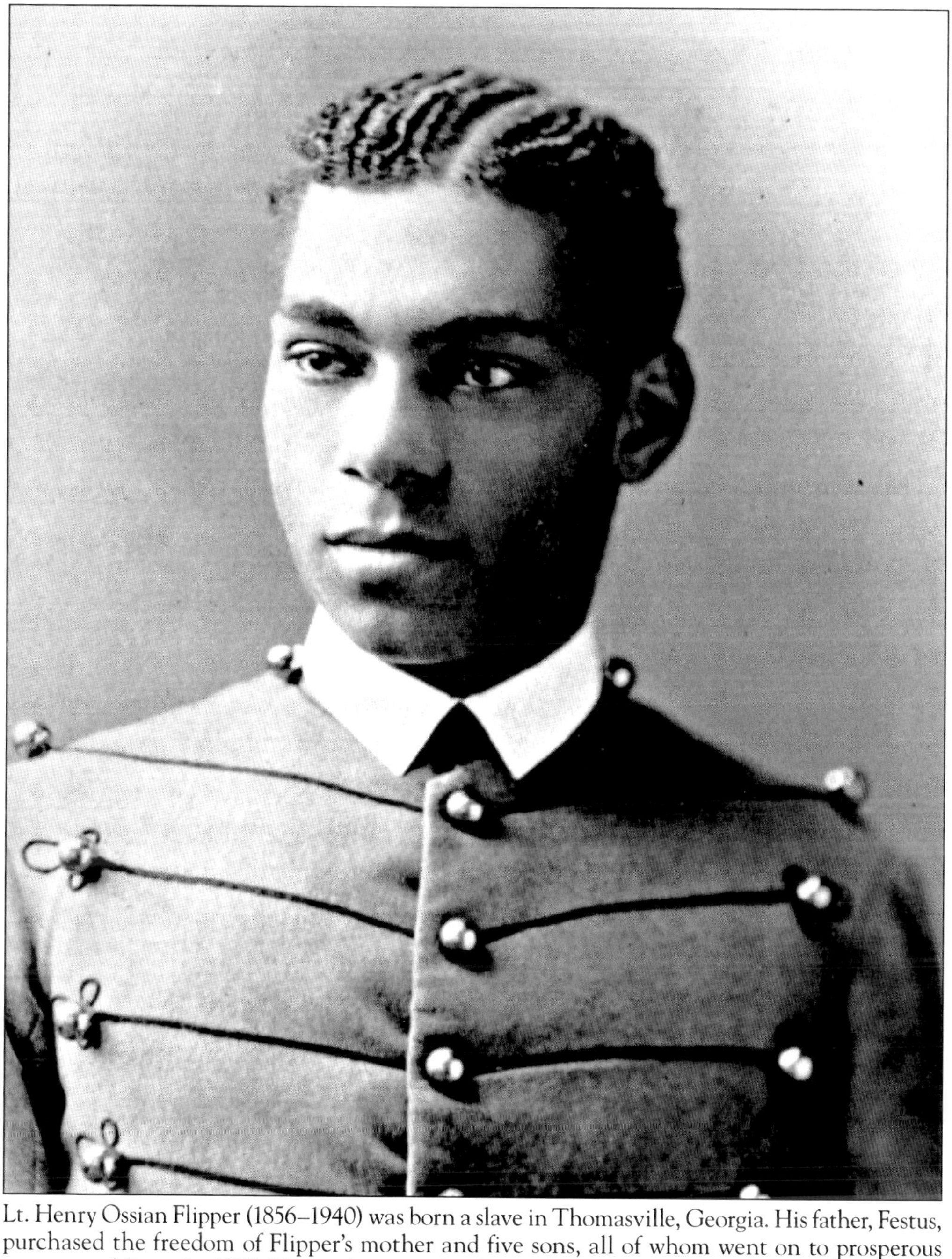

Lt. Henry Ossian Flipper (1856–1940) was born a slave in Thomasville, Georgia. His father, Festus, purchased the freedom of Flipper's mother and five sons, all of whom went on to prosperous careers and lives. In 1877, Flipper became the first African American to graduate from West Point. His military career was derailed with his questionable court-martial trial in 1881. Flipper came to El Paso in 1882, where he worked as an engineer and lived off and on for some 40 years. He chronicled his life in two publications, *The Colored Cadet at West Point* (1878) and *Negro-Frontiersman: The Western Memoirs of Henry O. Flipper* (1963). Flipper was pardoned posthumously on two occasions, once by the Army in 1976 and then by Pres. Bill Clinton in 1999. (Courtesy of US Military Academy at West Point.)

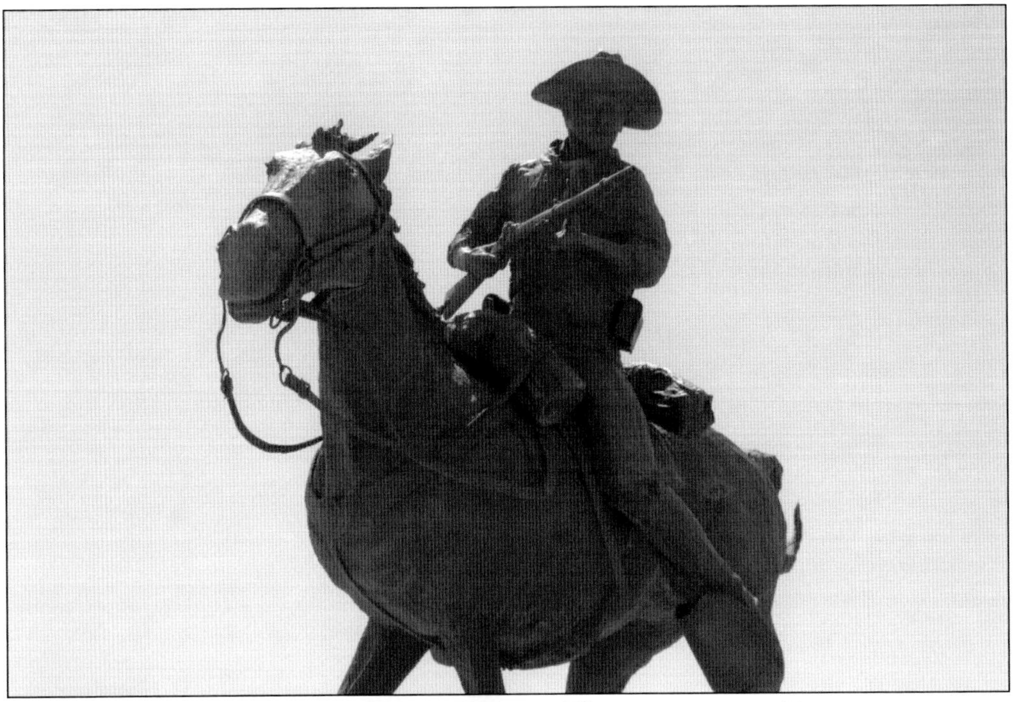

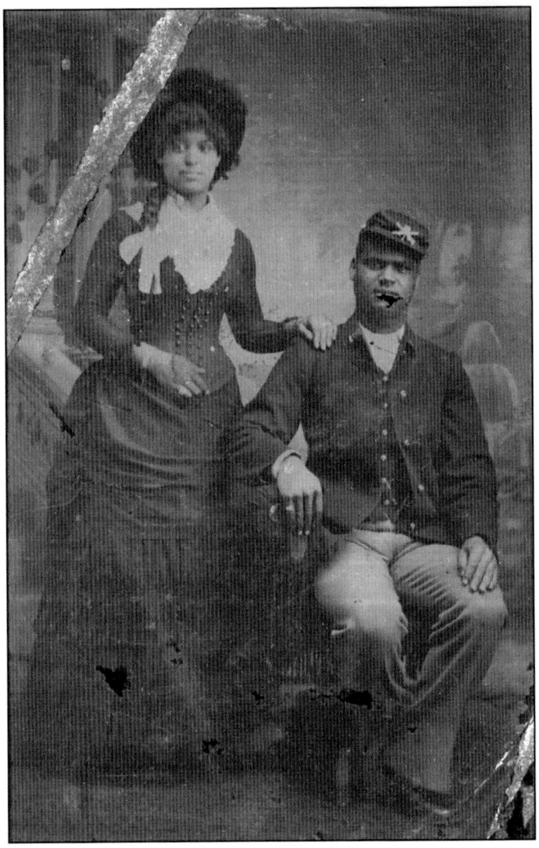

The inscription on this monument reads: "This Buffalo Soldier Monument erected at Fort Bliss in 1999 depicts Corp. John Ross, Troop I of the 9th US Cavalry. Several famed Buffalo Soldier regiments were garrisoned at Fort Bliss from 1866 to 1901. The term Buffalo Soldier was given to African American men serving the western frontier after the Civil War. El Paso is home to Fort Bliss which was established as a cavalry post in 1848 and is now the largest military installation in the United States." (Courtesy of Kathryn Smith-McGlynn.)

A Civil War soldier and probably his bride posed for this tintype photograph. The image shows the pride expressed by many black soldiers who fought during the Civil War. (Courtesy of Ada Tharp Photograph Collection, Department of Special Collections and Archives, University of Texas at El Paso Library.)

After the Civil War, many former slaves exercised their freedom by moving about the country to find loved ones or escape further persecution on the plantations on which they had worked. "Mother" Anne Clark, a former slave, moved to El Paso and posed for this picture near her home on May 26, 1937. This photograph was taken as part of the US Works Progress Administration's *Born in Slavery: Slave Narratives from the Federal Writers' Project, 1936–1938*. (Courtesy of Slave Narrative Collection, Library of Congress.)

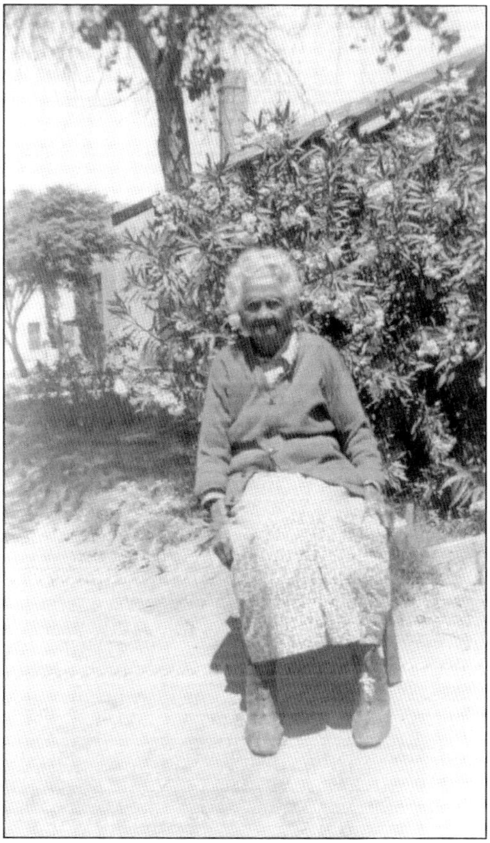

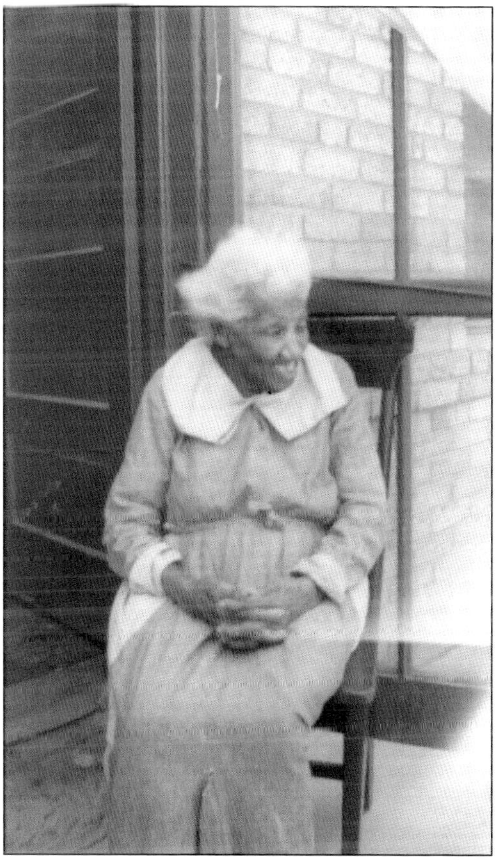

Rosa Washington, an ex-slave, also left the Deep South and moved West to El Paso. She posed for this picture on her front porch on May 5, 1937. (Courtesy of Slave Narrative Collection, Library of Congress.)

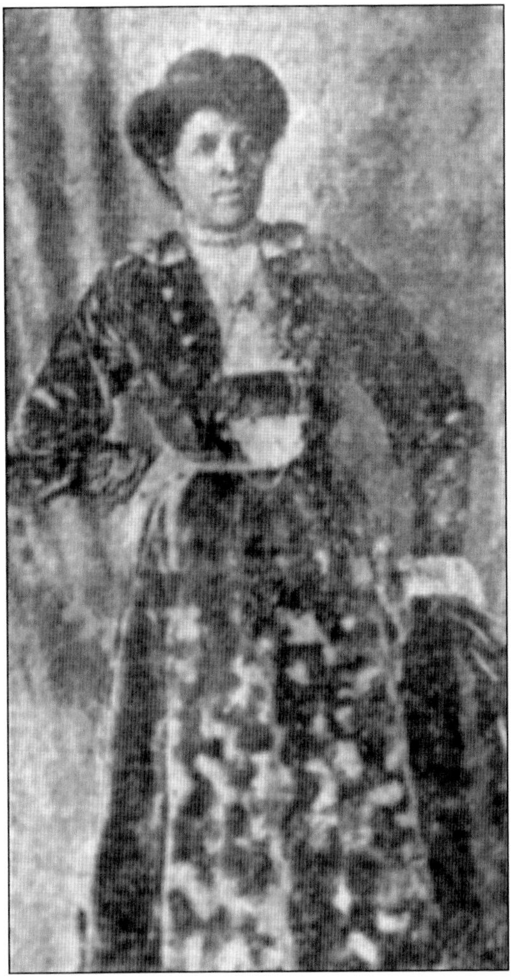

Florida J. Wolfe, also known as "Lady Flo," caused quite a stir during her lifetime. Exactly how she arrived in El Paso in the late 1800s is debatable, but she was well known on both sides of the border. Wolfe was the common-law wife and companion of Irish Lord Delaval James Beresford. She was credited with helping to salvage his lost fortune and building up his cattle ranches in Juarez, Mexico, where they lived due to more relaxed laws on interracial unions. Florida Wolfe attended the Second Baptist Church and was known for her generous donations to the El Paso Fire Department, Police Department, and other worthwhile community activities. (Courtesy of the Department of Special Collections and Archives, University of Texas at El Paso Library.)

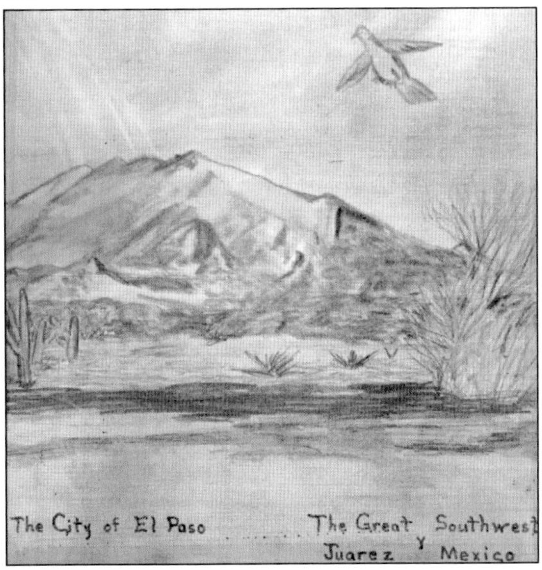

This desert scene by black artist Jonathan Jones depicts perfectly native El Pasoan Leona Ford Washington's self-composed song "The City of El Paso." The song speaks of the beauty of the land, the blending of cultures, and the great history surrounding the area. Mayor Jonathan Rogers adopted Leona Washington's song as the official song of El Paso, but many in the city see that honor as going to Martin Robinson, also known as "Marty Robbins," for his song "El Paso." Washington also collected African American documents and photographs that reveal the history of El Paso's black community. (Courtesy of Dr. William McIver and Edna Nixon McIver.)

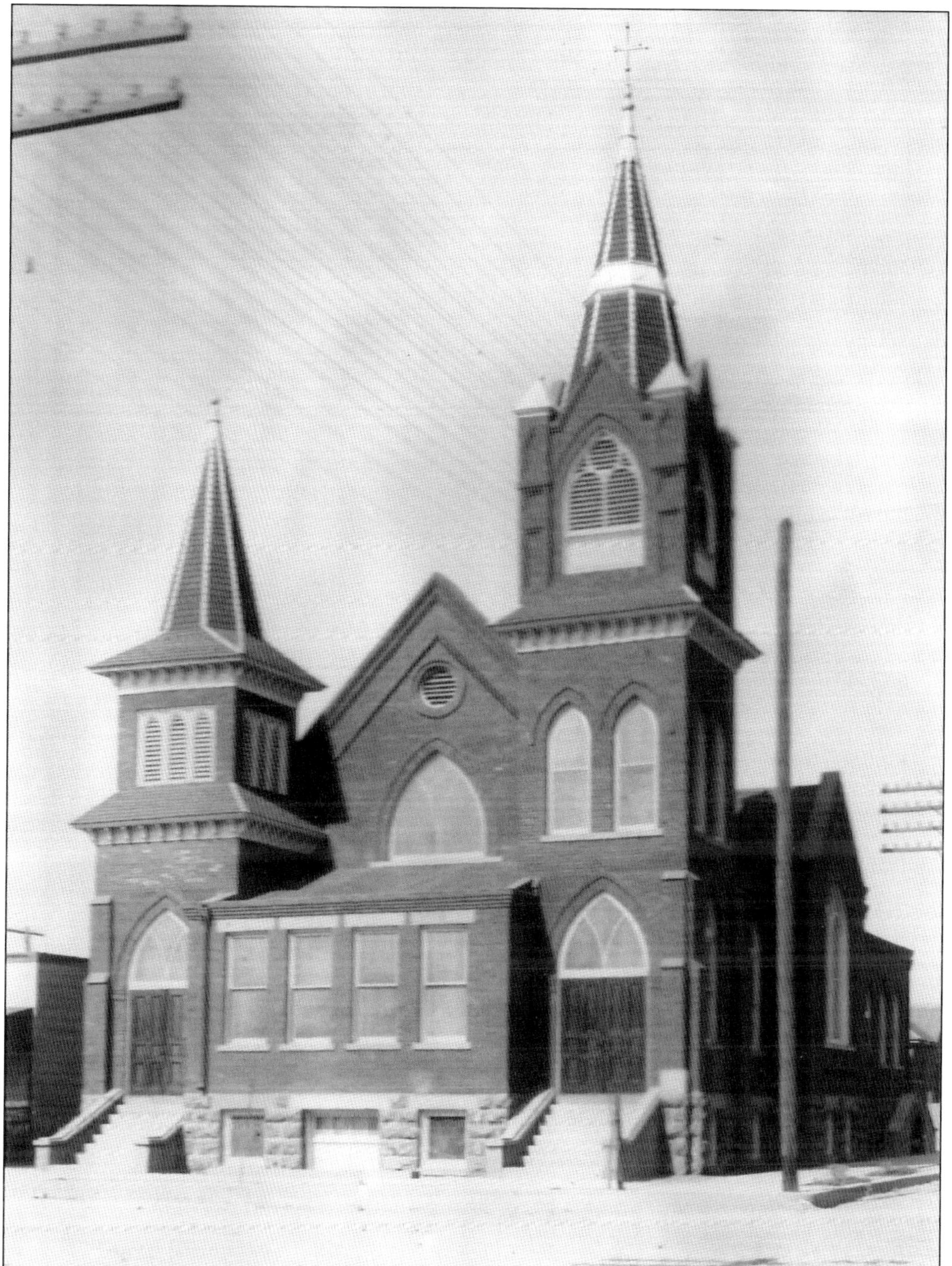

The Second Baptist Church was organized in 1884 through the efforts of the State Missionary Baptist Home Mission Board of New York, which sought to establish black churches in Texas. Rev. E.M. Griggs from Dallas arrived in El Paso and found five black Baptists in the community. This group rented a small one-room adobe on South Stanton Street between San Antonio and Overland in 1885 and established one of the major black congregations in El Paso. (Courtesy of Frances Grundy Hills.)

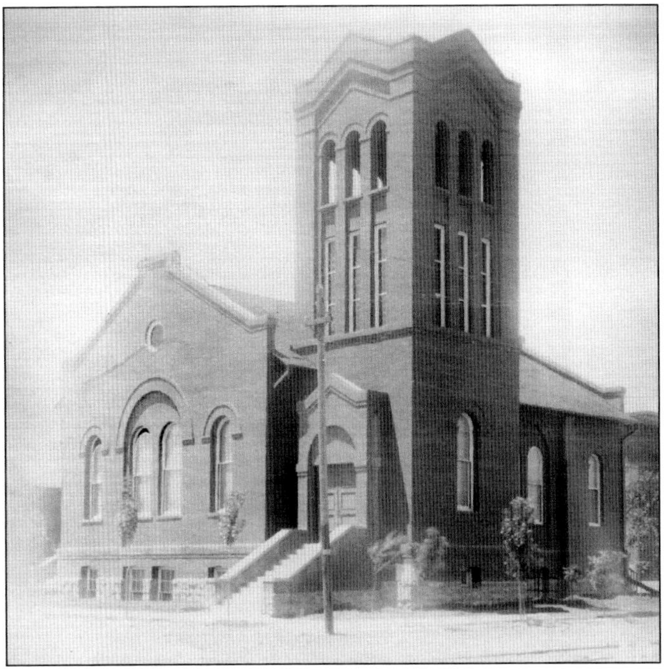

The African Methodist Episcopal (AME) Church was prohibited from practicing in the state of Texas prior to the Civil War. After the Emancipation, however, black Methodists were enticed to leave their former masters' churches to worship within the newly formed black congregations. The AME Church arrived in El Paso in 1885. (Courtesy of El Paso Public Library.)

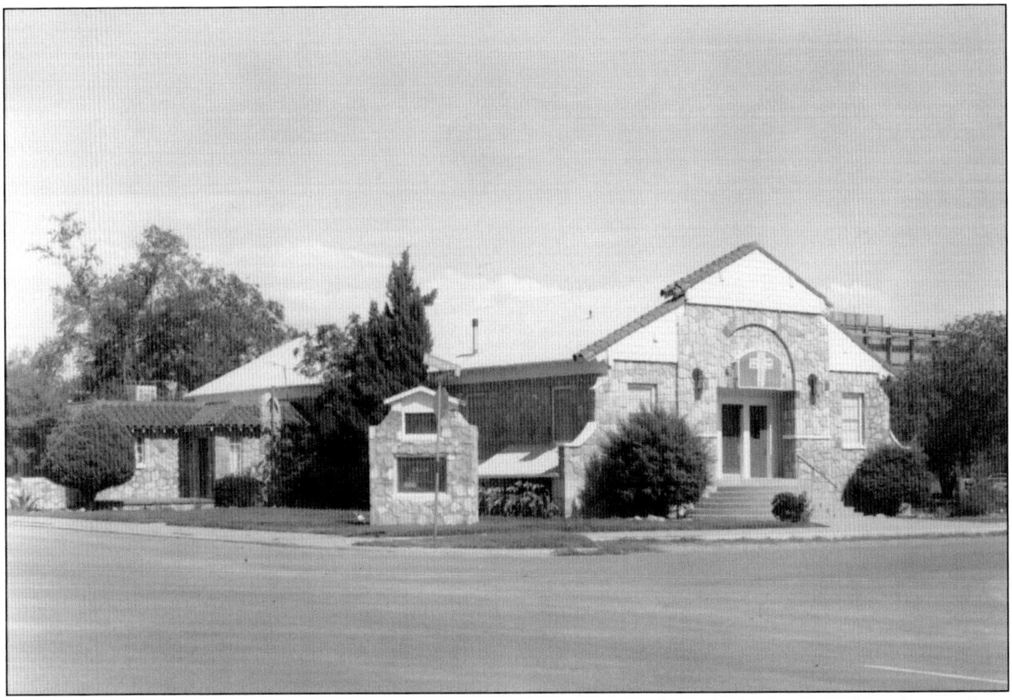

The Visitors Chapel African Methodist Episcopal Church, founded in 1885, first housed its congregation in the home of Joseph Smith, led by Rev. T. Grisby. As the number of members grew, they moved to the fire department's building on West Second and Santa Fe Streets, and in 1900, they built an adobe structure on South Florence Street. In 1907, they again moved to Tays and Third Streets, and in 1940, the congregation moved into its present structure. (Courtesy of Dr. Maceo Crenshaw Dailey Jr.)

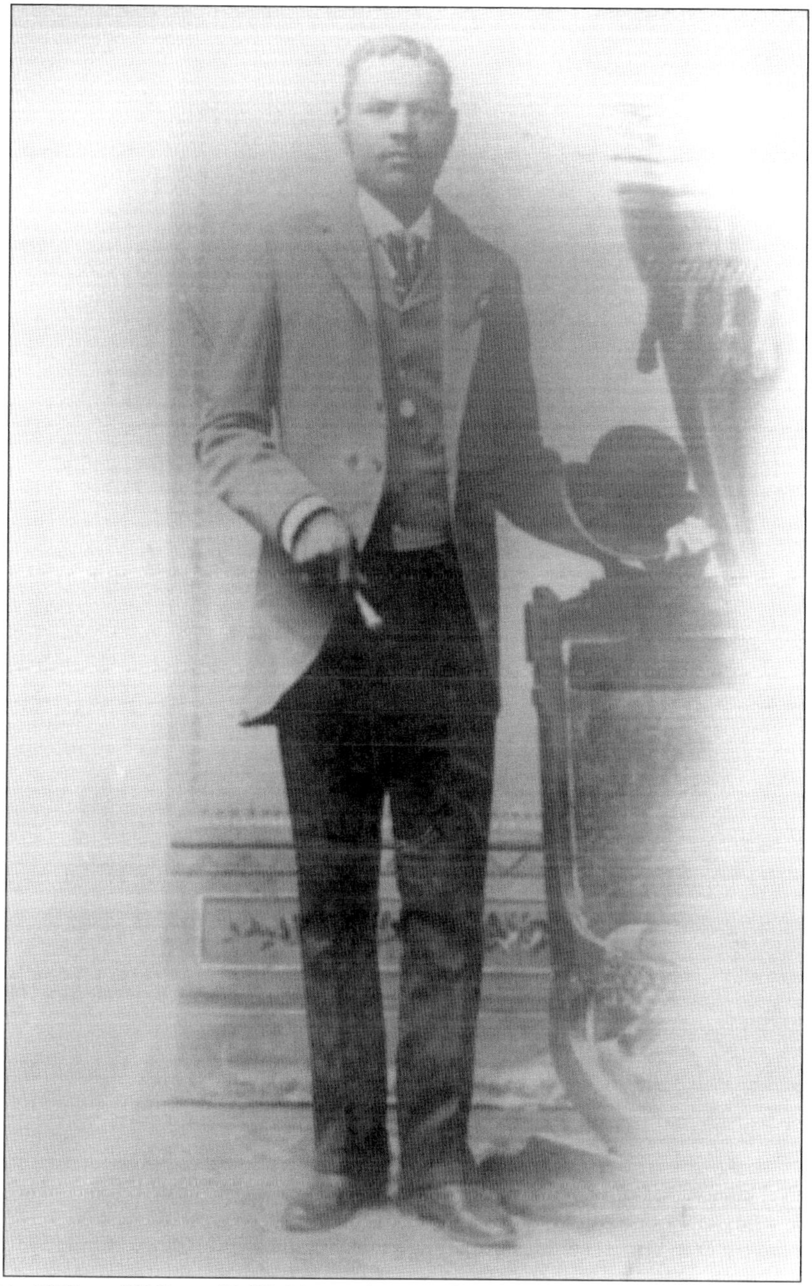

Stationed in El Paso, William "Bill" Alexander Henderson served in the 9th Cavalry during the Indian Wars from 1873 to 1878. Born in Virginia in 1850, he made El Paso his home until his death in 1934. Henderson and his family were members of the Second Baptist Church, where he later became deacon. The church was built in 1906 and was constructed with the bricks that Henderson made, as he was a popular brick maker in El Paso. He also made the bricks used to build El Paso's Masonic hall. Henderson was a member of Prince Hall Freemasonry, which is affiliated with the Masons, and served as the worshipful master of Sunset Lodge No. 76. He was fluent in Spanish and worked briefly for the Mexican government with another figure of note, Lt. Henry O. Flipper. (Courtesy of the Hills family.)

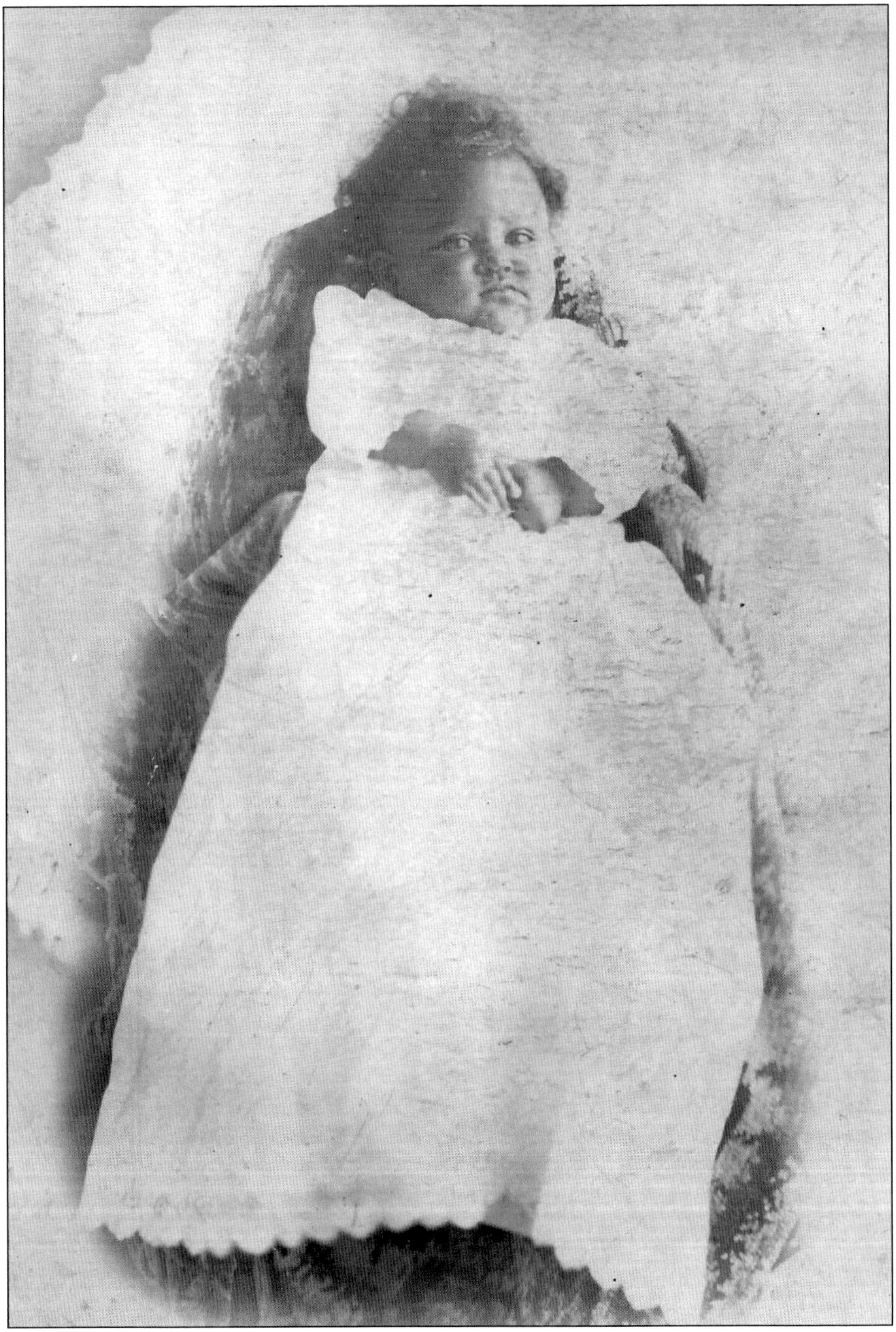

In 1896, William Alexander Henderson brought his new wife, Lucinda Godfrey, from Wharton, Texas, to his adopted home of El Paso. The couple had two children together. Their only surviving child, Blanche Ethel Henderson (pictured), was born in El Paso in 1898. (Courtesy of the Hills family.)

Three-year-old Ethel Foster, sitting on the swing, poses with her family on August 23, 1889. (Courtesy of Ada Tharp Photograph Collection, Department of Special Collections and Archives, University of Texas at El Paso Library.)

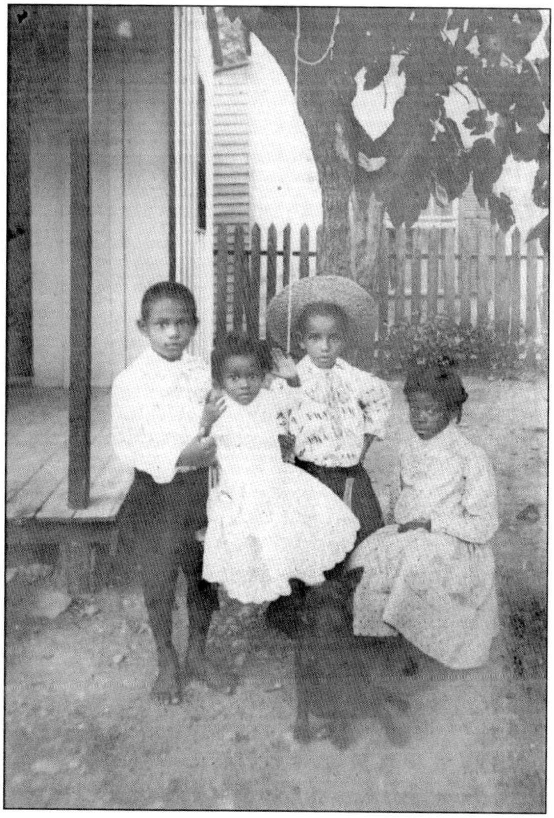

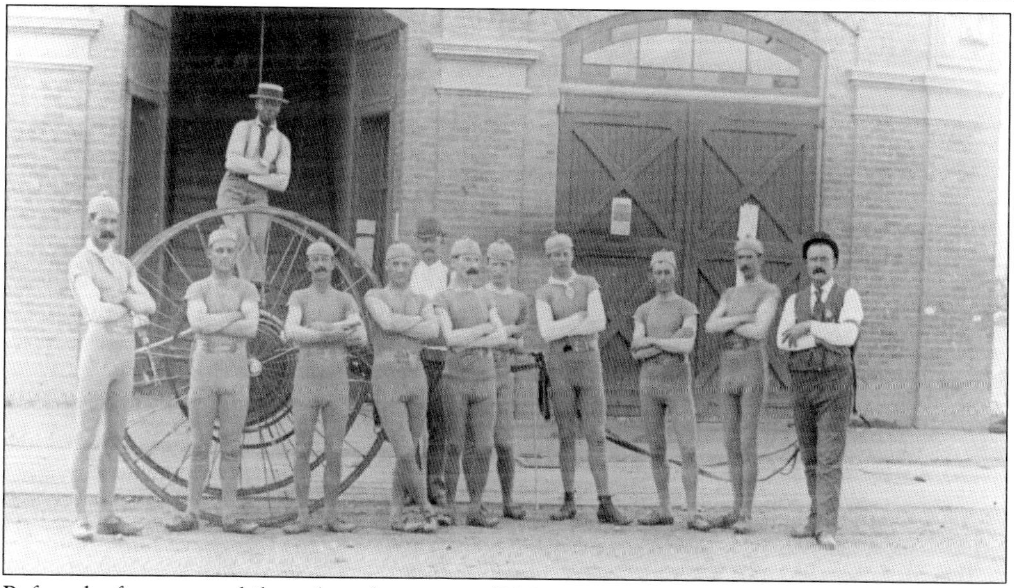

Before the first automobile took to the streets of El Paso in 1900, racing in various forms was quite popular. In this photograph, an African American man sits atop a fire truck that was apparently used for racing. The photograph is titled "Champions of the Southwest Straightaway." The team recorded a time of 22 seconds covering a distance of 200 yards. This photograph was taken in the 1890s. (Courtesy of El Paso Public Library.)

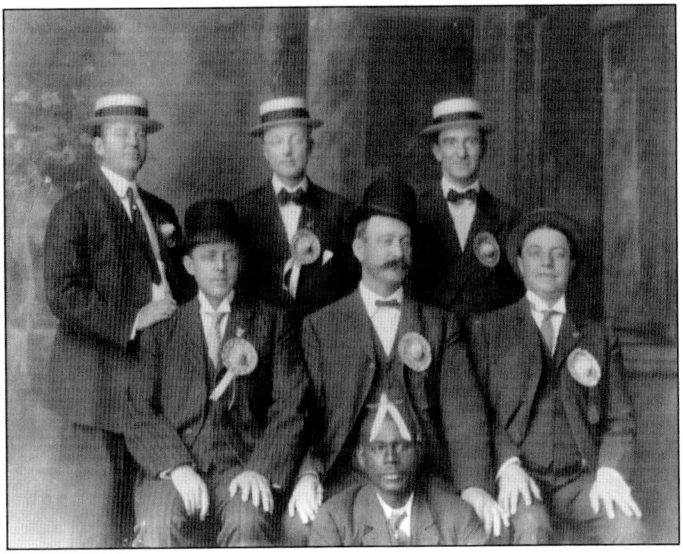

In the late 1800s, Felix Shelton, sitting on the ground, was widely known as "Felix the Bootblack," El Paso's resident shoe shiner. In 1893, all bootblacks were ordered off the streets of El Paso, and Felix appeared before city council to protest the removal of his place of business, saying that he "made his living blacking boots." Shelton had a thriving business and was reportedly robbed of cash and a railroad ticket. (Courtesy of El Paso Public Library.)

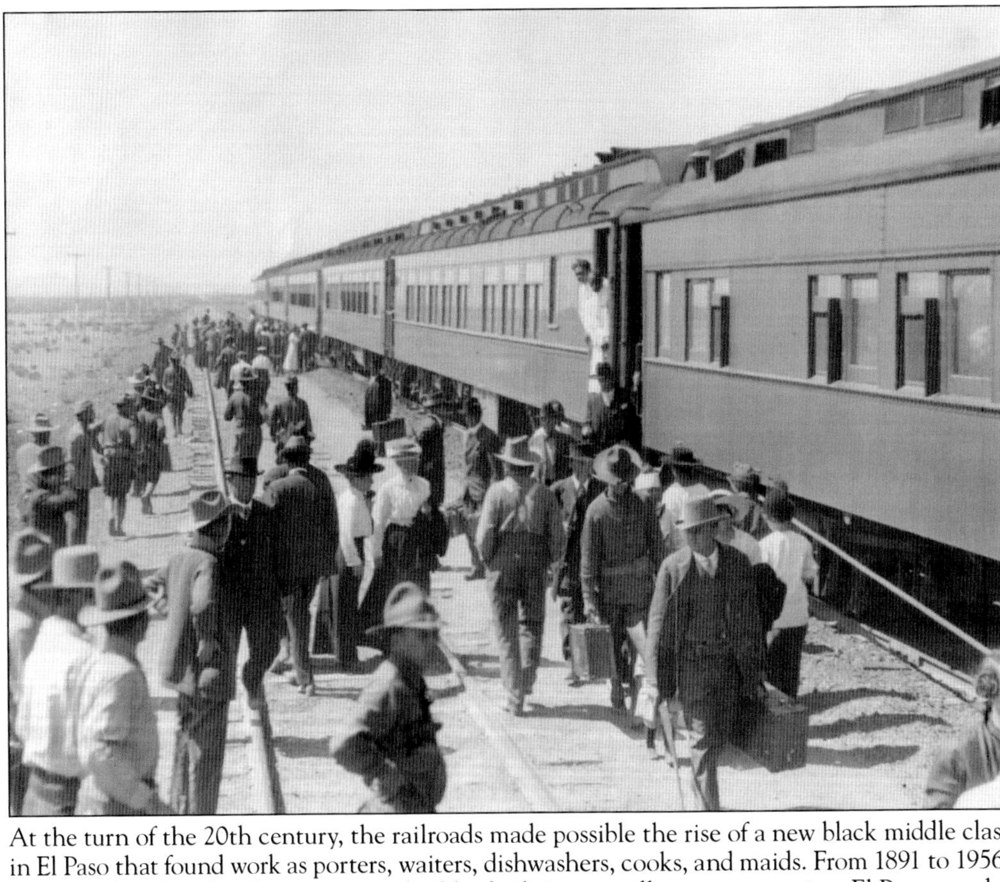

At the turn of the 20th century, the railroads made possible the rise of a new black middle class in El Paso that found work as porters, waiters, dishwashers, cooks, and maids. From 1891 to 1956, Jim Crow laws legislated segregation of public facilities, as well as transportation. El Paso was the transition point where all African Americans traveling through Texas moved to the Jim Crow car, the last car of the train. (Courtesy of El Paso Public Library.)

Two

The Enduring Community

1900–1927

The enduring community's formulation came amidst burning questions about the nature of democracy in both the United States and Mexico (with the latter nation soon to become embroiled in a revolution). The most evident signs of an enduring community are advocacy, coherent activities for development and growth, and a keen sense of preservation and legacy. Segregation fostered separation that turned into a motivational and purposeful sense of movement. From Second Ward residential space, black El Pasoans embraced a duty-and-diplomacy concept to develop their community from within, but also engaged with the larger city and nation in a struggle for dignity and human rights. The formation of the El Paso Branch of the NAACP, which evolved out of the El Paso Lyceum and Civic Improvement Society established in 1913, and Dr. Lawrence A. Nixon's launching of three voting rights lawsuits to be adjudicated by the US Supreme Court, highlighted the determination of black El Pasoans to obtain citizenship rights.

Thanks to black educators from elite Northern institutions of higher learning, such as Howard University and Brown University, a W.E.B. Du Bois Talented Tenth ethos, combined with a Booker T. Washington practical approach, was in place at Douglass High School. Booker T. Washington came to El Paso to speak in 1912 and inspired the celebration of Negro Health Week and the formation of the Negro Business League. At that time, the black population increased from 466 to 1,970, which was still less than three percent of all those residing in El Paso.

Douglass High School graduate and poet Bernice Love Wiggins's delightful book of poems, *Tuneful Tales*, captured the many aspects and aspirations of black El Pasoans and came out of the same kinds of concerns that gave rise to the Harlem Renaissance. African Americans had to use art to demonstrate and bring attention to progress that warranted additional considerations for first-class citizenship rights. Zephyr Chisom Carter, a talented young African American alumna of Douglass High School, attended Howard University, where she became one of the founding members of the Delta Sigma Theta sorority.

Black women were found in the forefront of community activities, especially the Negro Women's League, which took the lead in welcoming back to the United States the Buffalo Soldiers' 10th Cavalry Unit, which had been defeated and captured in 1916 in Mexico's Battle of Carrizal after an ill-fated attempt to capture Pancho Villa.

This period of expansion and coming together for African Americans in El Paso reflected solid and significant political, economic, and sociocultural progress befitting the accolade of an enduring community.

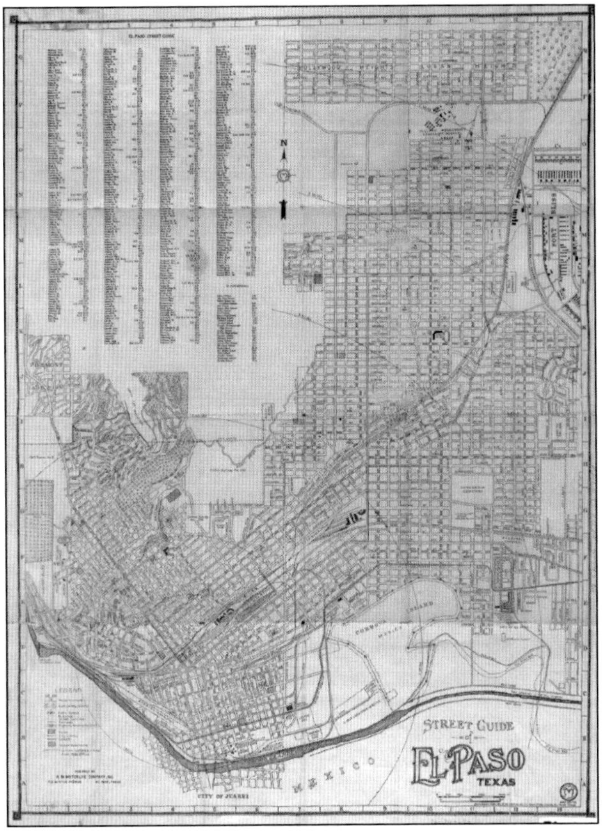

This early map of El Paso illustrates the area where African Americans lived in the city. (Courtesy of the Department of Special Collections and Archives, University of Texas at El Paso Library.)

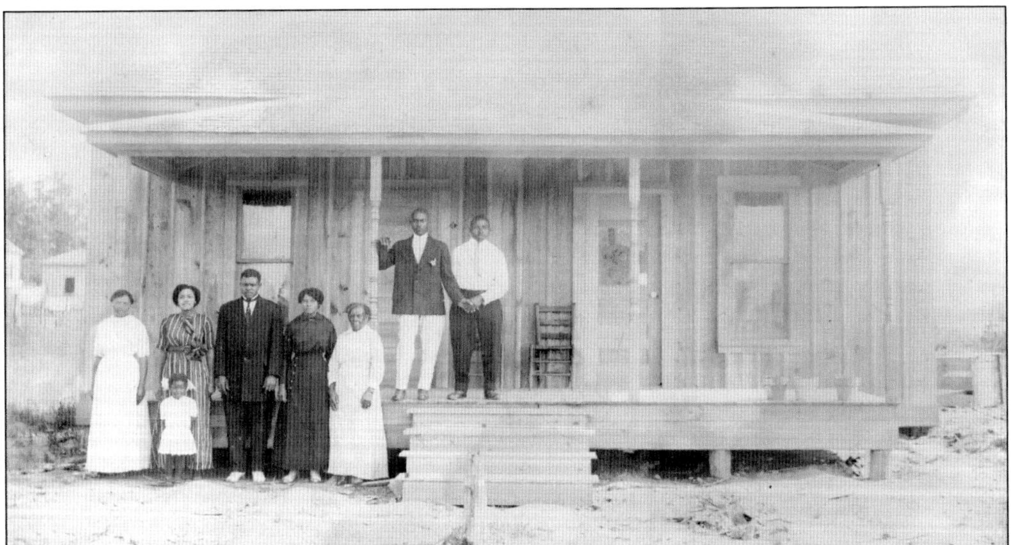

The Henderson family and friends posed outside this home. The family settled in El Paso in the 1890s and contributed to the community. (Courtesy of the Department of Special Collections and Archives, University of Texas at El Paso Library.)

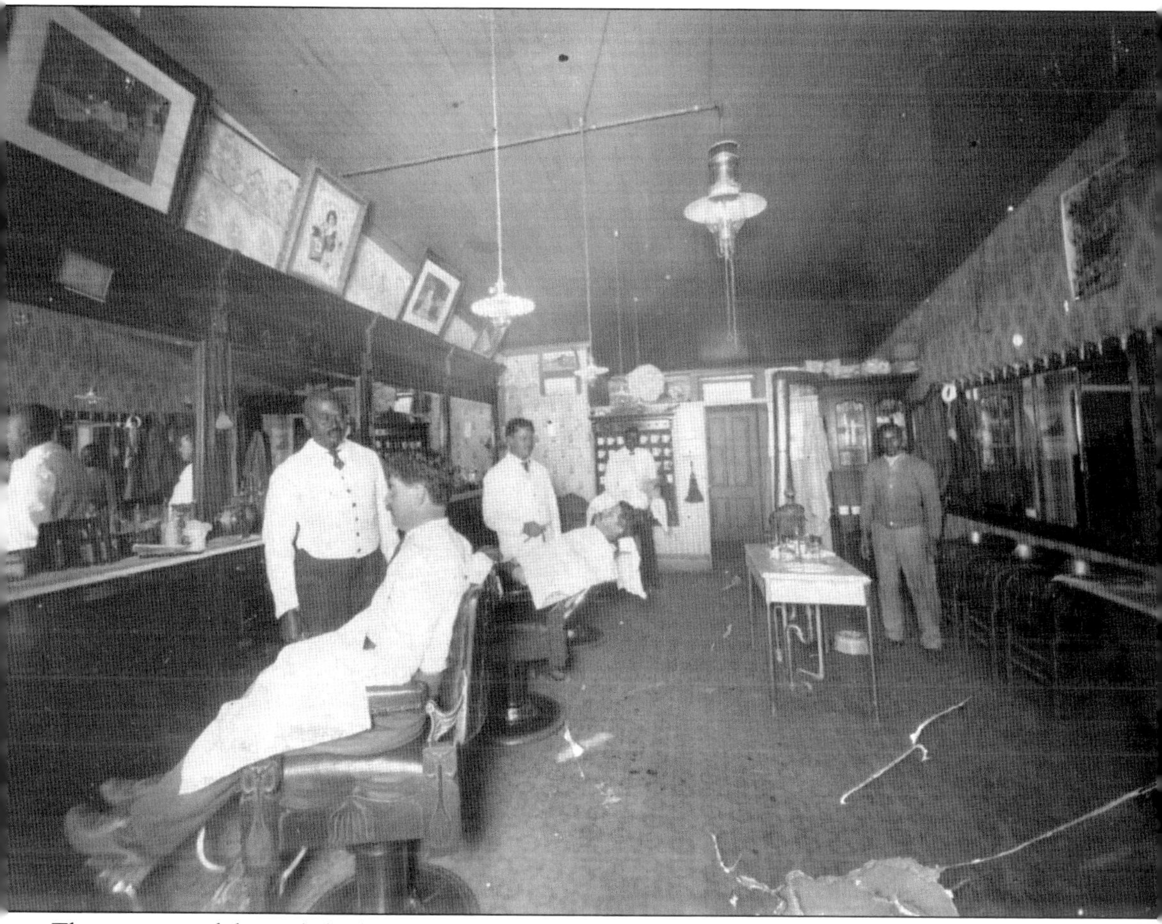

This was one of the early barbershops in El Paso that catered to African Americans. Men used this establishment to socialize and keep abreast of community happenings. (Courtesy of the Department of Special Collections and Archives, University of Texas at El Paso Library.)

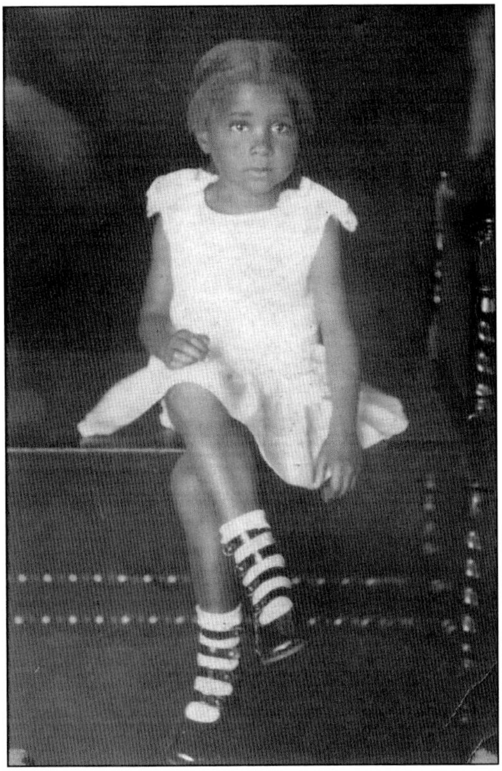

Blanche Henderson graduated from Douglass School in 1916 and returned to teach before earning her bachelor's and master's degrees in education at New Mexico State University. New Mexico State was the only nearby school of higher education available to African Americans at the time. Blanche saw an urgent need to educate the children of Fabens, Texas, who had fewer resources than those in El Paso. Blanche commuted from El Paso to Fabens each day to teach at the Washington Carver Colored School for 18 years. (Courtesy of the Hills family.)

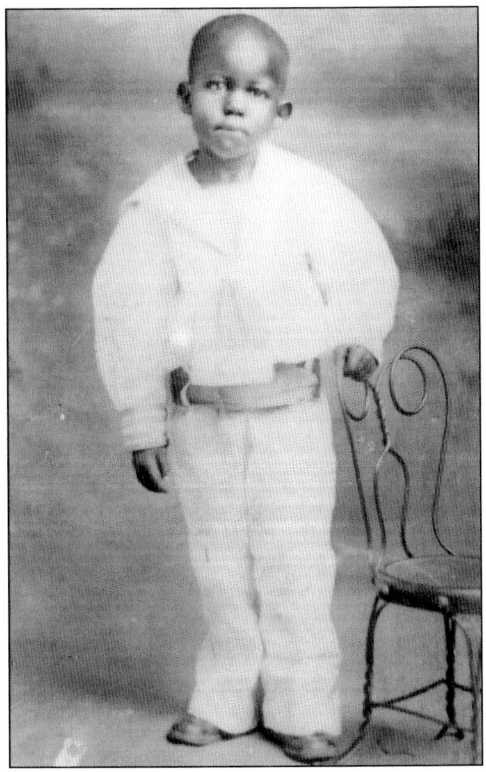

Blanche later married Sherman Grundy, pictured here as a child. He came to El Paso with his mother in 1915. Together, Blanche and Sherman raised their daughter Frances Marie Grundy Hills, born in El Paso in 1925. Sherman preceded Blanche in death; Blanche passed away in 1959. (Courtesy of the Hills family.)

Mother Lucinda Godfrey Henderson and daughter Blanche Ethel Henderson posed for this picture. Lucinda also gave birth to Lloyd, a boy who died as an infant. While infant mortality rates declined at the turn of the 20th century, they still remained high. At this time, black infants died at a rate of 170.3 deaths per 1,000 live births per annum, while white infant mortality was recorded at 110.8. Health disparities have always existed in the United States, and infant mortality was no exception. (Courtesy of the Hills family.)

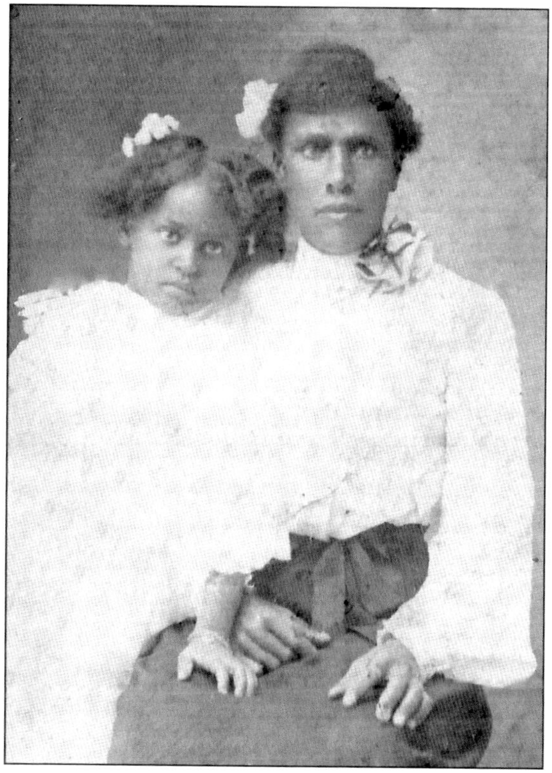

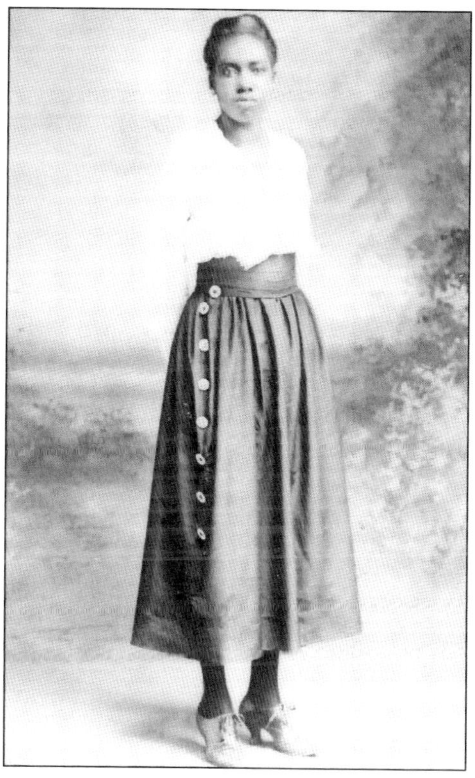

Ellen A. Gafford was the grandmother of Sherman Grundy and the great-grandmother of Frances Grundy Hills. She brought her grandson Sherman Grundy, along with her granddaughter Gertrude, to El Paso in 1915. (Courtesy of the Hills family.)

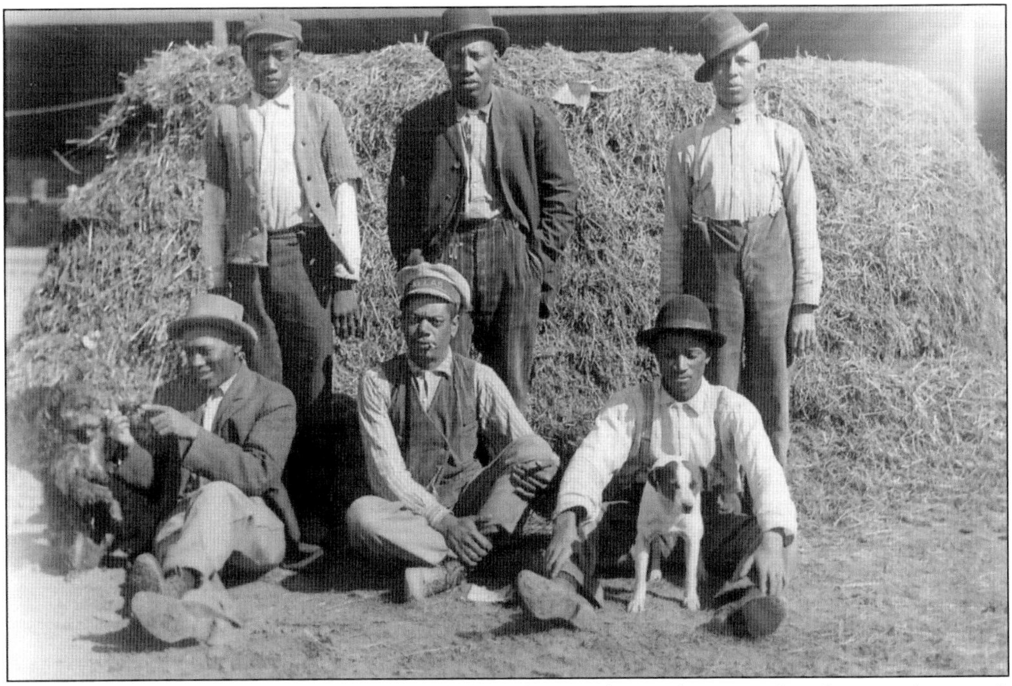

In the 1870s, African Americans, many of them former slaves, dominated jockeying, America's most popular sport at the time. The very first Kentucky Derby at Churchill Downs featured 13 African American jockeys out of 15. However, by 1904, institutional racism relegated African Americans to groomsmen, as depicted by the men in this photograph. Horse racing was a major sport in El Paso in the early 1900s, and El Pasoans flocked to the Juarez Racetrack. (Courtesy of El Paso Public Library.)

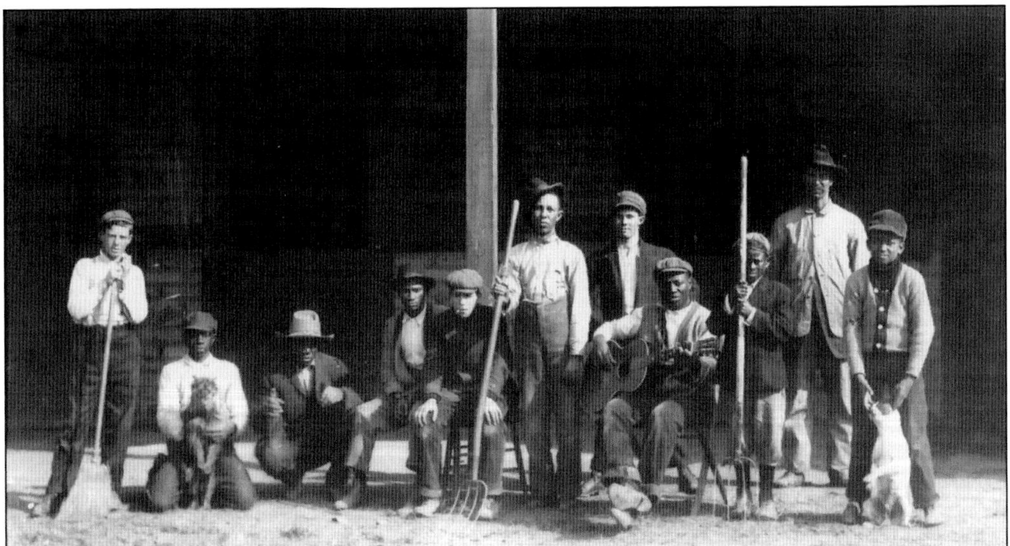

Horse racing drew crowds in Juarez, and several El Paso African Americans found employment there. These workers are seen in front of the racetrack stables around 1918. (Courtesy of El Paso Public Library.)

Students of the class of 1912, as well as their teachers, are pictured in front of Douglass School in their Sunday best. By this time, African Americans were building a strong community despite city turmoil, which brought several factions of Mexican revolutionaries to El Paso. African Americans established several churches, and the Douglass student body increased. (Courtesy of the Department of Special Collections and Archives, University of Texas at El Paso Library.)

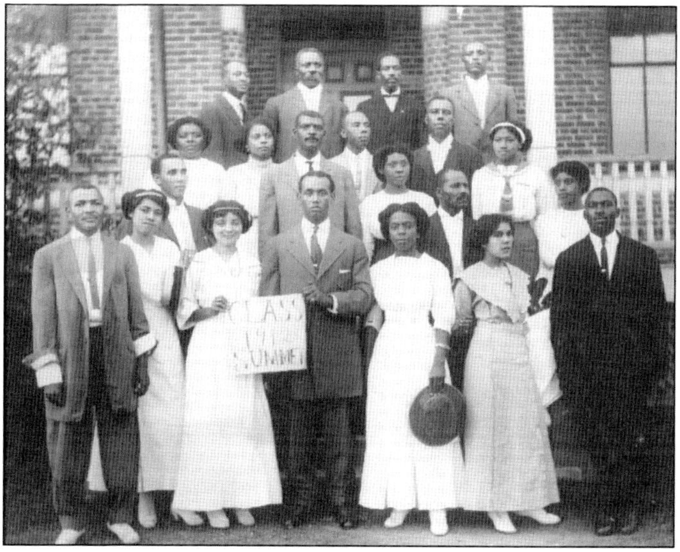

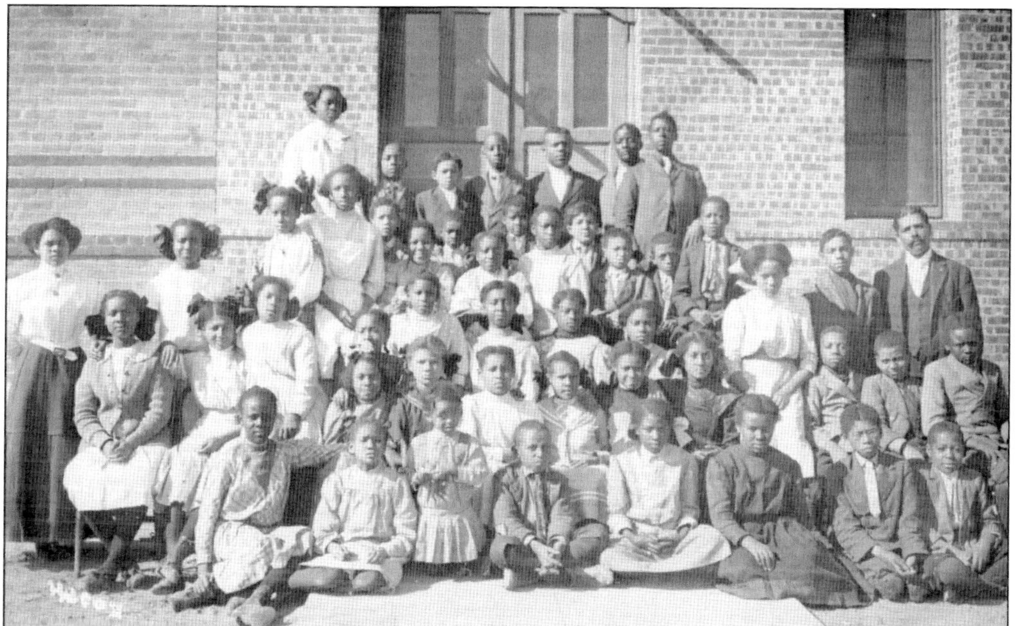

Prof. William Coleman (far right) posed with his class at Douglass School in the early 1900s. Georgia-born Coleman became a teacher of modern languages after graduating from Brown University in 1897, and eventually became principal of Douglass. In the school year of 1899–1900, there were approximately 87 students attending Douglass; by the following year, the number had increased to 122. (Courtesy of the Department of Special Collections and Archives, University of Texas at El Paso Library.)

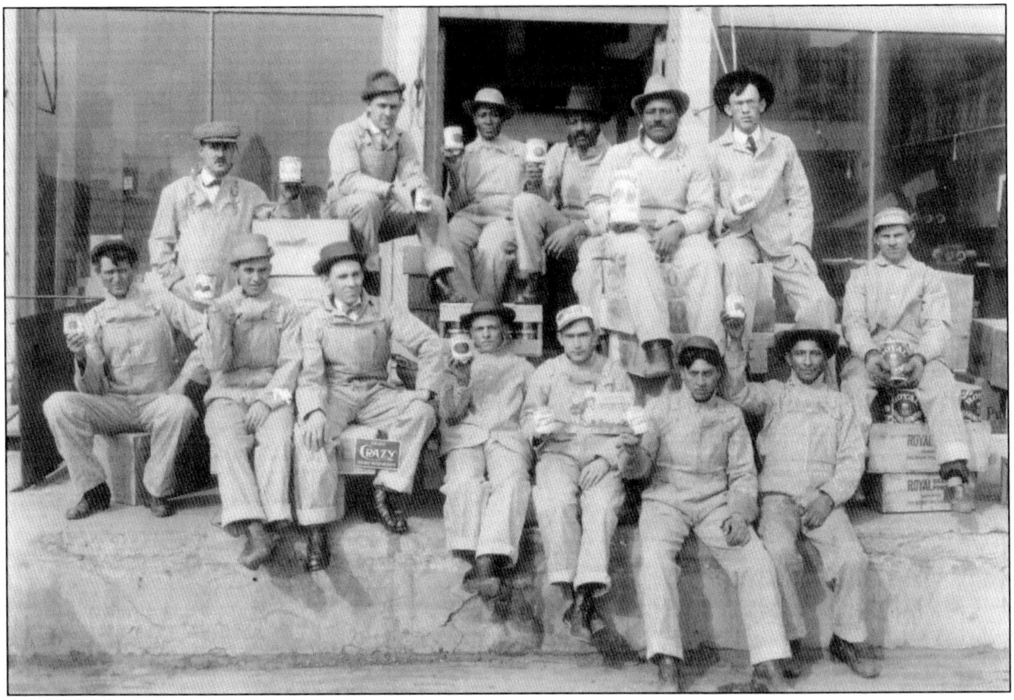

Established in El Paso in 1904, the James A. Dick Wholesale Grocery Co. began its operations by supplying the Army with beans, spices, and a popular ginger ale called Circle A. This c. 1913 photograph reveals that the company employed African Americans as part of its staff. (Courtesy of El Paso County Historical Society.)

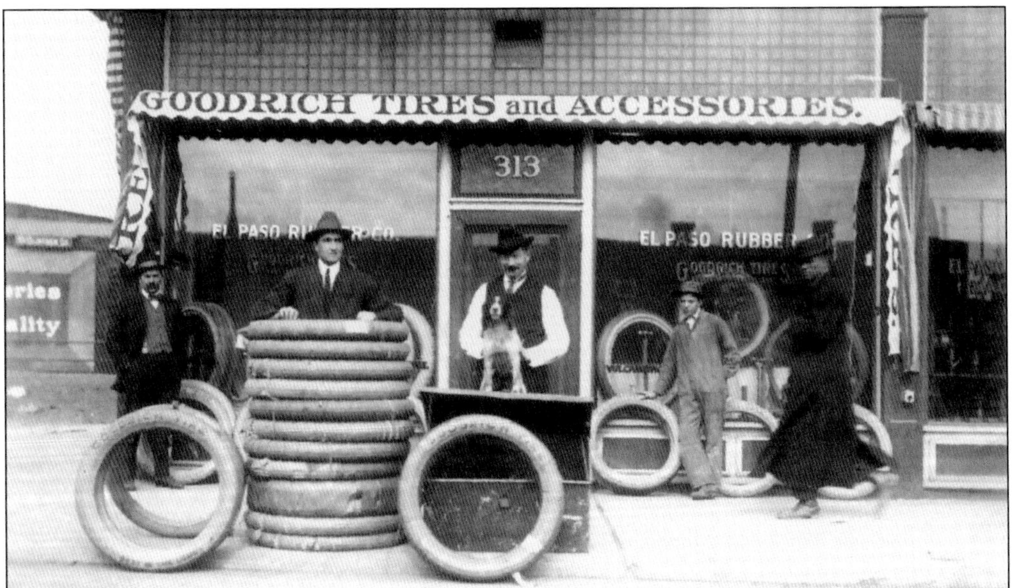

An unidentified African American male in a spiffy fedora passed by El Paso Rubber Co., located at 313 San Francisco Avenue, in this c. 1915 photograph. (Courtesy of Leona Washington Photograph Collection, Department of Special Collections and Archives, University of Texas at El Paso Library.)

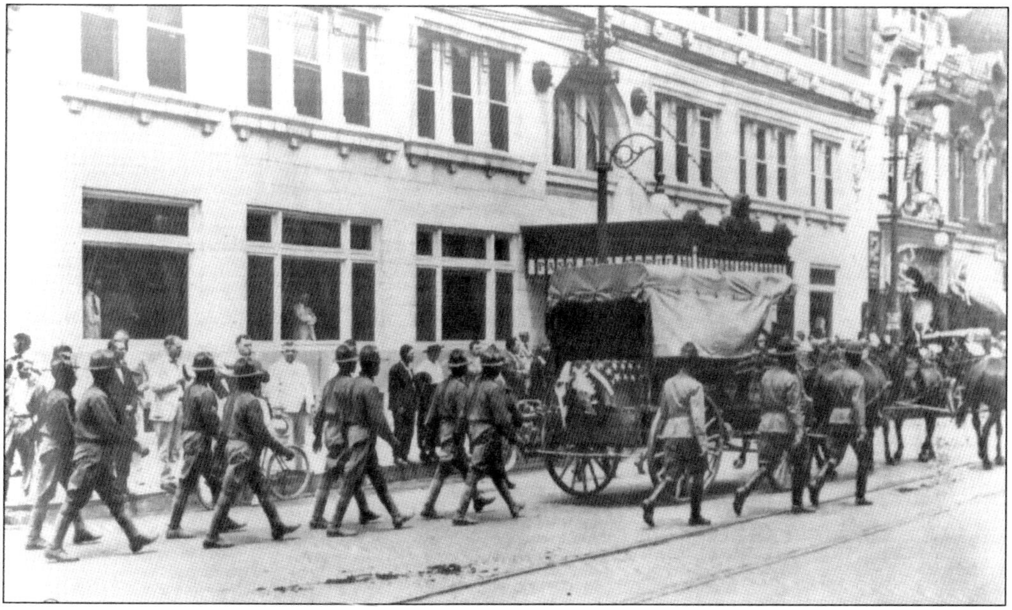

On June 21, 1916, Capt. Charles Trumbull Boyd led the 10th Cavalry Buffalo Soldiers troop into battle. Many troop members perished in the brutal Battle of Carrizal, Mexico, during the American expedition against Pancho Villa. The 10th Cavalry suffered heavy casualties, and Carrancistas took about 23 men prisoners; they were later returned to the United States. Captain Boyd was killed early in the battle, and this photograph was taken during his funeral procession. Note that the 10th Cavalry is following his casket. (Courtesy of Fort Bliss.)

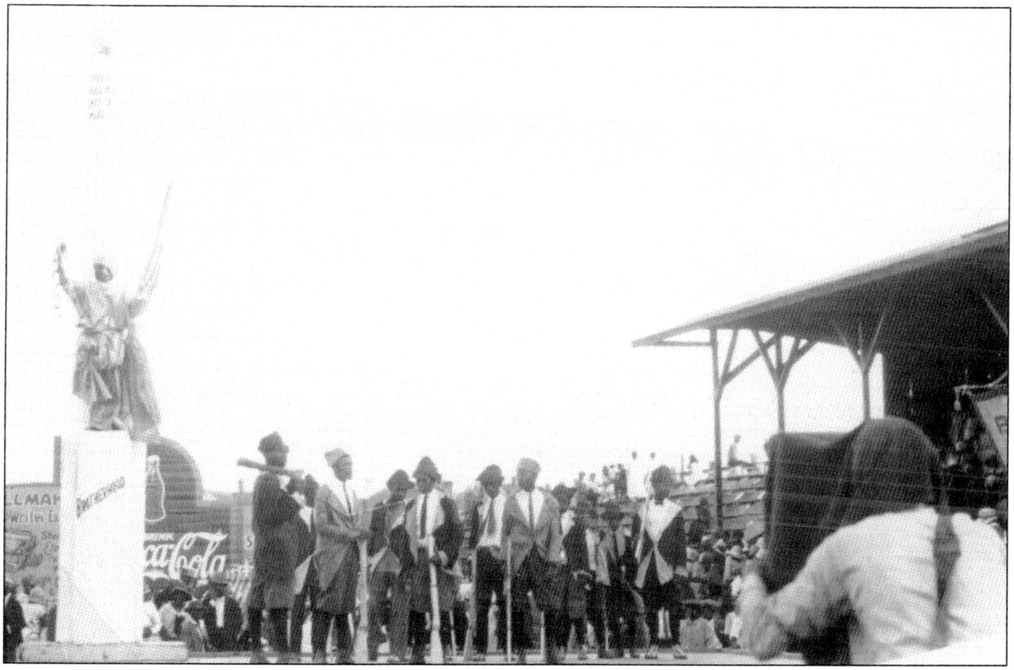

A group of men gather on an outdoor stage in the 1920s. They are posing with their rifles and hats for another photographer, visible at lower right. (Courtesy of the Department of Special Collections and Archives, University of Texas at El Paso Library.)

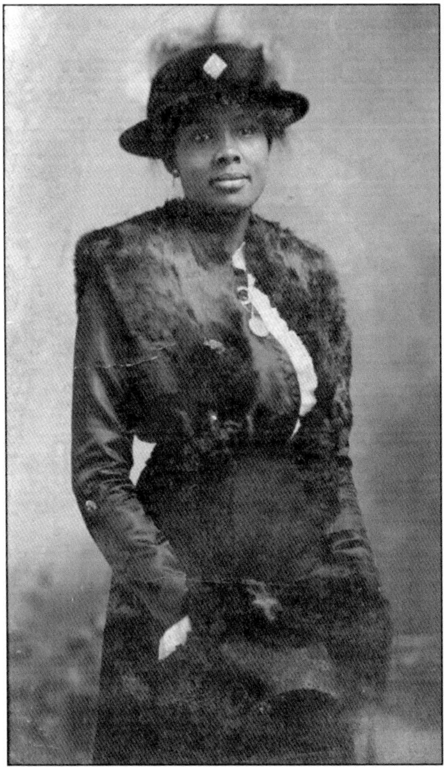

M.B. Aldridge posed in her stylish suit, hat, and fur stole in the 1930s. (Courtesy of the Department of Special Collections and Archives, University of Texas at El Paso Library.)

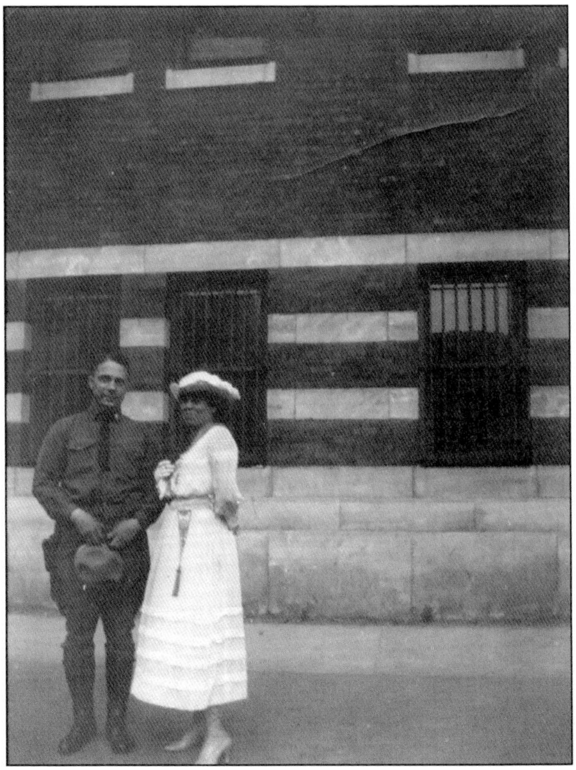

Blanche Bonner and a soldier are posing for the camera. During World War I, about 370,000 African Americans entered the service after the United States joined the conflict in 1917. More than half of the blacks fought with the French in the worst battles of this war. African Americans fought so gallantly that 107 soldiers received one of the highest French awards, the Croix de Guerre, from the French government. (Courtesy of the Department of Special Collections and Archives, University of Texas at El Paso Library.)

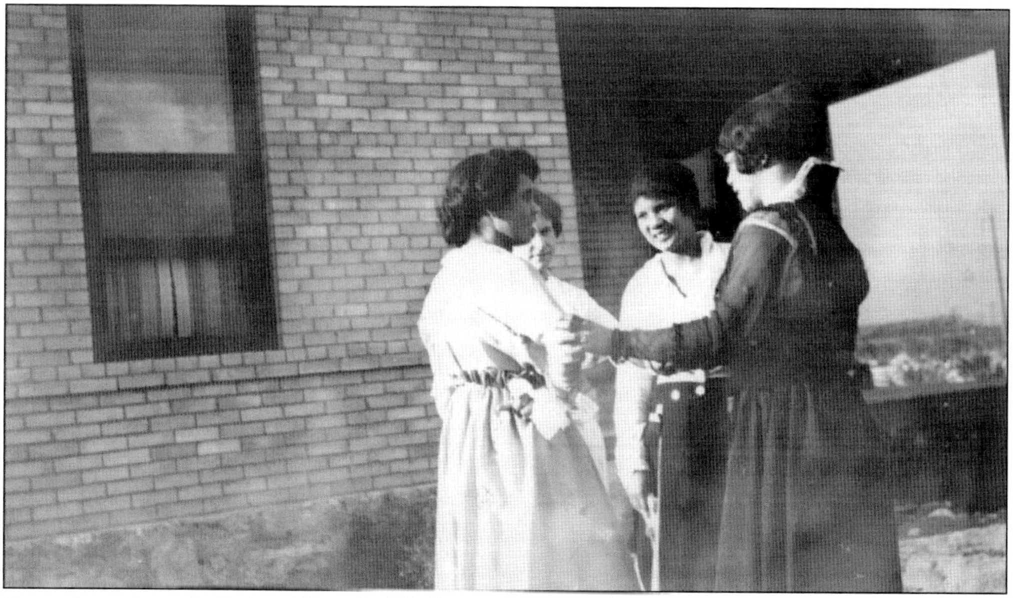

Several teachers, including Blanche Phillips, congregated in front of Douglass School in 1920. Since many African Americans sought the opportunity for education, many black women found teaching to be a wonderful chance to earn a living outside the home. (Courtesy of Leona Washington Photograph Collection, Department of Special Collections and Archives, University of Texas at El Paso Library.)

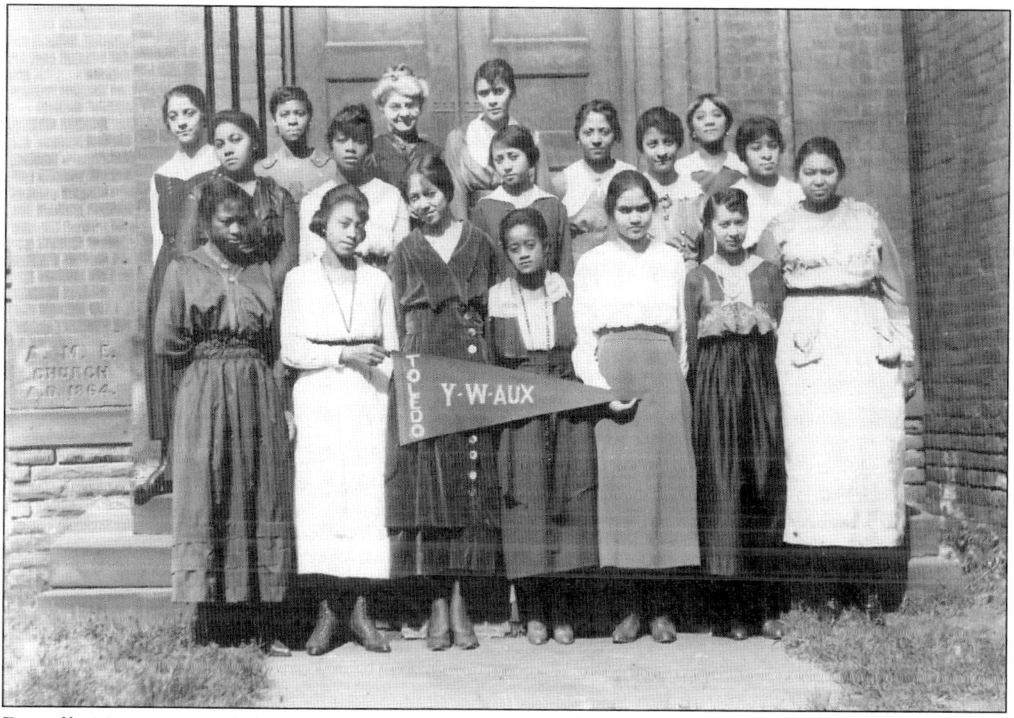

Drusilla Nixon started the Young Women's Christian Association (YWCA) auxiliary in El Paso and was the first African American woman to serve on the board of directors of the YWCA. (Courtesy of Dr. William McIver and Edna Nixon McIver.)

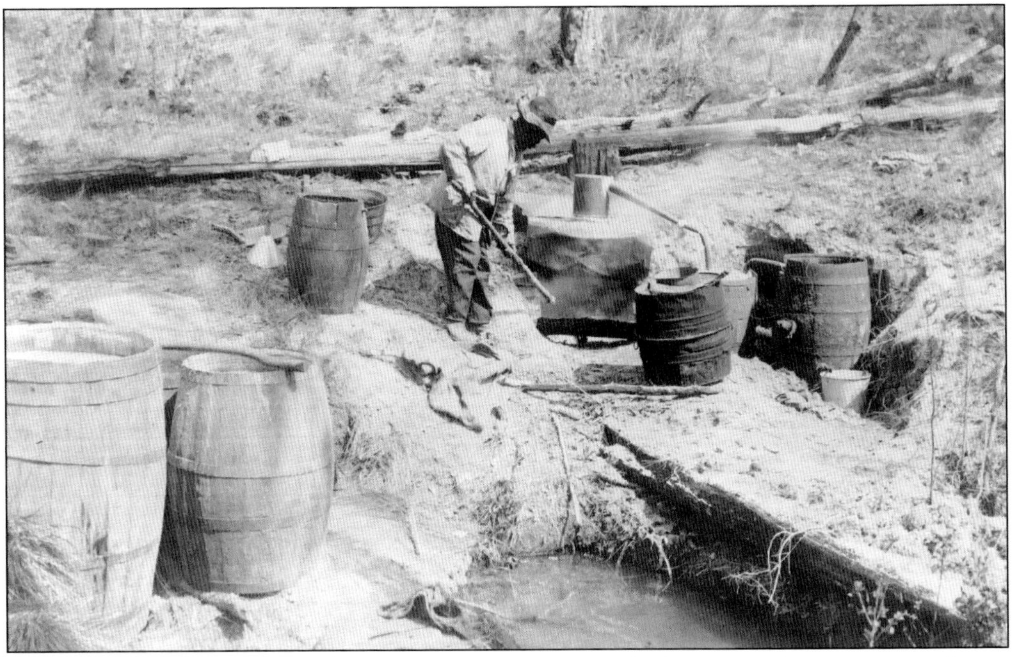

Making moonshine has a long history in Texas, and during Prohibition, stills popped up all over the state. Many procurers of spirits achieved respectability in the community for providing jobs, so their businesses proved "difficult to locate." Agents took to the air to find operating stills. This was one of the first stills shut down in the El Paso area. (Courtesy of the Library of Congress.)

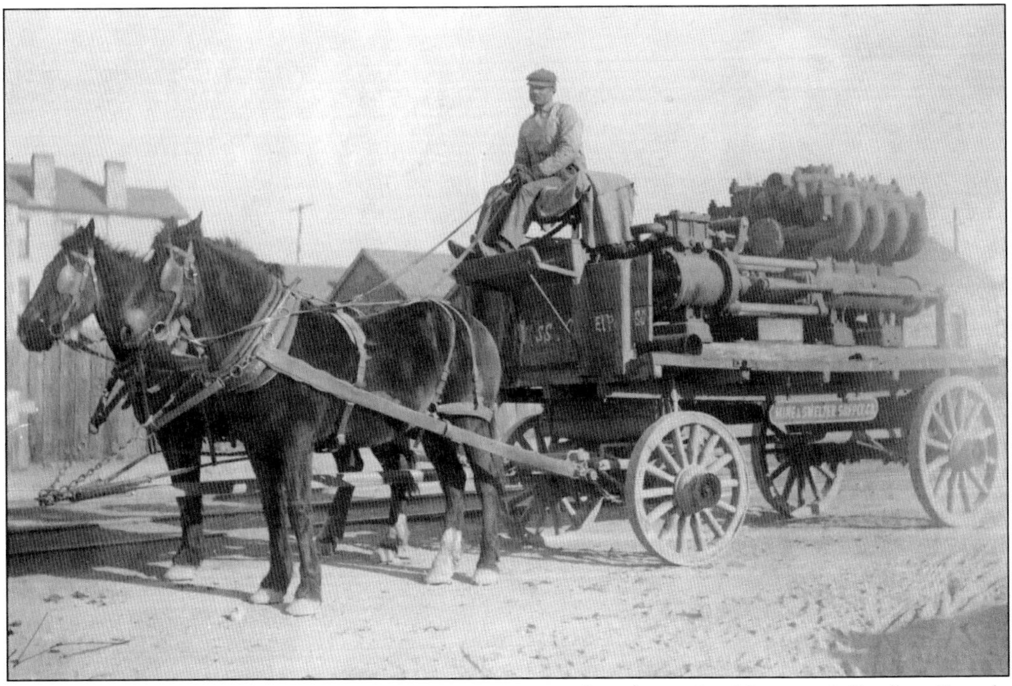

This man on a horse-drawn wagon was carrying supplies from the Mine and Smelter Supply Company. (Courtesy of the Department of Special Collections and Archives, University of Texas at El Paso Library.)

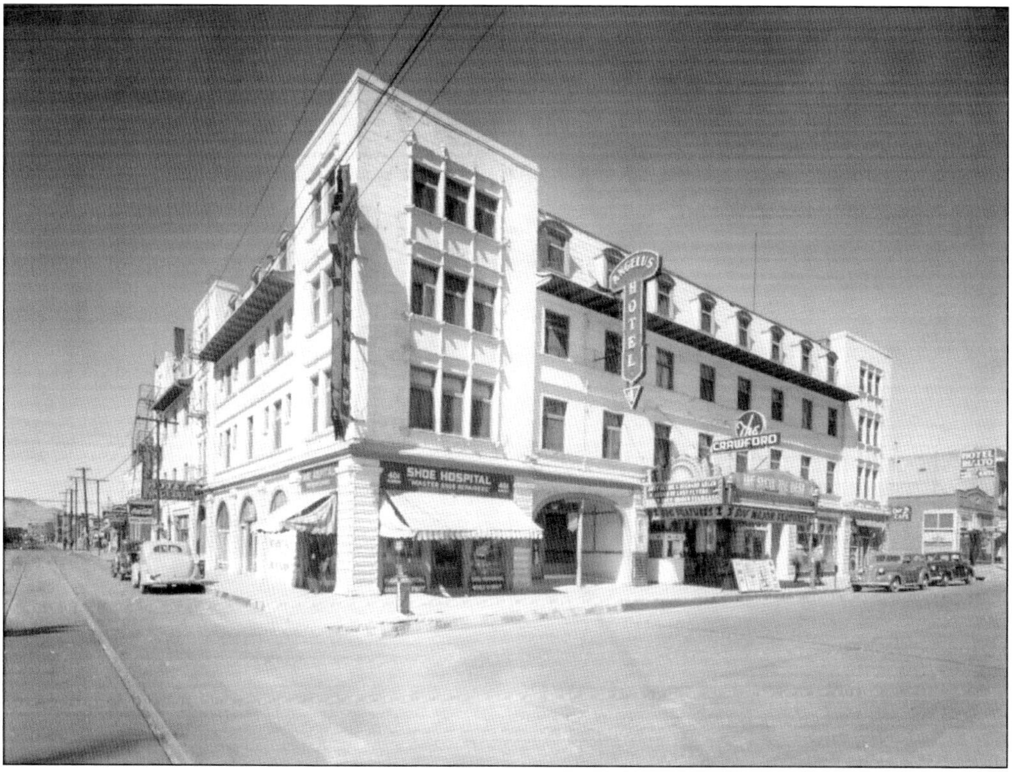

The Crawford Theater was one of the few that allowed African American patrons; however, they were relegated to the balcony's "colored-only" seating section. Frances Grundy Hills shared that this "reserved" seating area was sometimes called the "buzzard's roost." This theater was built in 1906 and converted to a movie theater before being razed in 1964. Other El Paso theaters that allowed blacks were the Alcazar, the Colón, and the Mission Theaters. (Courtesy of El Paso County Historical Society.)

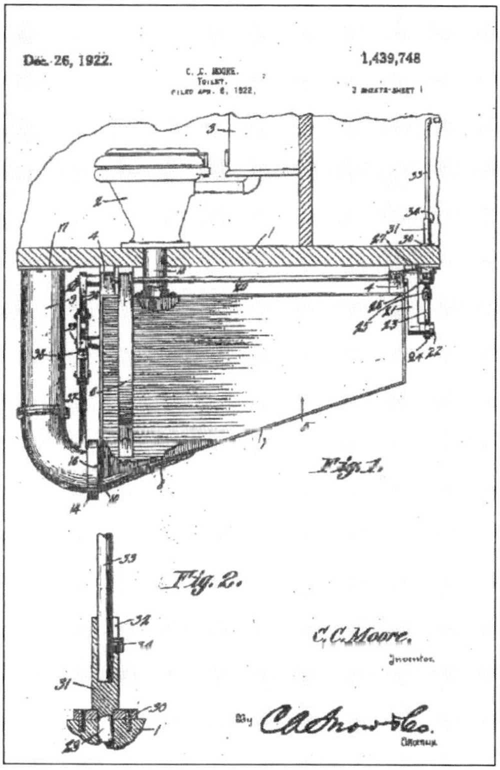

Charles C. Moore was an early inventor from El Paso. In 1922, he filed a patent for a new toilet to be utilized on trains. Subsequent inventors often referenced his patents, once for a vehicle sewage disposal system in 1947 and for a self-contained toilet unit and pump in 1952. (Courtesy of the US Patent office.)

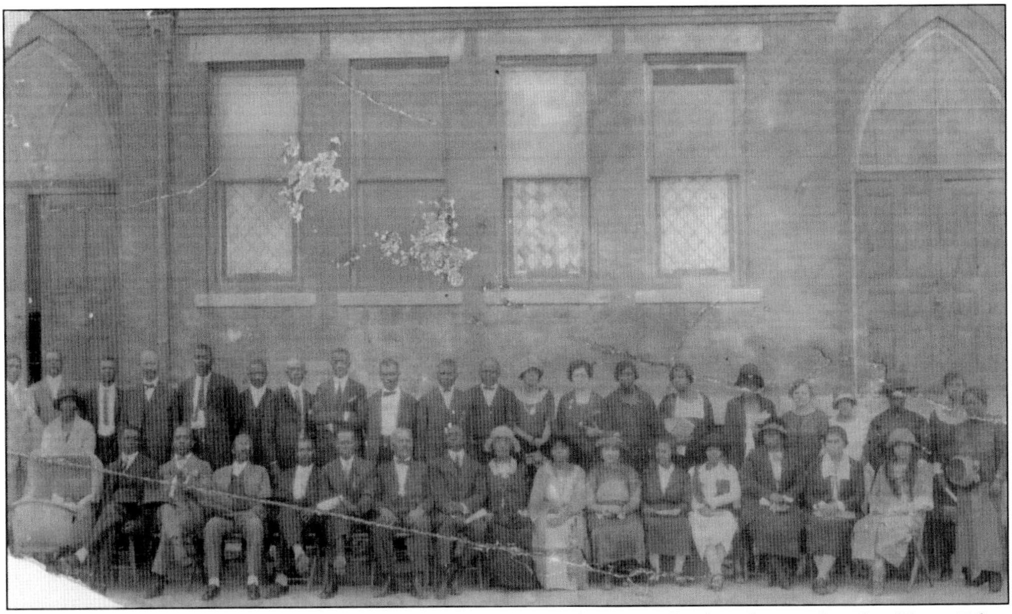

The congregation of the Second Baptist Church was photographed in front of its building. This church, established in 1884, continues to increase its membership and attracts many prominent citizens in El Paso. (Courtesy of Leona Washington Photograph Collection, Department of Special Collections and Archives, University of Texas at El Paso Library.)

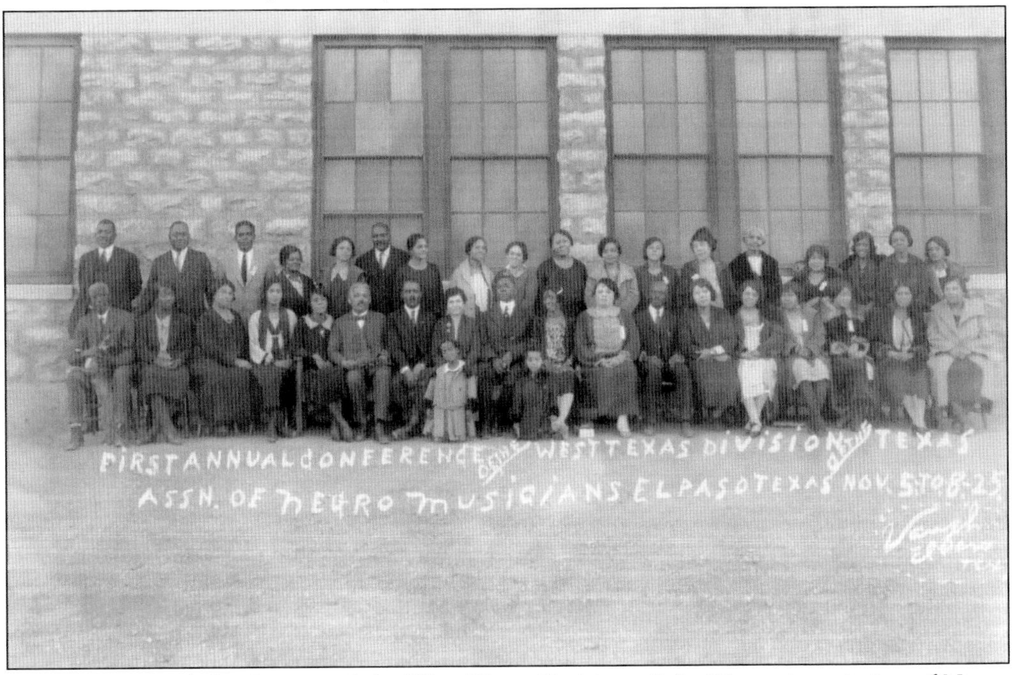

The First Annual Conference of the West Texas Division of the Texas Association of Negro Musicians met in the fall of 1925 and grouped themselves along the side of Douglass School. Included in the picture are Alice McGowan, Blanche Bonner, and Millie Bates, along with Professor Coleman. (Courtesy of Leona Washington Photograph Collection, Department of Special Collections and Archives, University of Texas at El Paso Library.)

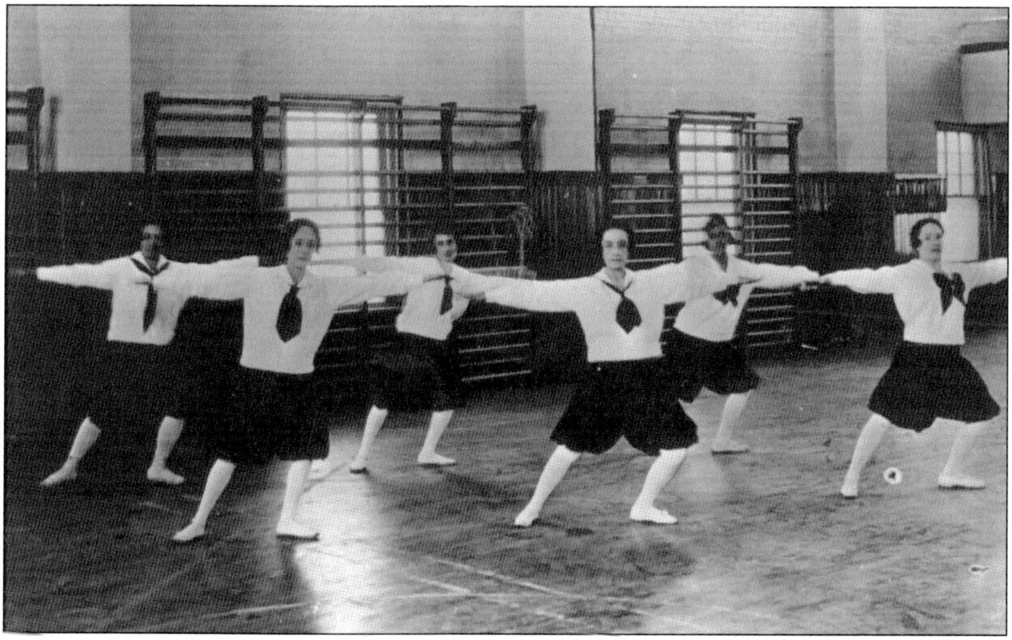

These stylishly coifed women in exercise gear are shown stretching at the Douglass High School gym. (Courtesy of *El Paso Times*.)

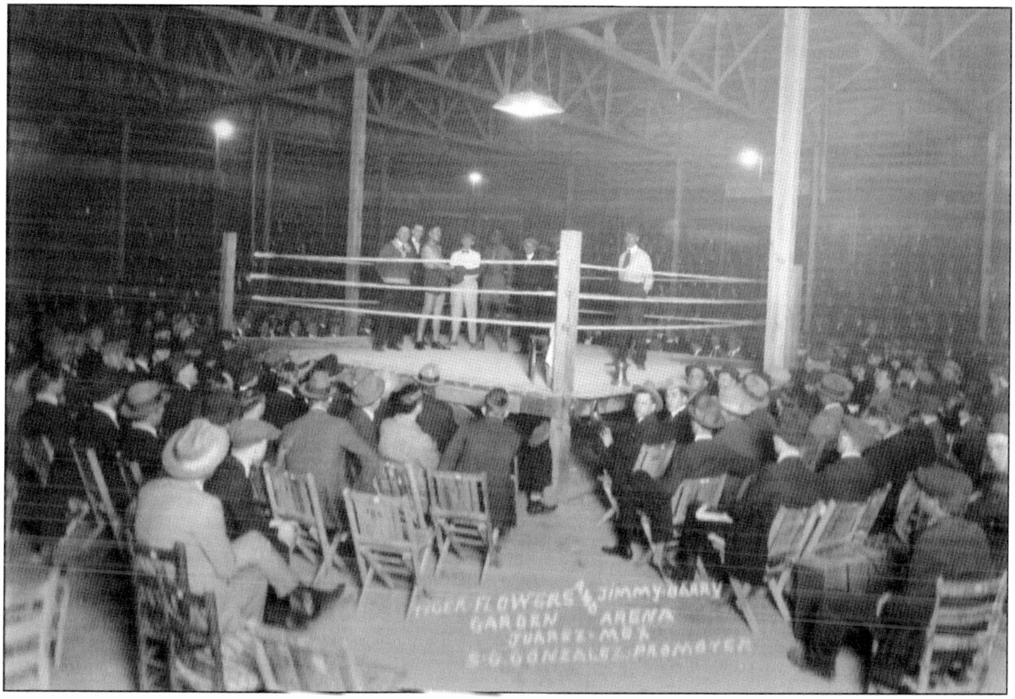

Theodore "Tiger" Flowers, pictured in the ring, was the first African American middleweight boxing champion; he sparred in a series of boxing matches in Juarez's Garden Arena. This c. 1922 photograph shows a match with Jimmy "Jim Jam" Barry. Their first match ended in a draw after 15 rounds, while a rematch three weeks later ended with Flowers winning in a knockout after five rounds. (Courtesy of El Paso Public Library.)

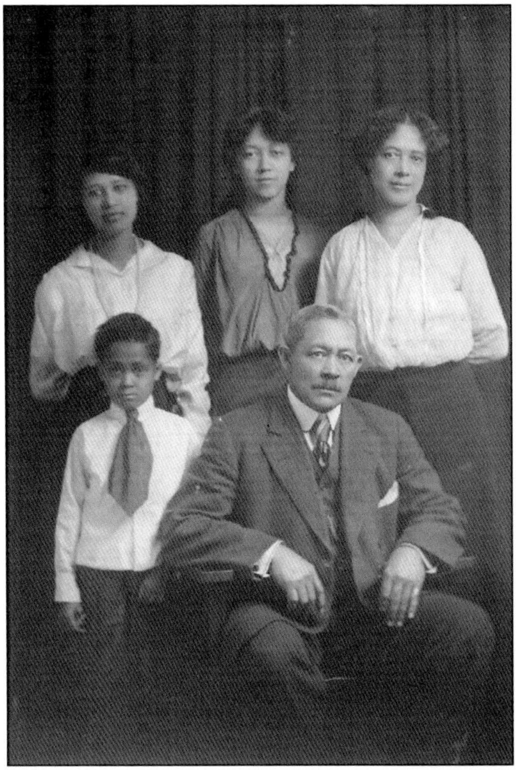

The Tandy family posed for this picture in 1917. Drusilla Tandy would go on to marry Lawrence Nixon in 1935, and they would become civil rights and community activists in the El Paso area. (Courtesy of Dr. William McIver and Edna Nixon McIver.)

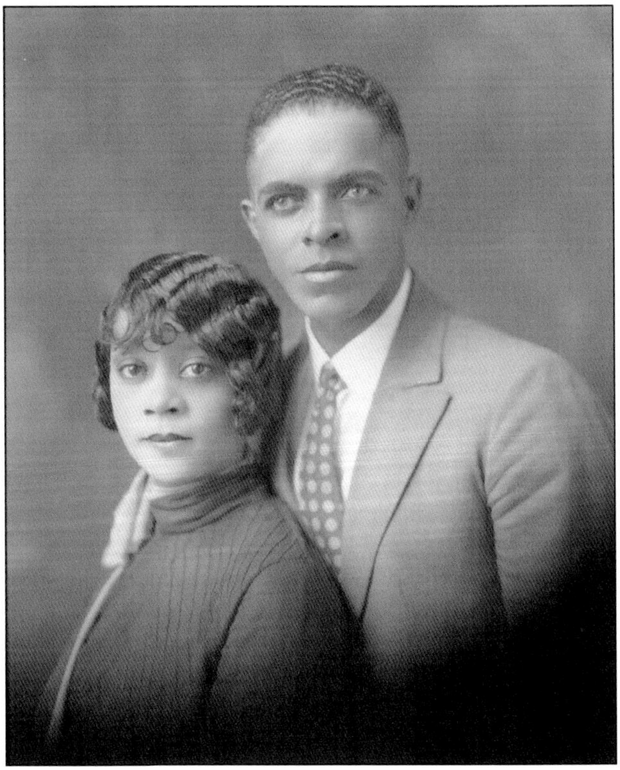

Ivory Leon Charlton is pictured in this 1927 portrait with his wife, Alma Tate Charlton. He was born in Beaumont, Texas, in 1898. He held several occupations including schoolteacher, letter carrier, railway worker, postal clerk, grocery store owner, cafeteria operator, Pullman porter, border patrolman, insurance underwriter, and civil service employee at Kelly Air Force Base. He was also active in many civic activities, including the Improved Benevolent Order of Elks of the World. In 1930, he served as exalted ruler of the African American Chapter of El Paso Elks Lodge. He was laid to rest in San Antonio on March 24, 1979. (Courtesy of Stout-Feldman Studio Photographs Collection, Department of Special Collections and Archives, University of Texas at El Paso Library.)

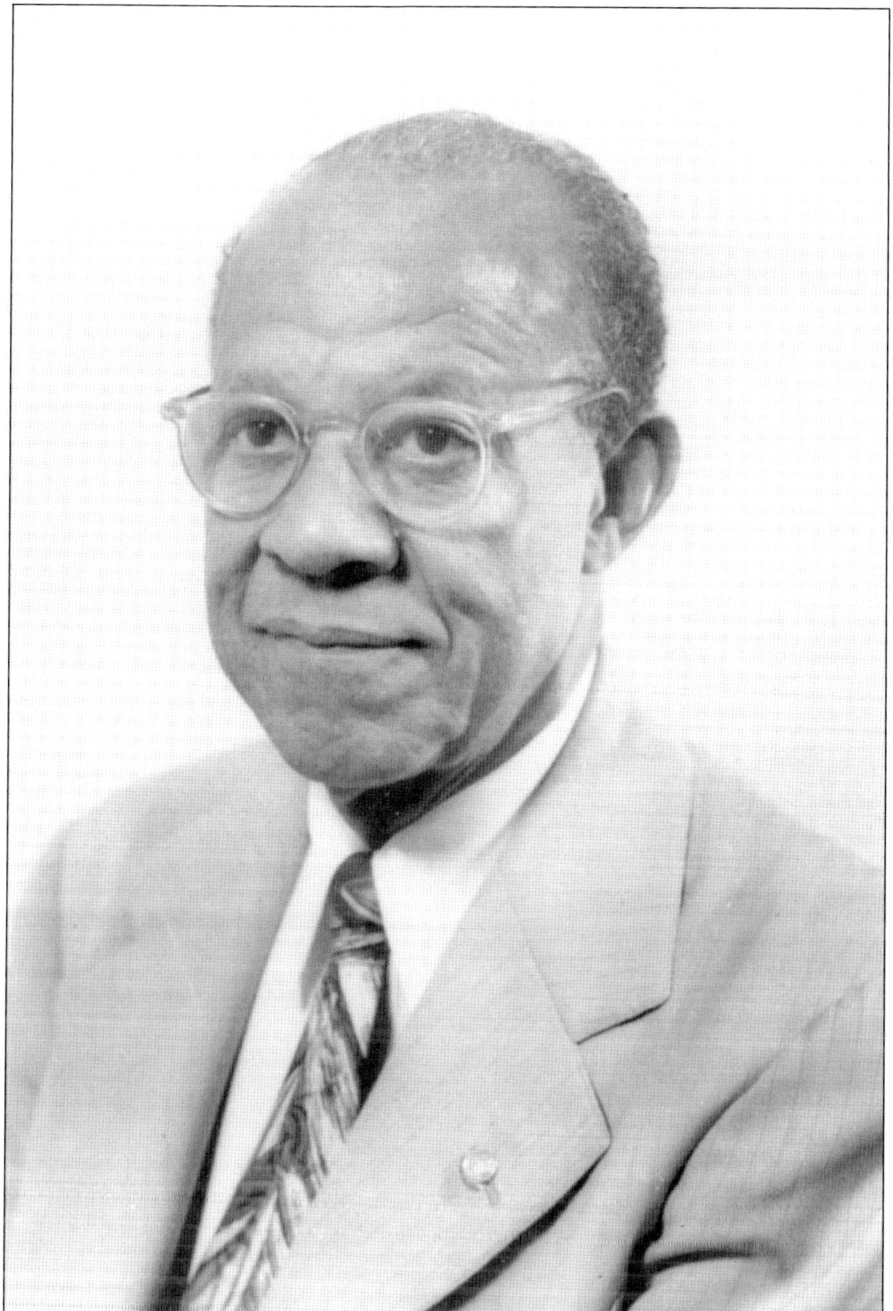

Dr. Lawrence Aaron Nixon was born on February 9, 1883, in Marshall, Texas. He graduated from Wiley College in 1902 and from Meharry Medical College in 1906. He began his career in Cameron, Texas, and moved to El Paso in 1909. He was a charter member of the El Paso Branch of the NAACP. Nixon brought three cases to the Supreme Court: *Nixon v. Herndon* (1927), *Nixon v. Condon* (1932), and *Nixon v. McCann* (1934). He retired in 1963 and died in 1966 from injuries sustained in a car accident. (Courtesy of the Department of Special Collections and Archives, University of Texas at El Paso Library.)

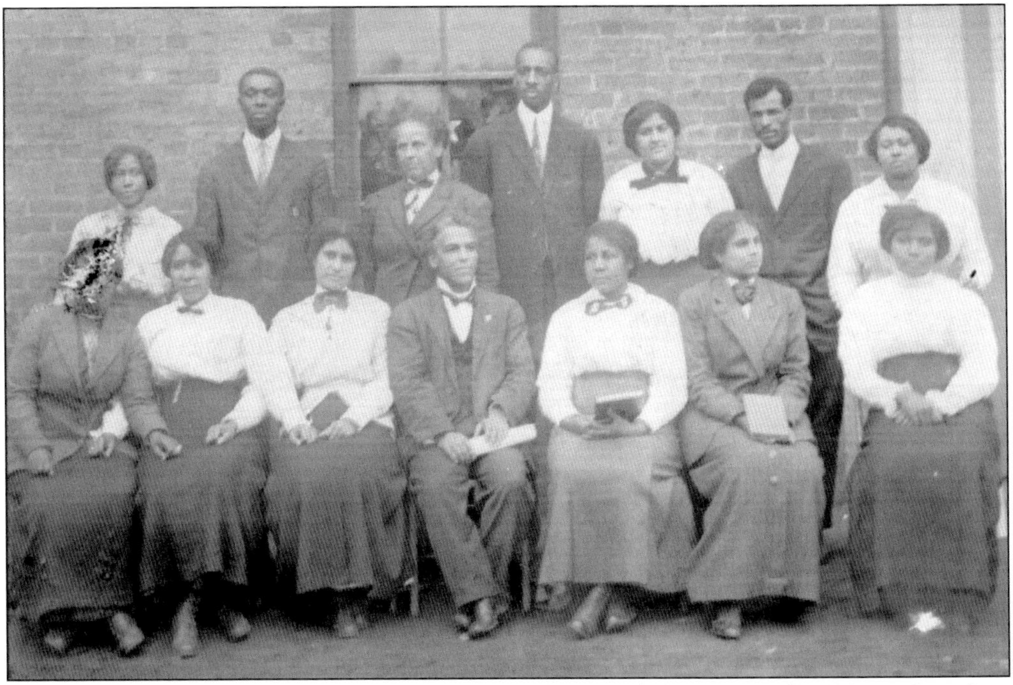

The teachers of Douglass School pose for this 1920s photograph. (Courtesy of Dr. Maceo Crenshaw Dailey Jr.)

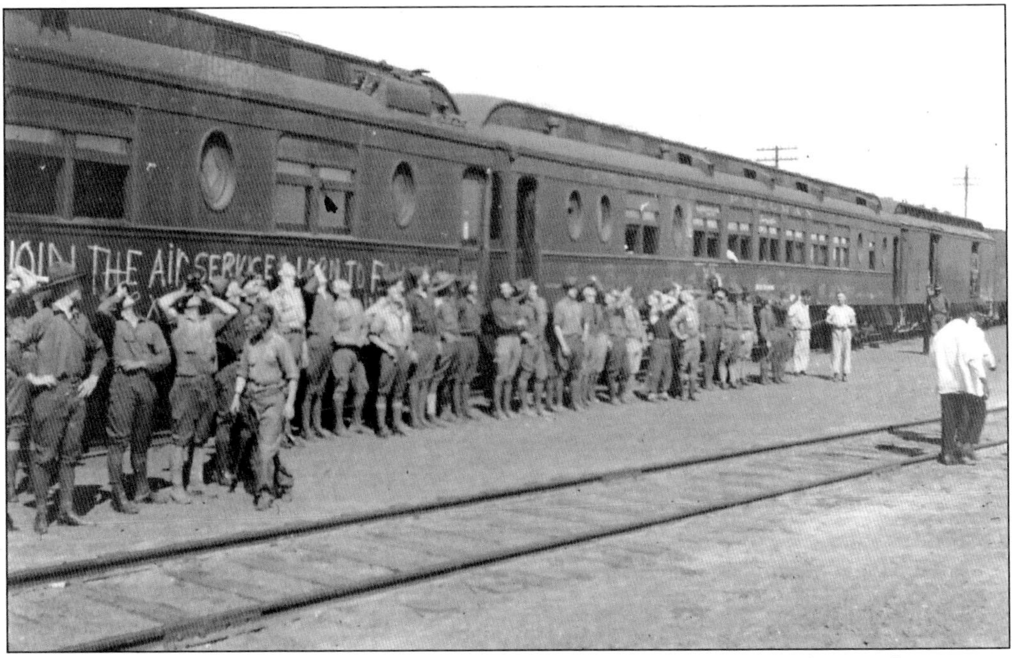

Porters are walking along the tracks in front of a large group of soldiers. These military men, attached to the Air Corps, arrived in this area in 1916 to search for Pancho Villa, who escaped after raiding Columbus, New Mexico. The Chicago-based Pullman Company, which provided sleeping cars for the railroads, employed several African Americans as cooks, servers, and maintenance personnel. (Courtesy of Ron Dawson.)

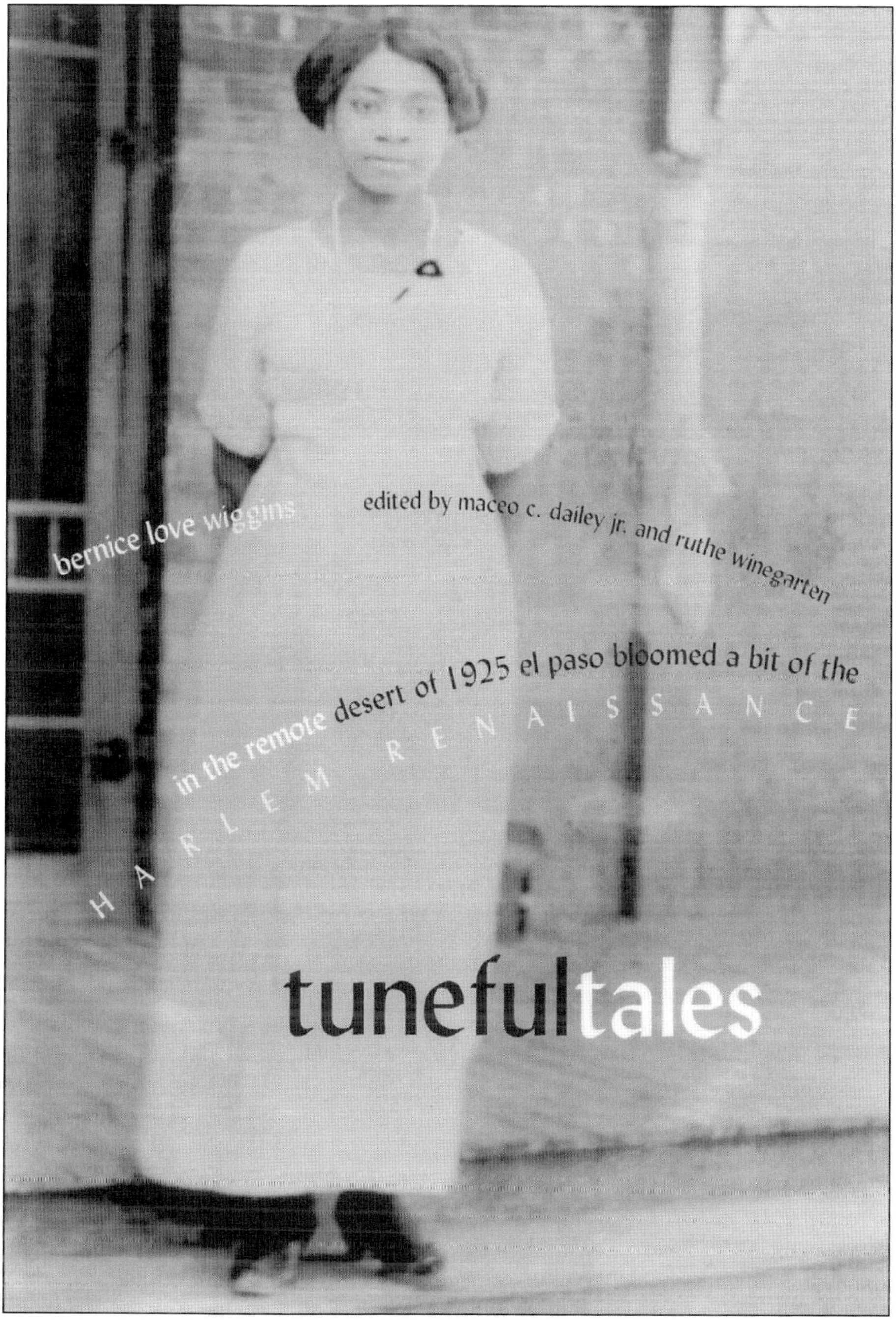

Bernice Love Wiggins was a gifted poet during the Harlem Renaissance. When Bernice was five years old, her mother died. She subsequently came to El Paso in 1903 to live with her aunt. A gifted student at Douglass School, Bernice was encouraged by her teacher Alice Lydia McGowan to pursue her writing. Wiggins died in 1936. Her self-published book, titled *Tuneful Tales*, was originally released in 1925 and given a second printing in 2002, bringing more attention to her writing as a contemporary of Langston Hughes, Zora Neale Hurston, and other writers of the Harlem Renaissance. (Courtesy of Dr. Maceo Crenshaw Dailey Jr.)

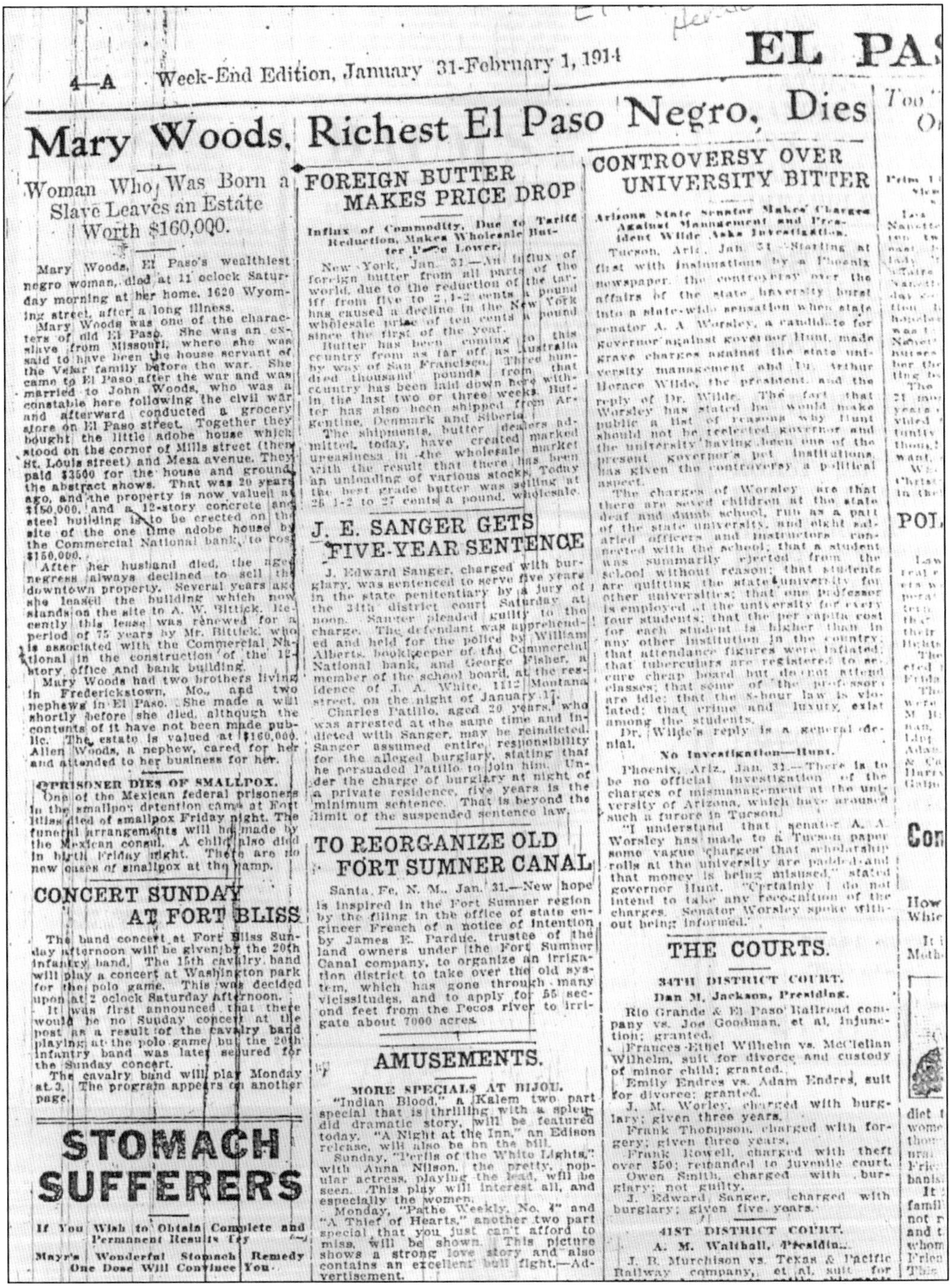

4—A Week-End Edition, January 31-February 1, 1914 EL PAS

Mary Woods, Richest El Paso Negro, Dies

Woman Who Was Born a Slave Leaves an Estate Worth $160,000.

Mary Woods, El Paso's wealthiest negro woman, died at 11 oclock Saturday morning at her home, 1620 Wyoming street, after a long illness.

Mary Woods was one of the characters of old El Paso. She was an ex-slave from Missouri, where she was said to have been the house servant of the Vafar family before the war. She came to El Paso after the war and was married to John Woods, who was a constable here following the civil war and afterward conducted a grocery store on El Paso street. Together they bought the little adobe house which stood on the corner of Mills street (then St. Louis street) and Mesa avenue. They paid $3500 for the house and ground, the abstract shows. That was 20 years ago, and the property is now valued at $150,000, and a 12-story concrete and steel building is to be erected on the site of the one time adobe house by the Commercial National bank, to cost $150,000.

After her husband died, the aged negress always declined to sell the downtown property. Several years ago she leased the building which now stands on the site to A. W. Bittick. Recently this lease was renewed for a period of 75 years by Mr. Bittick, who is associated with the Commercial National in the construction of the 12-story office and bank building.

Mary Woods had two brothers living in Frederickstown, Mo., and two nephews in El Paso. She made a will shortly before she died, although the contents of it have not been made public. The estate is valued at $160,000. Allen Woods, a nephew, cared for her and attended to her business for her.

PRISONER DIES OF SMALLPOX.

One of the Mexican federal prisoners in the smallpox detention camp at Fort Bliss died of smallpox Friday night. The funeral arrangements will be made by the Mexican consul. A child also died in birth Friday night. There are no new cases of smallpox at the camp.

CONCERT SUNDAY AT FORT BLISS

The band concert at Fort Bliss Sunday afternoon will be given by the 20th infantry band. The 15th cavalry band will play a concert at Washington park for the polo game. This was decided upon at 2 oclock Saturday afternoon. It was first announced that there would be no Sunday concert at the post as a result of the cavalry band playing at the polo game, but the 20th infantry band was later secured for the Sunday concert.

The cavalry band will play Monday at 3. The program appears on another page.

STOMACH SUFFERERS

If You Wish to Obtain Complete and Permanent Results Try

Mayr's Wonderful Stomach Remedy One Dose Will Convince You

FOREIGN BUTTER MAKES PRICE DROP

Influx of Commodity, Due to Tariff Reduction, Makes Wholesale Butter Price Lower.

New York, Jan. 31.—An influx of foreign butter from all parts of the world, due to the reduction of the tariff from five to 2 1-2 cents a pound, has caused a decline in the New York wholesale price of ten cents a pound since the first of the year.

Butter has been coming to this country from as far off as Australia by way of San Francisco. Three hundred thousand pounds from that country has been laid down here within the last two or three weeks. Butter has also been shipped from Argentine, Denmark and Siberia.

The shipments, butter dealers admitted, today, have created marked uneasiness in the wholesale market with the result that there has been an unloading of various stocks. Today the best grade butter was selling at 26 1-2 to 27 cents a pound, wholesale.

J. E. SANGER GETS FIVE-YEAR SENTENCE

J. Edward Sanger, charged with burglary, was sentenced to serve five years in the state penitentiary by a jury of the 34th district court Saturday at noon. Sanger pleaded guilty to the charge. The defendant was apprehended and held for the police by William Alberts, bookkeeper of the Commercial National bank, and George Fisher, a member of the school board, at the residence of J. A. White, 1112 Montana street, on the night of January 17.

Charles Patillo, aged 20 years, who was arrested at the same time and indicted with Sanger, may be reindicted. Sanger assumed entire responsibility for the alleged burglary, stating that he persuaded Patillo to join him. Under the charge of burglary at night of a private residence, five years is the minimum sentence. That is beyond the limit of the suspended sentence law.

TO REORGANIZE OLD FORT SUMNER CANAL

Santa Fe, N. M., Jan. 31.—New hope is inspired in the Fort Sumner region by the filing in the office of state engineer French of a notice of intention by James E. Pardue, trustee of the land owners under the Fort Sumner Canal company, to organize an irrigation district to take over the old system, which has gone through many vicissitudes, and to apply for 55 second feet from the Pecos river to irrigate about 7000 acres.

AMUSEMENTS.

MORE SPECIALS AT BIJOU.

"Indian Blood," a Kalem two part special that is thrilling with a splendid dramatic story, will be featured today. "A Night at the Inn," an Edison release, will also be on the bill.

Sunday, "Perils of the White Lights," with Anna Nilson, the pretty, popular actress, playing the lead, will be seen. This play will interest all, and especially the women.

Monday, "Pathe Weekly, No. 4" and "A Thief of Hearts," another two part special that you just can't afford to miss, will be shown. This picture shows a strong love story and also contains an excellent bull fight.—Advertisement.

CONTROVERSY OVER UNIVERSITY BITTER

Arizona State Senator Makes Charges Against Management and President Wilde Asks Investigation.

Tucson, Ariz., Jan. 31.—Starting at first with insinuations by a Phoenix newspaper, the controversy over the affairs of the state university burst into a state-wide sensation when state senator A. A. Worsley, a candidate for governor against governor Hunt, made grave charges against the state university management and Dr. Arthur Horace Wilde, the president, and the reply of Dr. Wilde. The fact that Worsley has stated he would make public a list of reasons why Hunt should not be reelected governor and the university having been one of the present governor's pet institutions, has given the controversy a political aspect.

The charges of Worsley are that there are seven children at the state deaf and dumb school, run as a part of the state university, and eight salaried officers and instructors connected with the school; that a student was summarily ejected from the school without reason; that students are quitting the state university for other universities; that one professor is employed at the university for every four students; that the per capita cost for each student is higher than in any other institution in the country; that attendance figures were inflated; that tuberculars are registered to secure cheap board but do not attend classes; that some of the professors are idle; that the 8-hour law is violated; that crime and luxury exist among the students.

Dr. Wilde's reply is a general denial.

No Investigation—Hunt.

Phoenix, Ariz., Jan. 31.—There is to be no official investigation of the charges of mismanagement at the university of Arizona, which have aroused such a furore in Tucson.

"I understand that senator A. A. Worsley has made to a Tucson paper some vague charges that scholarship rolls at the university are padded and that money is being misused," stated governor Hunt. "Certainly I do not intend to take any recognition of the charges. Senator Worsley spoke without being informed."

THE COURTS.

34TH DISTRICT COURT.

Dan M. Jackson, Presiding.

Rio Grande & El Paso Railroad company vs. Joe Goodman, et al, injunction; granted.

Frances Ethel Wilhelm vs. McClellan Wilhelm, suit for divorce and custody of minor child; granted.

Emily Endres vs. Adam Endres, suit for divorce; granted.

J. M. Worley, charged with burglary; given three years.

Frank Thompson, charged with forgery; given three years.

Frank Rowell, charged with theft over $50; remanded to juvenile court.

Owen Smith, charged with burglary; not guilty.

J. Edward Sanger, charged with burglary; given five years.

41ST DISTRICT COURT.

A. M. Walthall, Presiding.

J. B. Murchison vs. Texas & Pacific Railway company, et al, suit for

Although Mary Woods was born a slave, when she died in 1914 she was the richest African American in El Paso, leaving an estate worth $160,000. Mary migrated to El Paso from Missouri after the Civil War. Her husband, John Woods, was a constable in El Paso, and later the proprietor of a grocery store on El Paso Street. Around 1894, the couple bought a house on the corner of Mills Avenue and Mesa Street in the heart of downtown El Paso. (Courtesy of El Paso County Historical Society.)

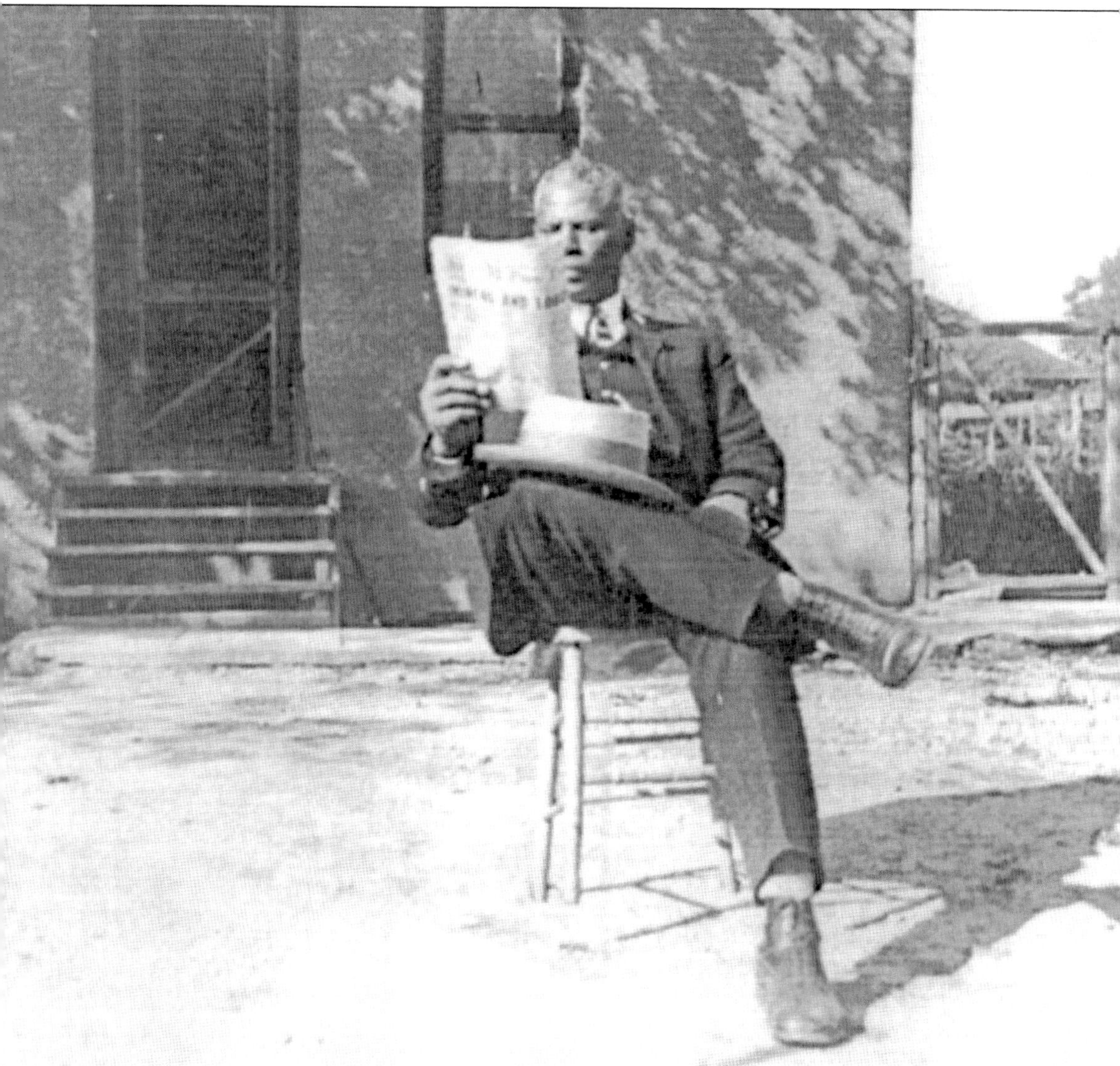

Ben Aldridge was a railroad employee in El Paso and a member of the Second Baptist Church. (Courtesy of Dr. Maceo Crenshaw Dailey Jr.)

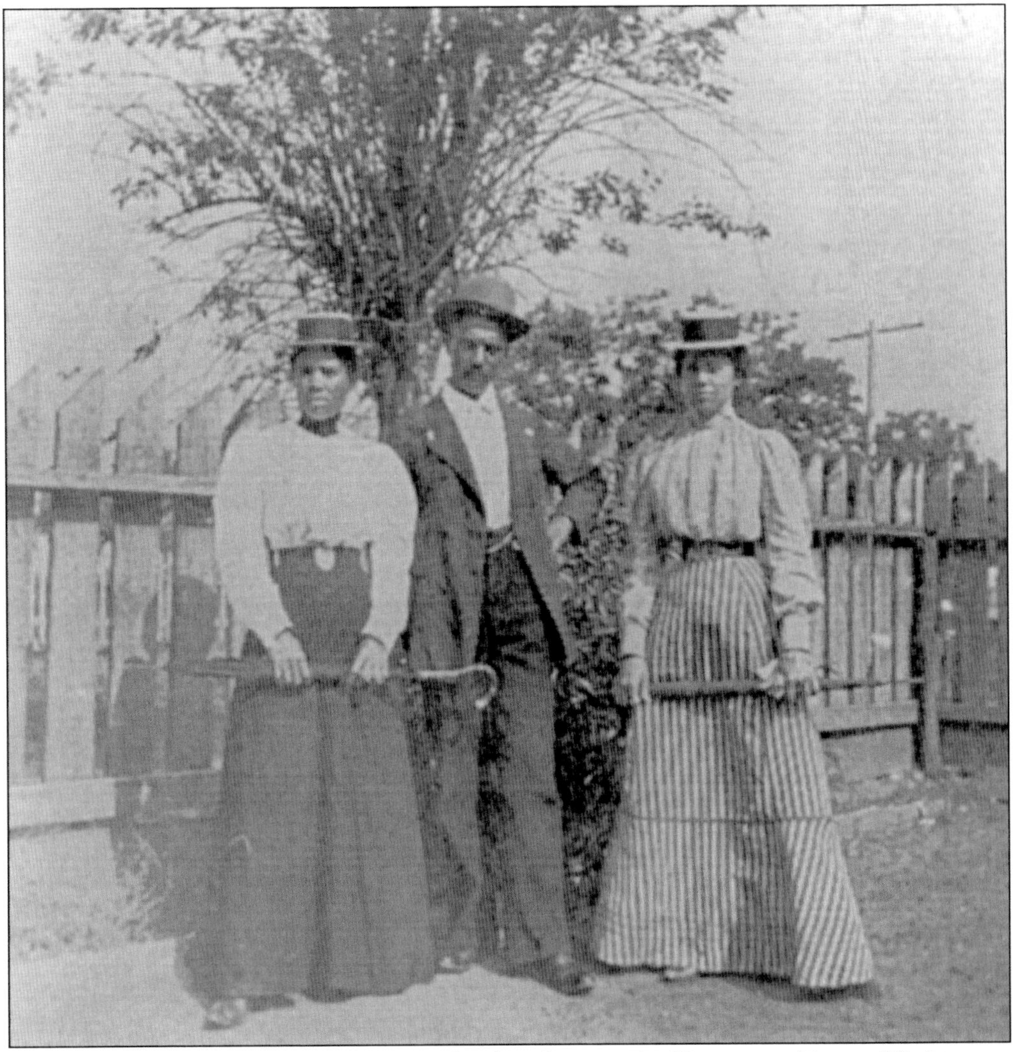

Ward and Della are dressed in fine attire for this photograph. (Courtesy of Leona Washington Photograph Collection, Department of Special Collections and Archives, University of Texas at El Paso Library.)

Three

A POISED COMMUNITY

1928–1955

Despite the Depression and World War II, the African American El Paso community remained focused on racial progress. The El Paso Black Chamber of Commerce's *Negro Business Directory of 1947* reveals black-owned hotels, beauty salons, barbershops, restaurants, and a taxicab company. The Murray Theatre, opened in 1949, showed movies ranging from *Tarzan's New York Adventure* to *Harlem on Parade*, but also noted in its advertisement that "It will be the future policy of this theater to present one all-colored cast picture each Sunday-Monday-Tuesday in connection with other first-class Pictures."

The theater's owner, G.H. Murray, was identified in the souvenir pamphlet issued on the occasion of the opening of the theatre in 1949 as an "outstanding businessman and Real Estate Broker [who] has given unstintingly of his time, money, and talent to his church." Murray's mindset was indicative of many blacks in El Paso, including Mr. and Mrs. J.M. Washington, owners of the Golden Moon Hotel Bar and Café; Olalee McCall, principal of Douglass High School; and Marvin E. Williams, founder of the *Southwest Torch* newspaper.

Though distant and seemingly disconnected from mainstream black America, the African American El Paso community found itself knowledgeable and in step with uplift activities by bringing in, to speak or perform, nationally known blacks such as poet Langston Hughes and divas Marian Anderson and Philippa Schuyler.

The community's efforts to open El Paso African Americans to wider opportunities is evident in the hiring of the first black uniformed patrol officer, Roscoe Roberts, by the police department. Undoubtedly, the major achievement of the city's black community was its successful challenge to the segregationist law that prevented Douglass High School alumna and valedictorian Thelma White from entering Texas Western College (now the University of Texas at El Paso). The lawsuit, handled capably by the local and state branches of the NAACP, resulted in 12 black students entering the formerly all-white institution of higher learning in 1955.

Having obtained resources and skills to contest their déclassé situation in the city, black El Pasoans continued to develop their community as well as challenge, more formidably, segregationist views that restricted and marginalized them.

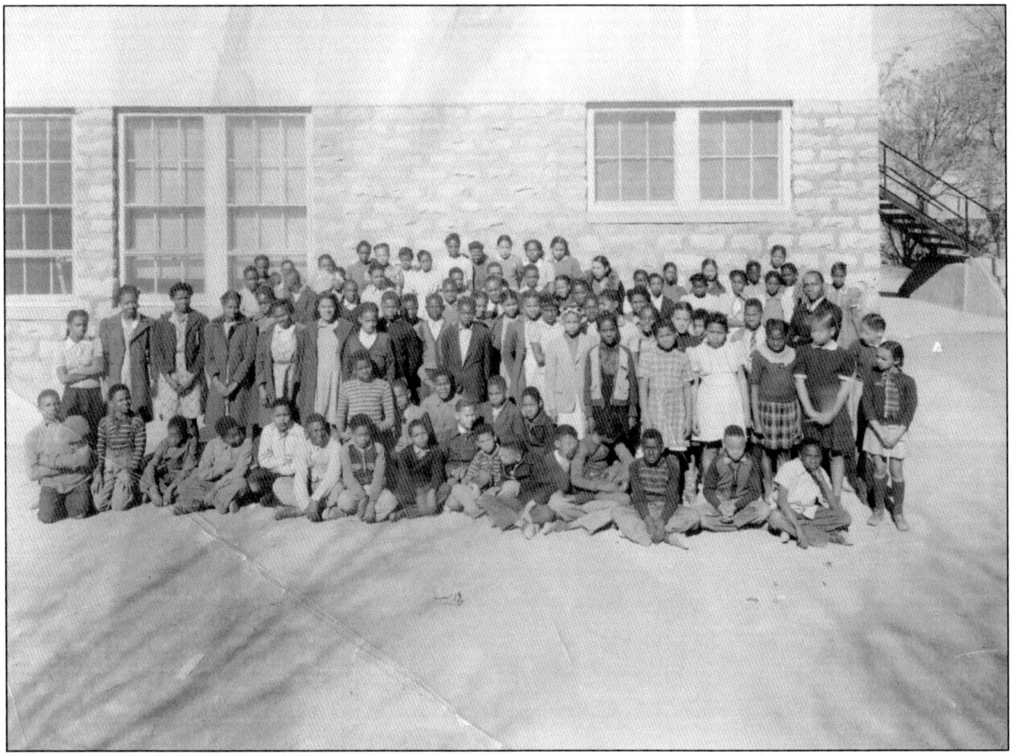

Principal Olalee McCalls, George Chandler, and Estine Davis posed with their students in front of Douglas school. By this time, in the 1940s, the number of students had increased to 383. (Courtesy of the Department of Special Collections and Archives, University of Texas at El Paso Library.)

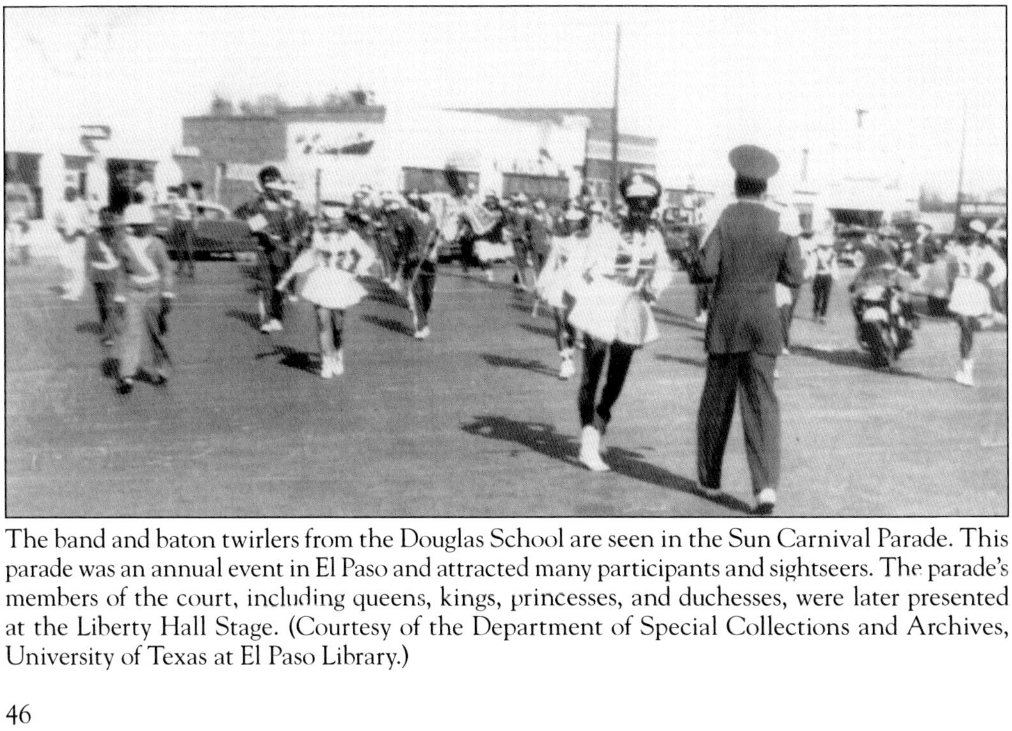

The band and baton twirlers from the Douglas School are seen in the Sun Carnival Parade. This parade was an annual event in El Paso and attracted many participants and sightseers. The parade's members of the court, including queens, kings, princesses, and duchesses, were later presented at the Liberty Hall Stage. (Courtesy of the Department of Special Collections and Archives, University of Texas at El Paso Library.)

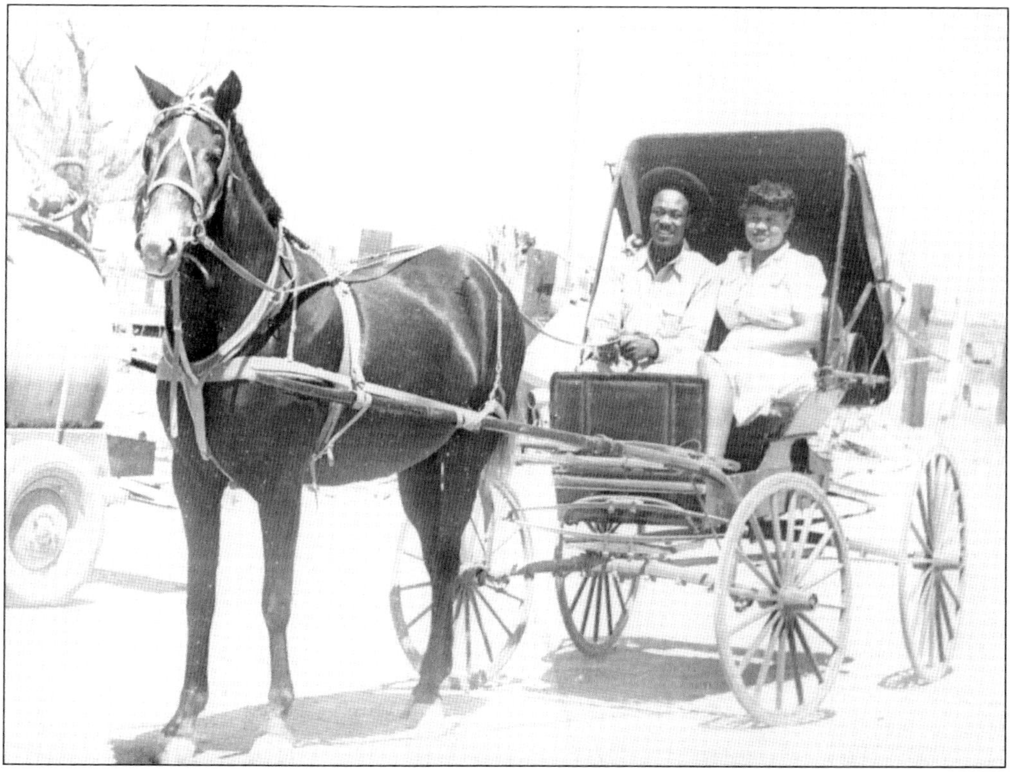

Ernie and Mary Aldridge took a ride around town in this horse-drawn cart in the 1940s. While automobiles sped through the streets of El Paso at this time, the horse-and-buggy hailed back to previous decades when the pace was slower. (Courtesy of the Department of Special Collections and Archives, University of Texas at El Paso Library.)

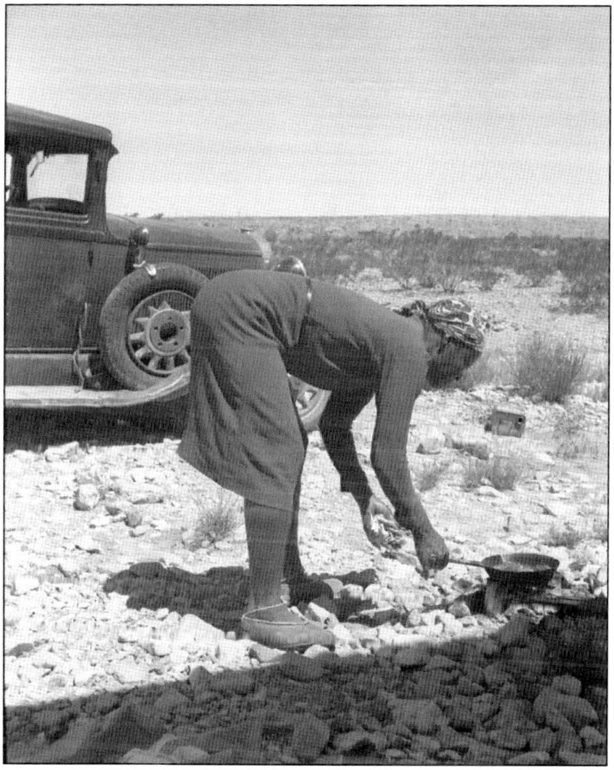

This 1938 Dorothea Lange photograph shows a woman cooking a meal for her family outside of El Paso. Since many African Americans were relegated to low-paying jobs, they often moved in with family or became transients for a time before they could afford a home. (Courtesy of the Library of Congress.)

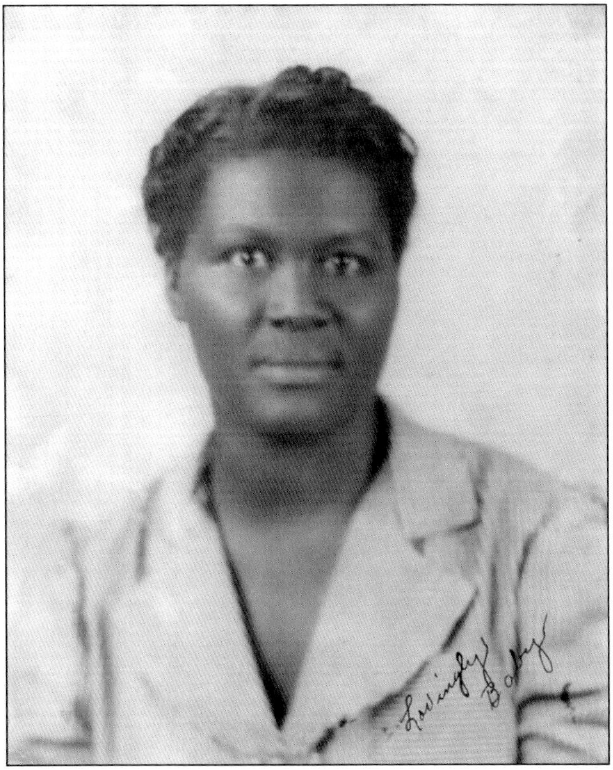

Gertrude Gafford McGrew came to El Paso in 1915 when she was four years old with her grandmother Ellen Gafford, her aunt Etta, and her father. Gertrude worked at the El Paso Woolworth store, and in 1941, she married Jesse B. McGrew, who was a doughboy in France during World War I. After the war, the couple moved to Vado, New Mexico, a community just 31 miles north of El Paso. After Jesse McGrew passed away, Gertrude moved back to El Paso in 1999, where she resided until her death in 2006. (Courtesy of the Hills family.)

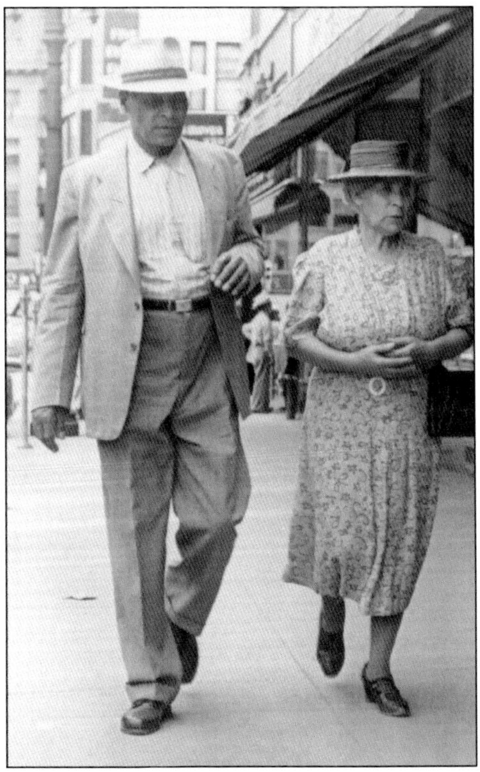

B.H. and Amelia Aldridge stroll downtown in this 1941 photograph. (Courtesy of the Department of Special Collections and Archives, University of Texas at El Paso Library.)

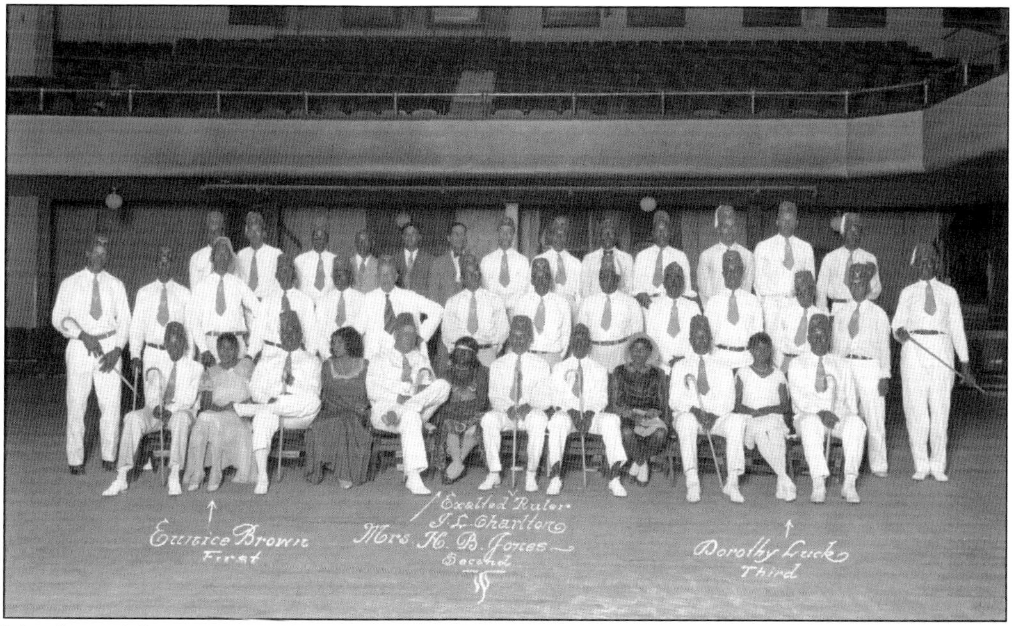

Members of the Gateway Elks Lodge posed for this photograph in 1930. The Elks Club nationally harks back to 1898 with founders Arthur J. Riggs and Benjamin Franklin Howard. The Improved Benevolent Protective Order of the Elks catered to issues concerning African Americans, namely segregation. This group sought racial uplift and cultural pride for its members and provided leadership and educational opportunities. They espoused patriotism and aided those in need within the community. (Courtesy of Stout-Feldman Studio Photographs Collection, Department of Special Collections and Archives, University of Texas at El Paso Library.)

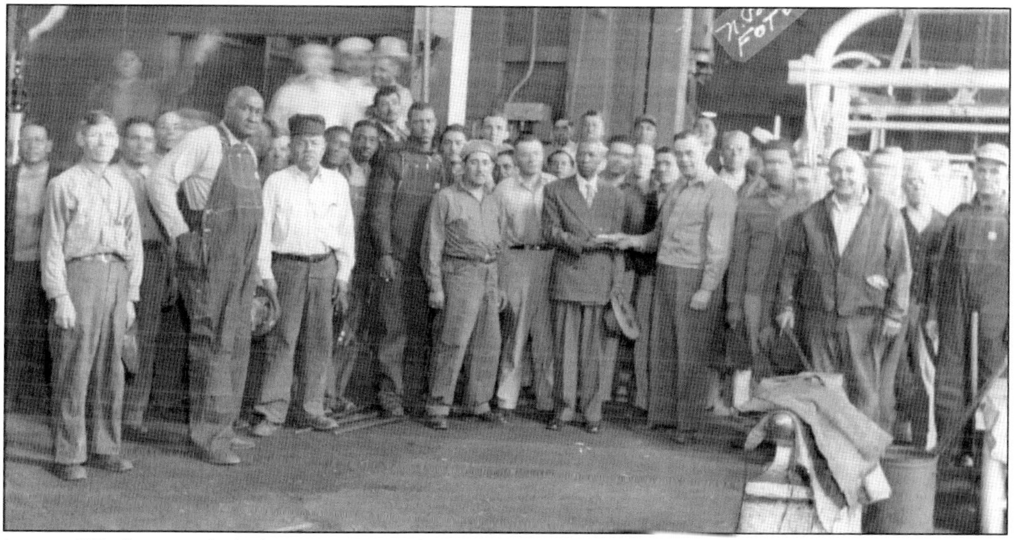

Leona Washington's father, in suit and tie, received his retirement award from the Southern Pacific Railroad for his long service as a blacksmith. The Southern Pacific station was located on Franklin Street between Stanton and Kansas Streets. In 1904, the railroad and the city built Union Station. Many African Americans arrived in El Paso because of the railroad. They found jobs as porters, cooks, and maintenance workers. (Courtesy of the Department of Special Collections and Archives, University of Texas at El Paso Library.)

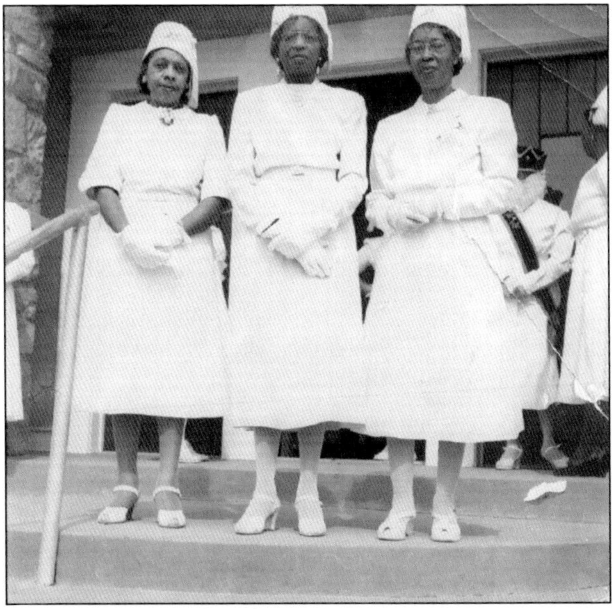

From left to right, Minnie Hayworth, Mrs. King Phillips, and Marie Bloodworth were members of the Star of the West Chapter No. 51 of the Order of the Eastern Star. This organization for blacks began nationally in 1874 as a women's organization affiliated with the male Masons. Each chapter hosted two male members, a patron and his assistant. Female membership for this group was contingent on their relationship with a Mason. (Courtesy of the Department of Special Collections and Archives, University of Texas at El Paso Library.)

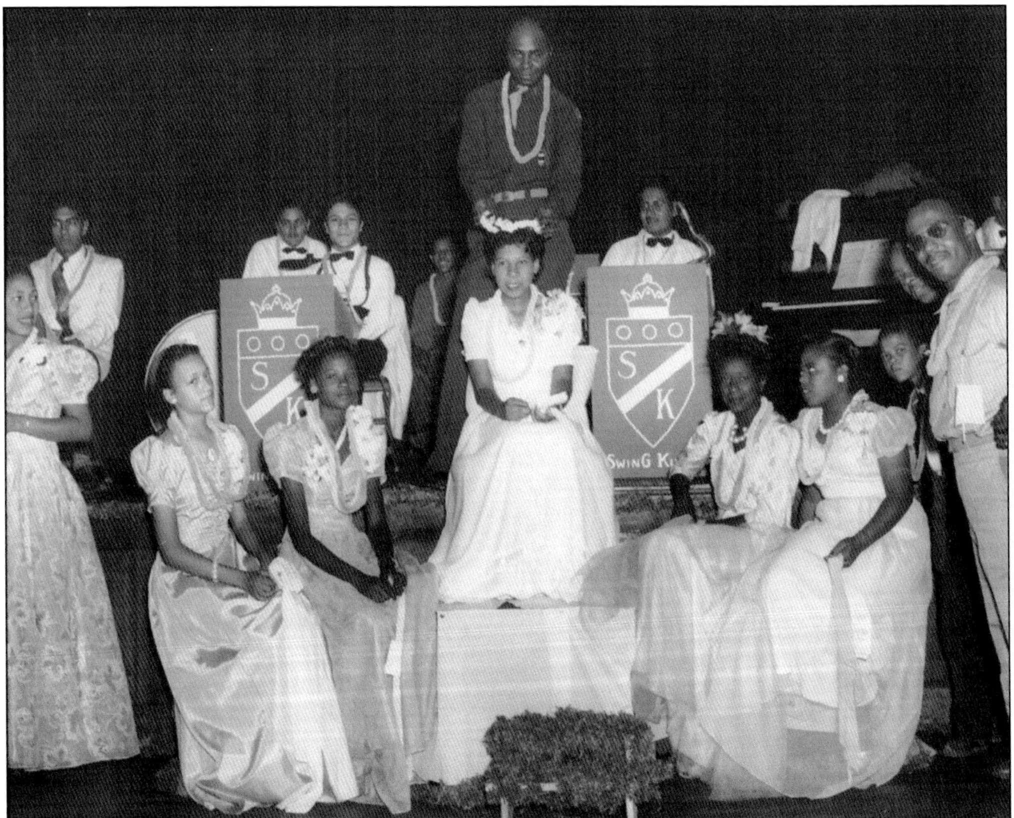

In 1940, the United Service Organization (USO) crowned its queen. Seated are Monty Earl Mattias, Maryanne Butler, Constance Anderson, Kathy Lee Patton, and Ruby Joe Williams. (Courtesy of the Department of Special Collections and Archives, University of Texas at El Paso Library.)

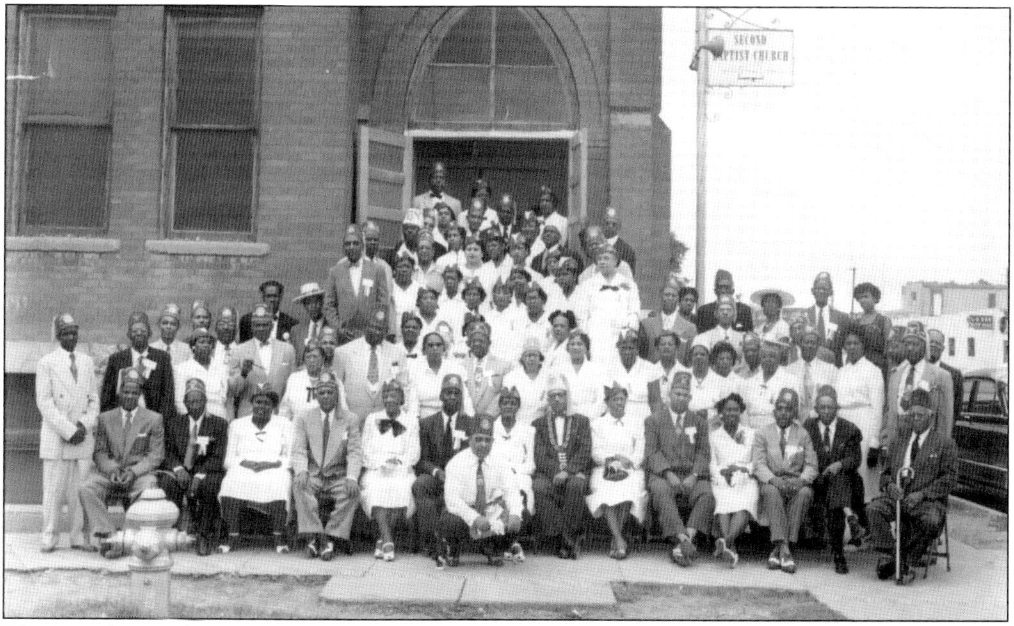

The Daughters of Iris, Oro Temple No. 9 is pictured with members of the Second Baptist Church on Virginia Street. The Daughters of Iris began nationally in 1901 and espoused principles of patriotism, loyalty, and faithfulness. They served their community through acts of charity. (Courtesy of the Department of Special Collections and Archives, University of Texas at El Paso Library.)

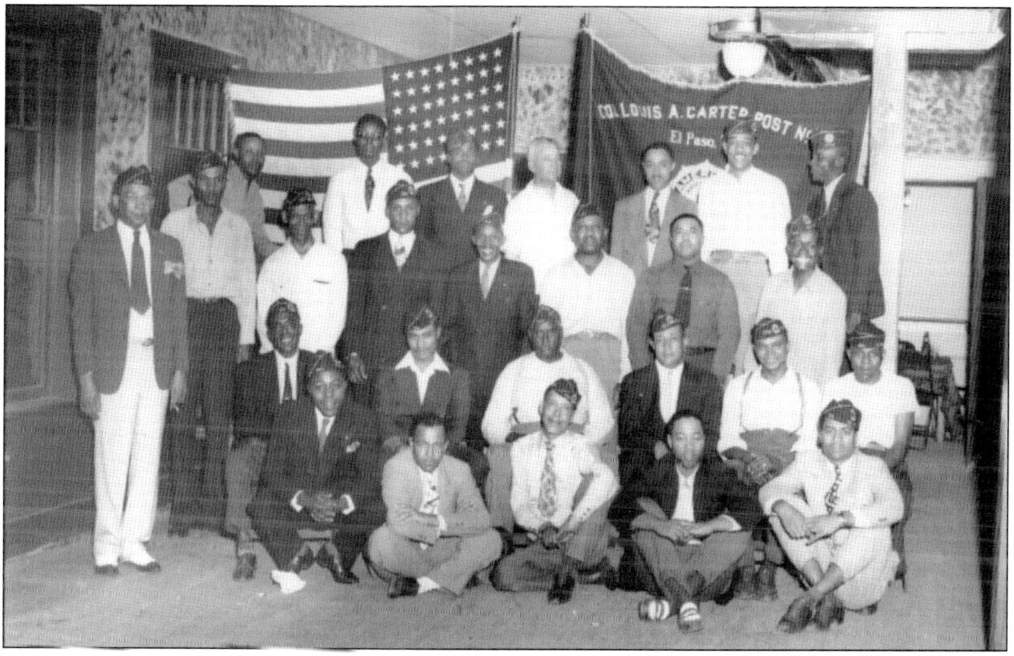

Members of the Col. Louis A. Carter Post No. 58A of the American Legion Club pose in their meeting room. The American Legion in Texas is a nonpolitical organization started after World War I, which aided veterans through legislation to secure access to hospitals, rehabilitation programs, and finding employment. (Courtesy of the Department of Special Collections and Archives, University of Texas at El Paso Library.)

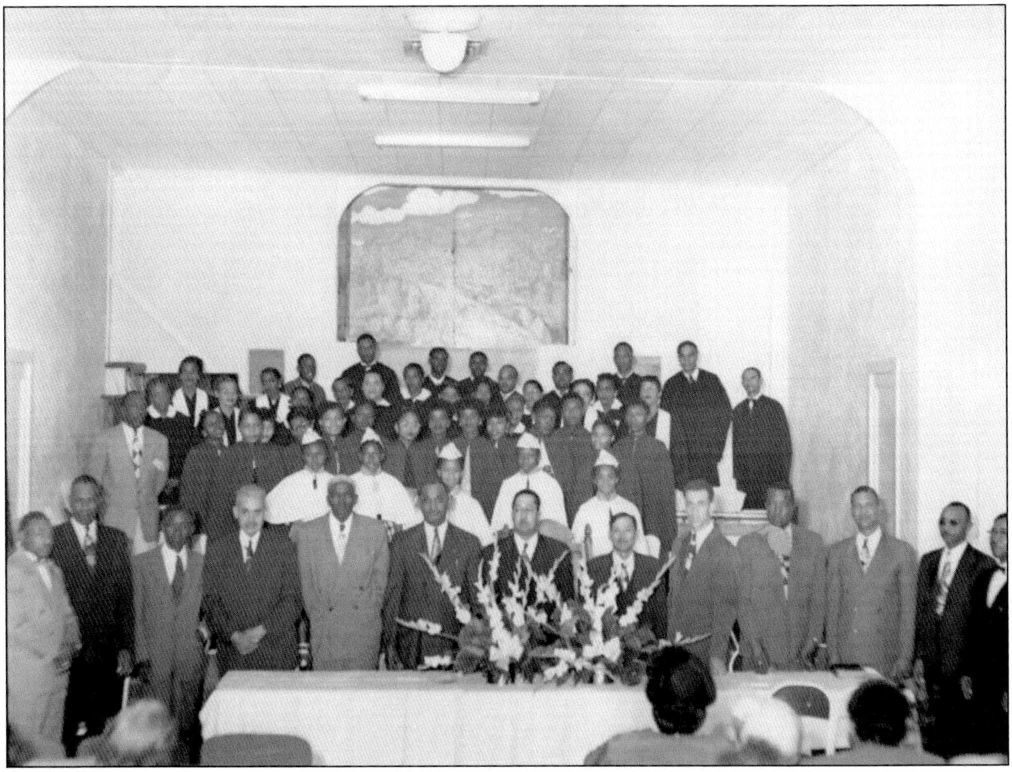

Reverend Butler, pictured at center behind the flowers, posed for this picture with some of the congregation of the Shiloh Baptist Church. Shiloh Baptist Church was organized in 1910 by Rev. G.W. Gradington and met in the pastor's home before moving to Magoffin Avenue, where they worshipped for almost 10 years. Under the leadership of Rev. F.O. Brown, the congregation relocated to 3201 Frutas Avenue in 1921. (Courtesy of the Department of Special Collections and Archives, University of Texas at El Paso Library.)

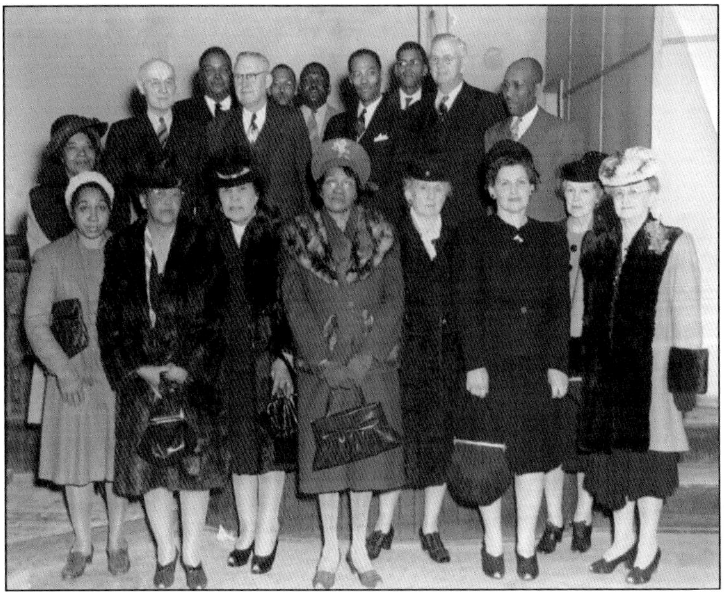

The McCall Day Center board is pictured here in the 1940s. Among those in the first row are Sadie Collins and Anita Bush. In the third row are Dr. Collins, William Davis, Reverend Crenshaw, Immanuel Campbell, Reverend Dale, and the principal of Douglass School, Honesbury. (Courtesy of the Department of Special Collections and Archives, University of Texas at El Paso Library.)

YWCA program committee members (from left to right) Aguilla Jones, program assistant; Drusilla Nixon, chairman; and Sadie Collins are pictured here. Ruth G. Jackson was the "director of Negro work" at this time. (Courtesy of Dr. William McIver and Edna Nixon McIver.)

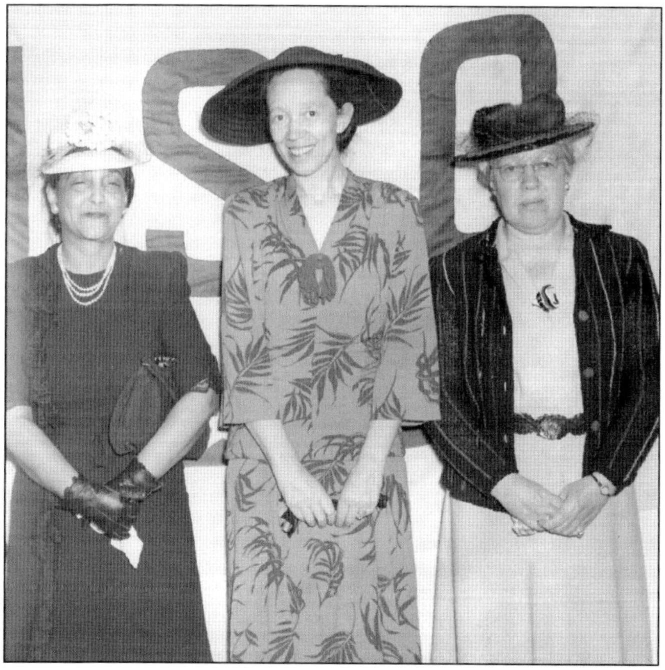

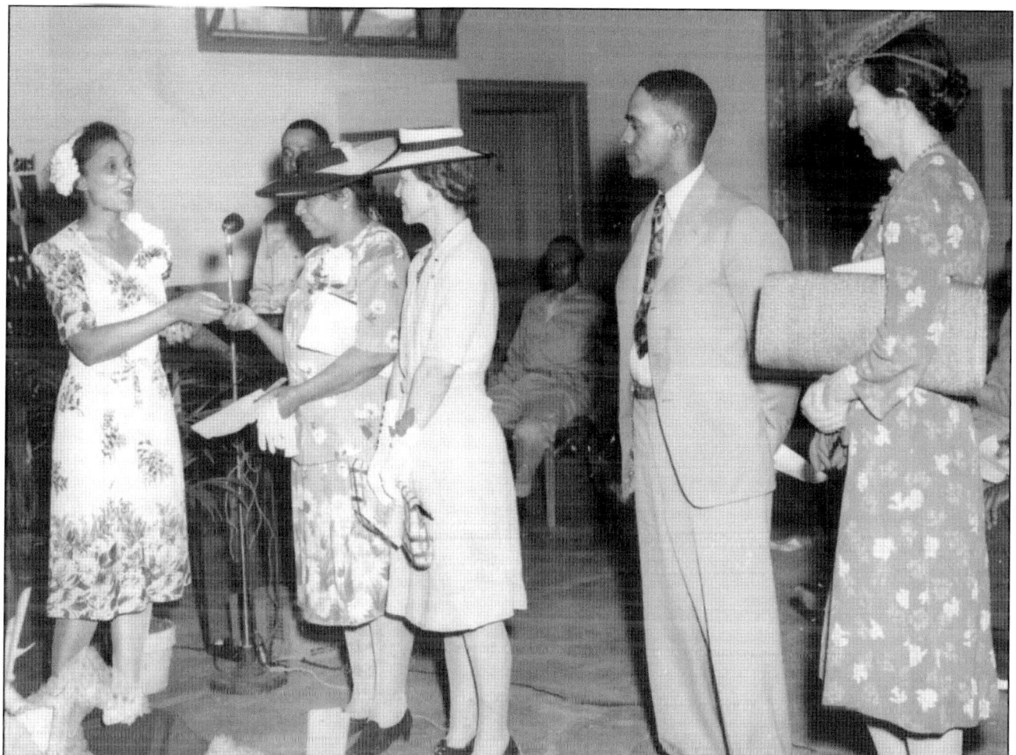

Lollie Ford (second from left), Leona Ford Washington's mother, received an award witnessed by Mrs. Matthis and Drusilla Nixon. (Courtesy of the Department of Special Collections and Archives, University of Texas at El Paso Library.)

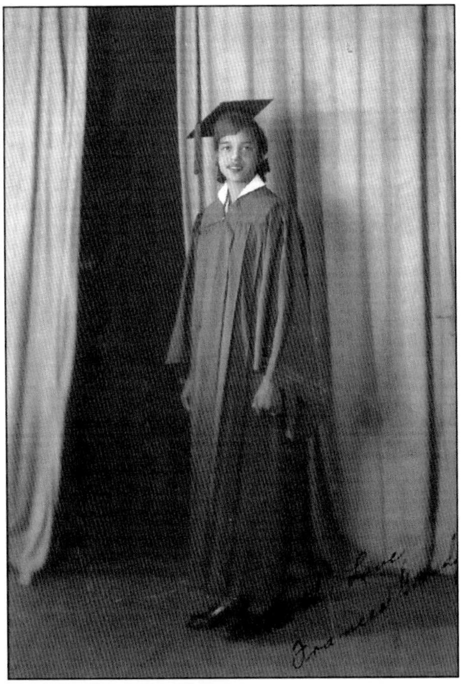

Frances Marie Grundy Hills, born in 1925, is a third-generation El Pasoan. Her earliest memories as a child were of playing on Park Street and attending Second Baptist Church. Frances attended Douglass School, which she loved, and received numerous perfect attendance records. After she received her bachelor's degree, she returned to Douglass to teach, and later taught at Talladega College. During her summers, she worked for the USO. She received a mathematics degree from the University of New Mexico and worked as a civilian ballistic computer at Fort Bliss. (Courtesy of Hills family.)

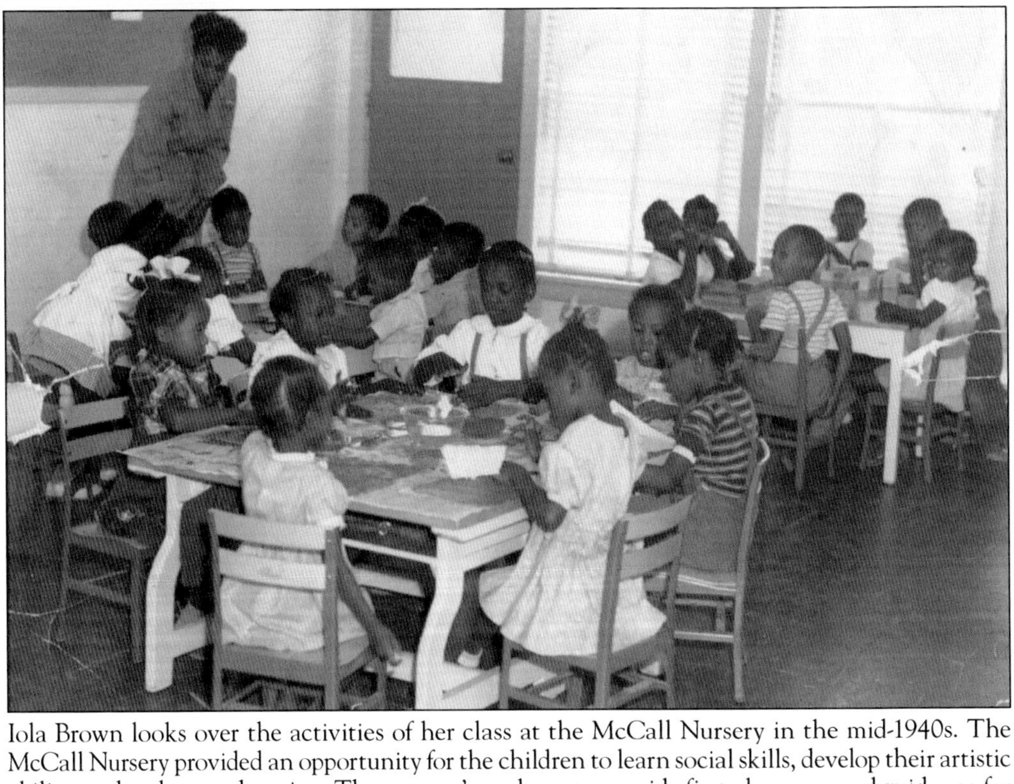

Iola Brown looks over the activities of her class at the McCall Nursery in the mid-1940s. The McCall Nursery provided an opportunity for the children to learn social skills, develop their artistic ability, and embrace education. The nursery's goal was to provide first-class care and guidance for children of working parents. (Courtesy of the Department of Special Collections and Archives, University of Texas at El Paso Library.)

This serviceman danced for the camera. Many military personnel were stationed at Fort Bliss during World War II. Many of them came back to the area after the war's end, contributing to the growth of the African American community in El Paso. (Courtesy of the Department of Special Collections and Archives, University of Texas at El Paso Library.)

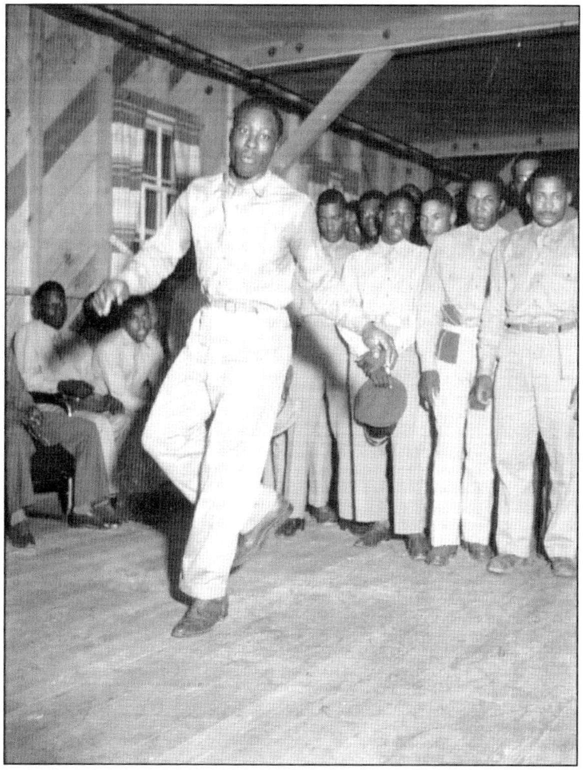

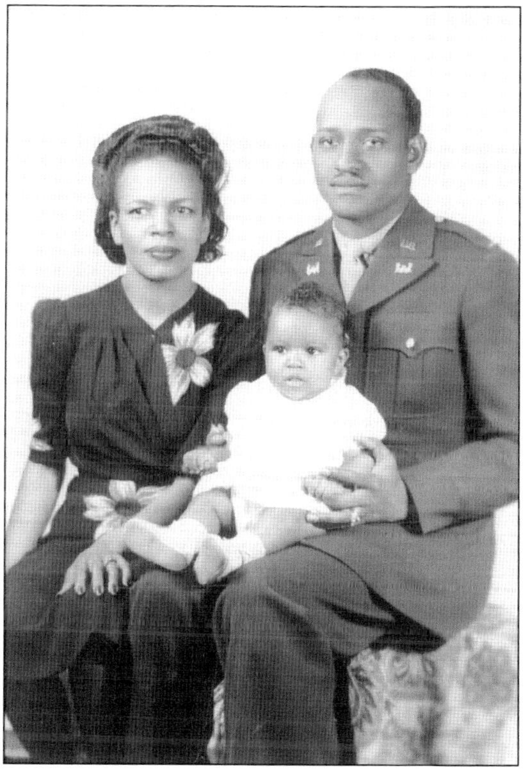

Rose, George, and baby Gerolyn Chandler sat for this photograph in the 1940s. George Chandler served in World War II and returned to El Paso after the war. He taught English and choir at Douglass School. (Courtesy of the Department of Special Collections and Archives, University of Texas at El Paso Library.)

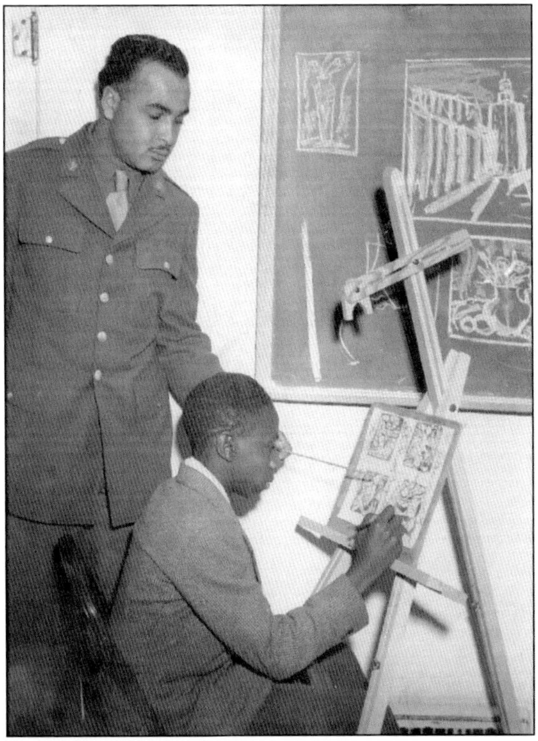

This photograph, taken between 1947 and 1949, shows a USO art class student being instructed by his professor. (Courtesy of Dr. Maceo Crenshaw Dailey Jr.)

Ruth Sumpter posed with soldiers. (Courtesy of Leona Washington Photograph Collection, Department of Special Collections and Archives, University of Texas at El Paso Library.)

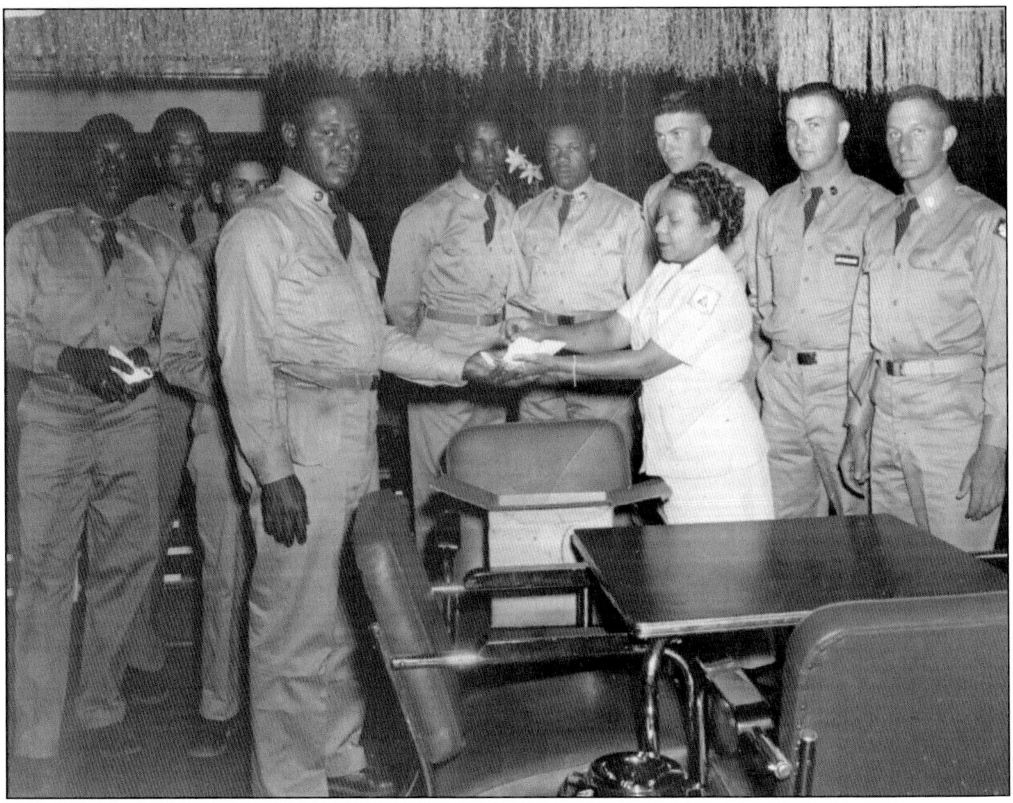

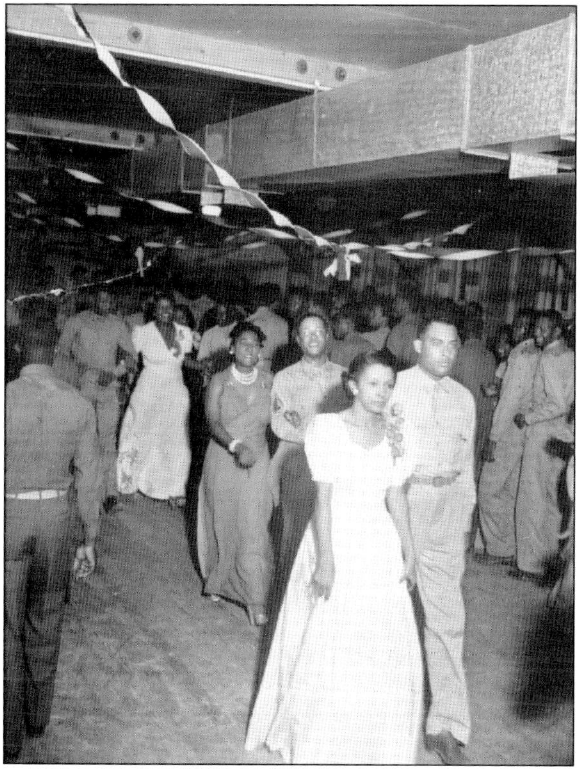

Servicemen and their dates are pictured enjoying a night of dancing and relaxing in their formal attire at the USO YWCA Negro Center on Myrtle Avenue. (Courtesy of the Department of Special Collections and Archives, University of Texas at El Paso Library.)

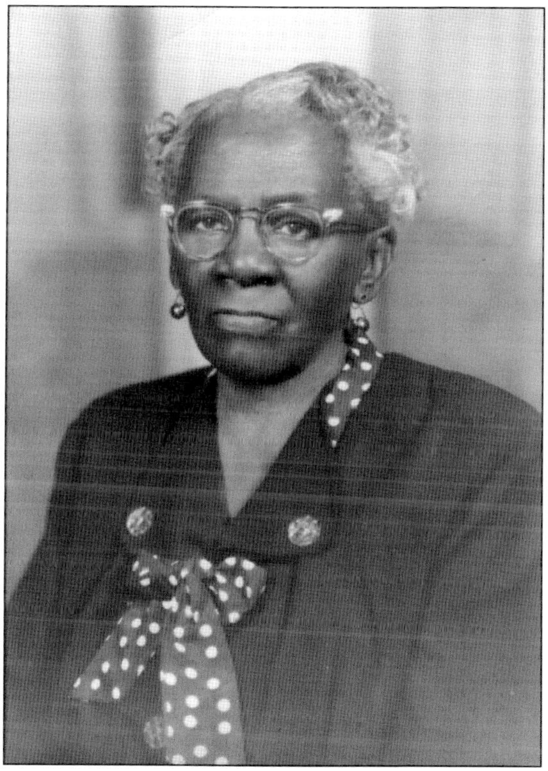

Mattie Gafford Grundy was Ellen A. Gafford's daughter and Frances Grundy Hills's paternal grandmother. She was born around 1874. In 1940, she lived on Bassett Avenue in El Paso with her mother, Ellen, and her sisters Etta Gafford and Lillian Cole. (Courtesy of the Hills family.)

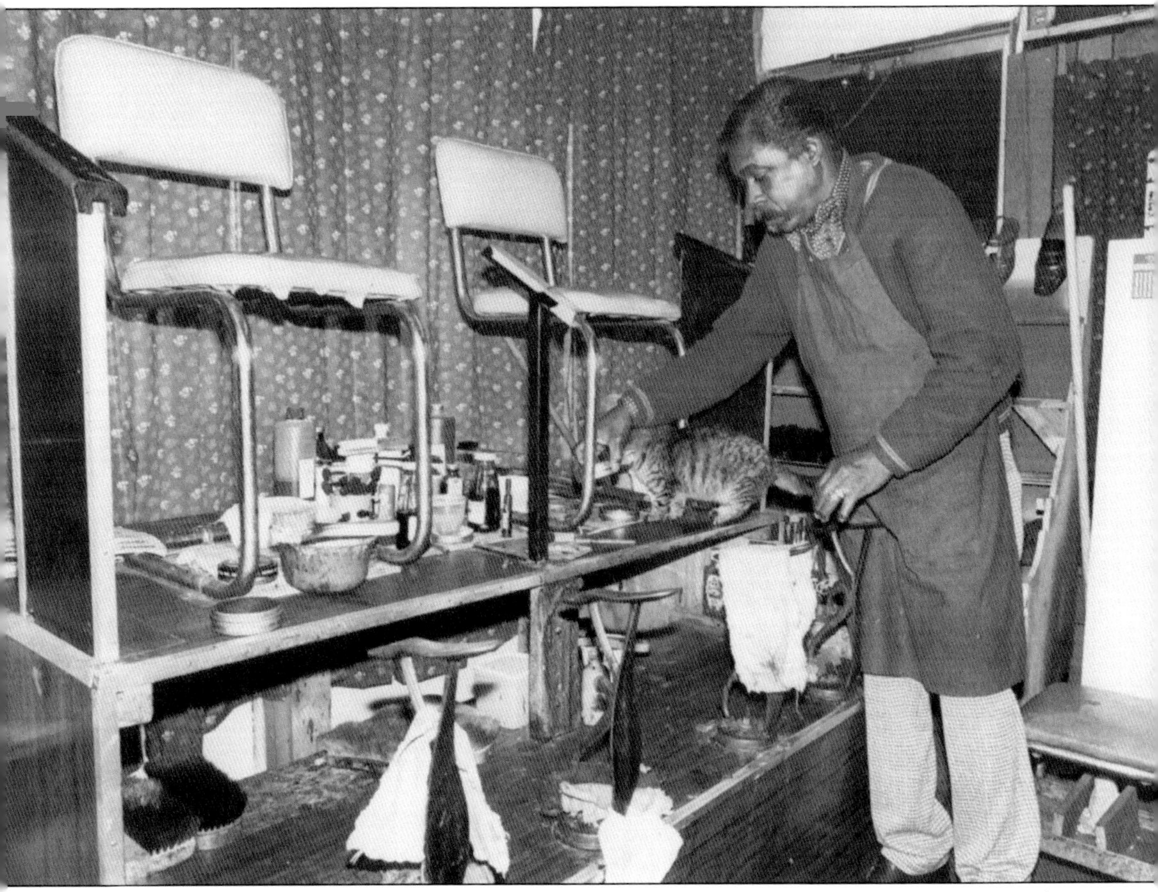

James Kelly feeds his cat in this photograph. Kelly owned and operated a shoe shine parlor on Oregon Street. He shined shoes for 15 years in El Paso and later brought in his two sons, who helped him during the summer and after school. (Courtesy of the Department of Special Collections and Archives, University of Texas at El Paso Library.)

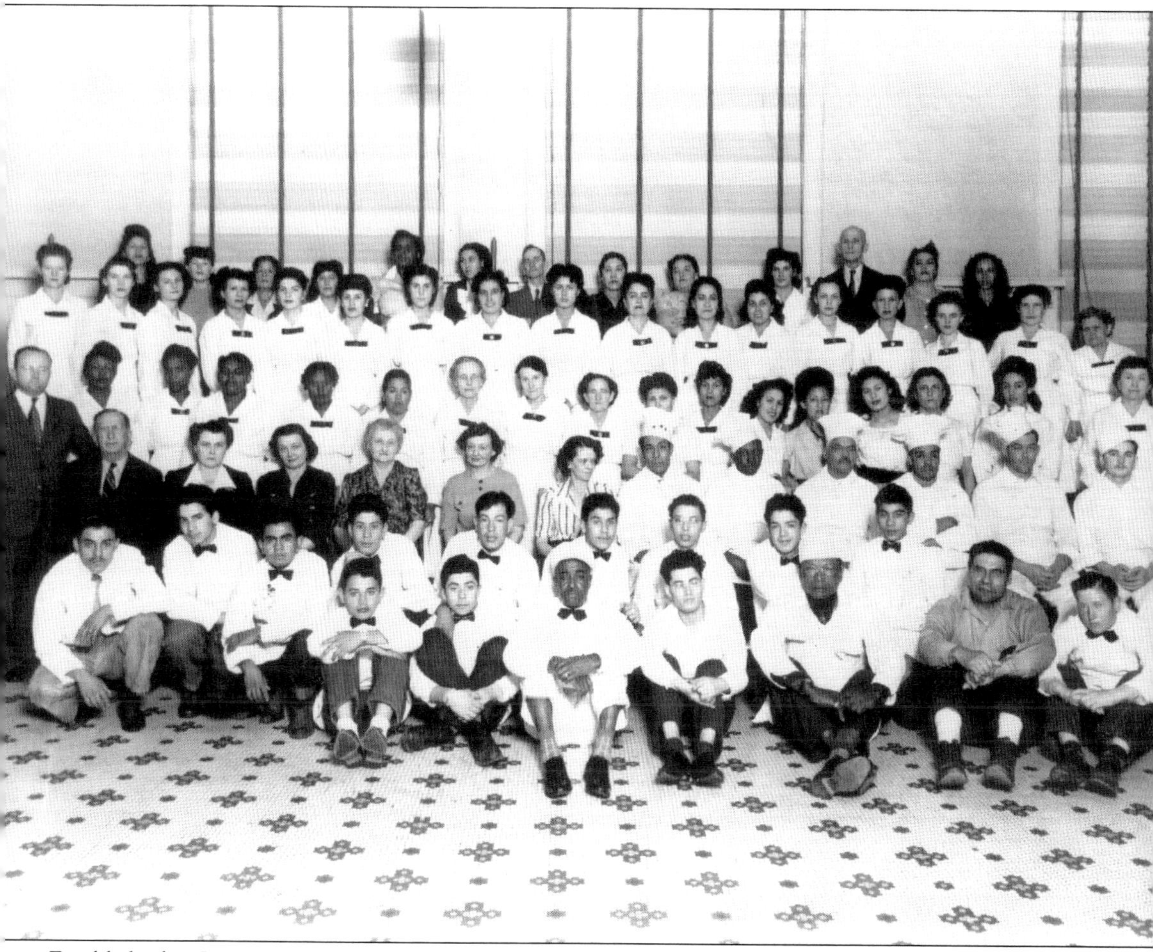

Established in January 1876 in Topeka, Kansas, as the first train depot restaurant, the Fred Harvey Company operated eateries along railway lines throughout the West. After racial skirmishes in New Mexico, Harvey relegated blacks to the kitchen and out of the public eye. This photograph of the Atchison, Topeka & Santa Fe Railway Company's Fred Harvey House staff in El Paso, dated between 1945 and 1959, reveals that black men and women were employed, contrary to published reports that there were never any black "Harvey Girls," the moniker given to females employed by the company. (Courtesy of the Kansas Historical Society.)

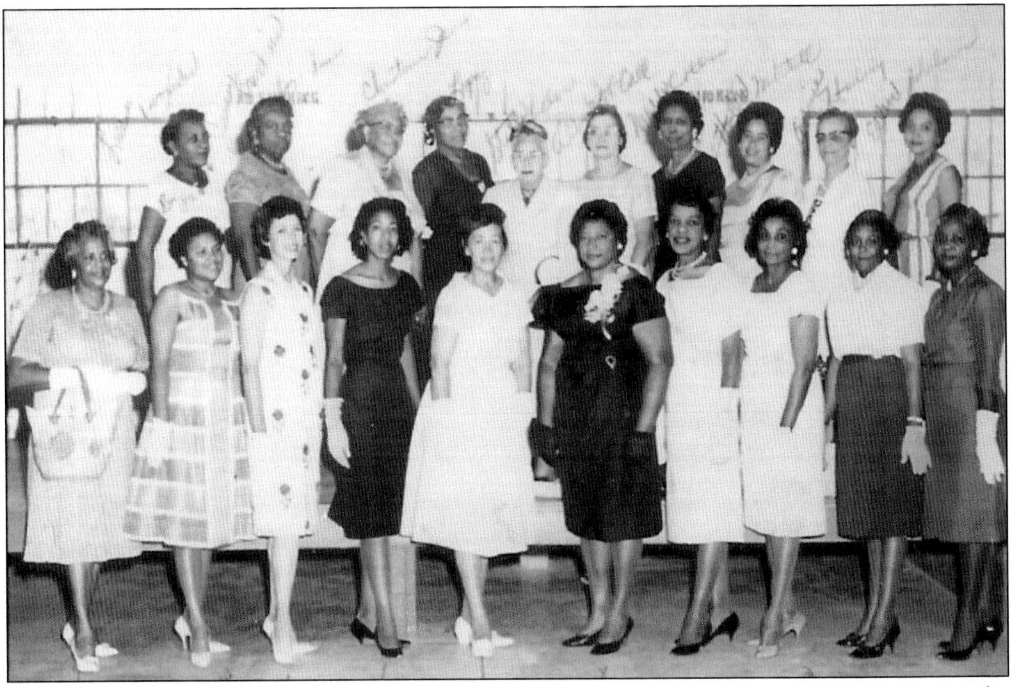

The Phillis Wheatley Club in El Paso was established in 1933 as a center of civic activities for women of color. The club was named in honor of Phillis Wheatley, a slave poet who lived from 1753 to 1784. (Courtesy of McCall Neighborhood Center.)

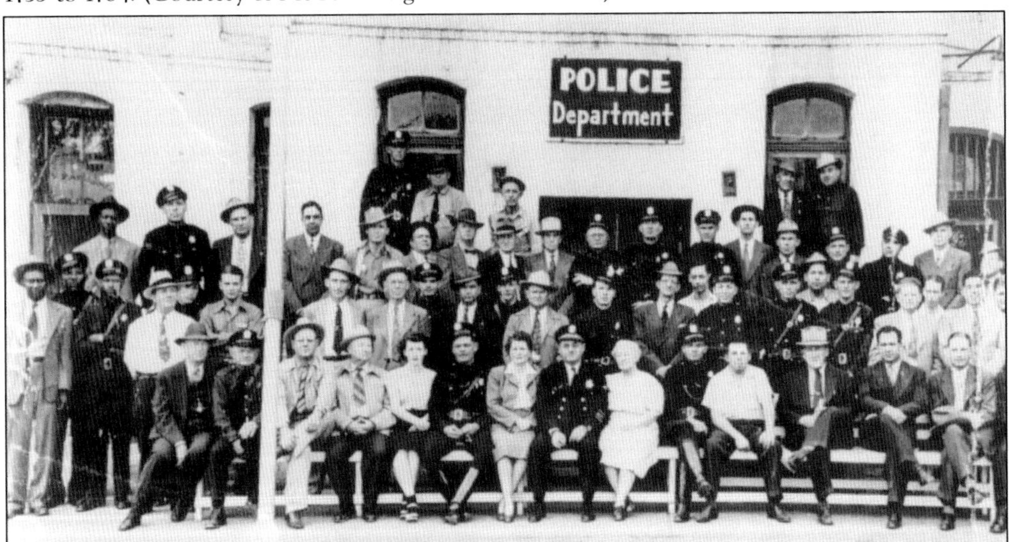

Given the disruption involving black military personnel in El Paso in the early 1940s, white city leaders engaged in discussion with El Paso's black ministers regarding changing employment policies and practices. In 1946, upon the recommendation of Rev. Osborne A. Crenshaw of Second Baptist Church, Roscoe Roberts and John Golston became the first two of four black recruits of the El Paso Police Department. Anita Person Dailey at American Airlines in 1965 and Rufus Wilson and Dexter Huff in the El Paso Fire Department in 1971 were two of the more notable results of these civil rights changes. (Courtesy of Dr. Maceo Crenshaw Dailey Jr.)

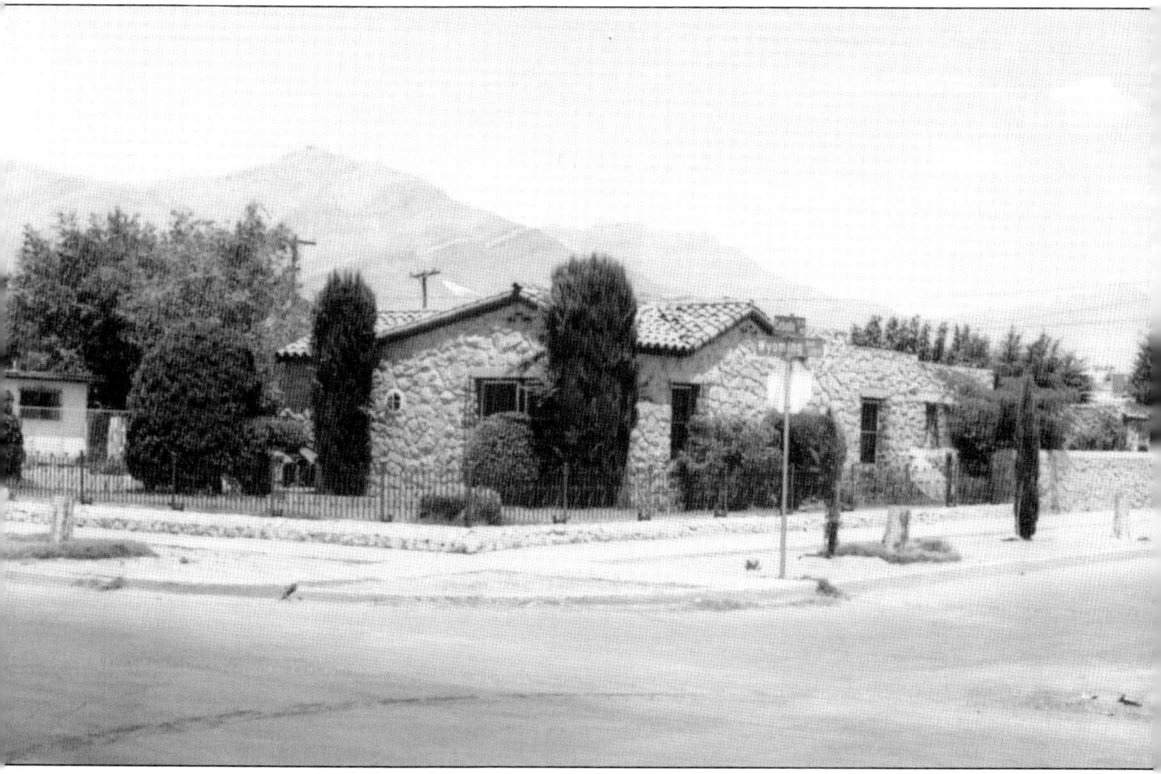

McCall Neighborhood Center was the home of Marshall McCall and Olalee McCall. The couple built their home at 3231 East Wyoming Avenue out of stone and rock. The sturdy structure and property was purchased in 1985 by the city, and it became the McCall Neighborhood Center. The building has been expanded and is home to a historical marker for Henry O. Flipper and Dr. Lawrence Nixon. (Courtesy of the Department of Special Collections and Archives, University of Texas at El Paso Library.)

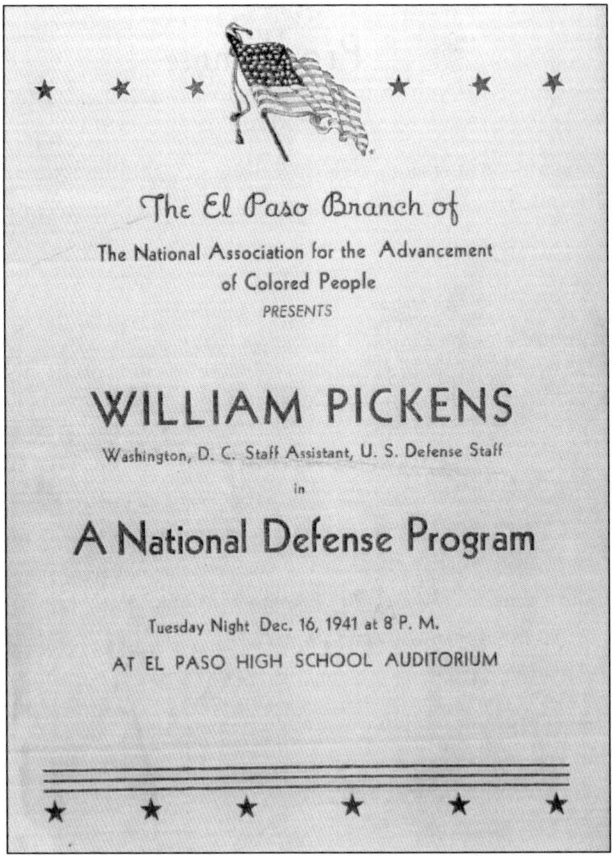

The El Paso Branch of
The National Association for the Advancement
of Colored People
PRESENTS

WILLIAM PICKENS
Washington, D. C. Staff Assistant, U. S. Defense Staff
in

A National Defense Program

Tuesday Night Dec. 16, 1941 at 8 P. M.
AT EL PASO HIGH SCHOOL AUDITORIUM

Local members of the NAACP held a meeting in 1913 to organize a branch for this city. In June 1914, members held their first meeting. Their most prescient leaders were Dr. Lawrence A. Nixon, Le Roy White, and L.W. Washington, who all saw the need for blacks to organize to deal with oppression. The El Paso branch remains an informed and vigorous group. Its executive committee during the 1940s represented a "Who's Who" list of the city's African American population. They brought William L. Pickens, former field secretary of the NAACP, who served in the early 1940s in the US treasury department, to speak about progressive politics, civil rights concerns, and patriotism. (Both, courtesy of Dr. Maceo Crenshaw Dailey Jr.)

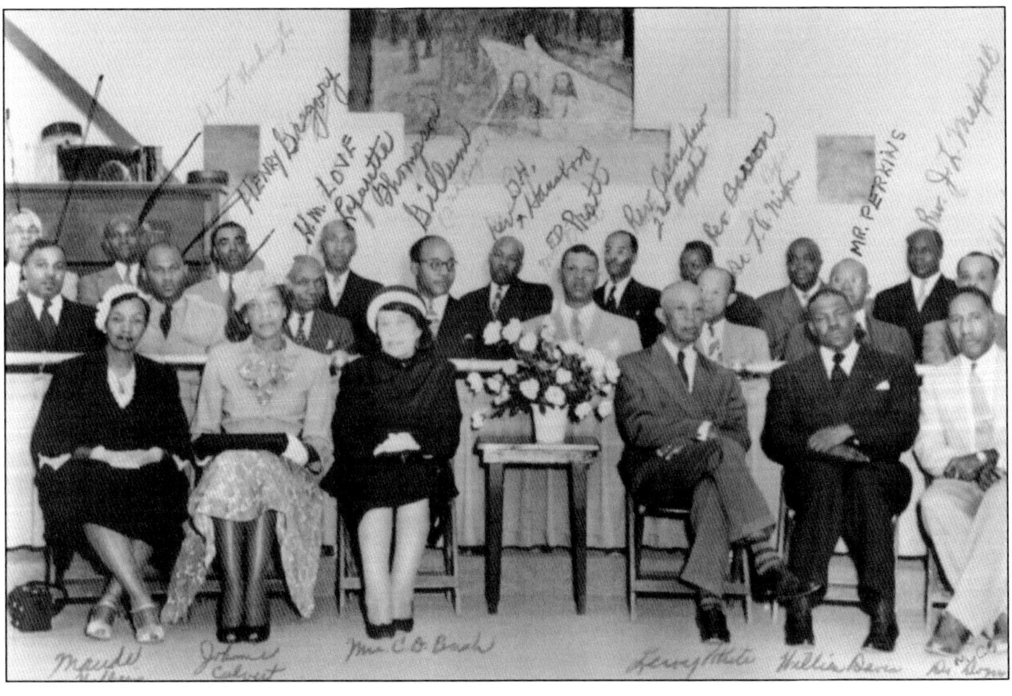

Restrictive covenants were agreements new-home purchasers, who were primarily white, signed in which they agreed not to resell their properties to various other ethnic groups, such as African Americans, Asian Americans, and Hispanic Americans. This one is from the Deed Records of El Paso County in 1939, forbidding property from being "sold to nor occupied by Negroes." The practice was declared "unenforceable" in the Supreme Court case *Shelley v. Kraemer* in 1948. (Courtesy of El Paso County Public Records.)

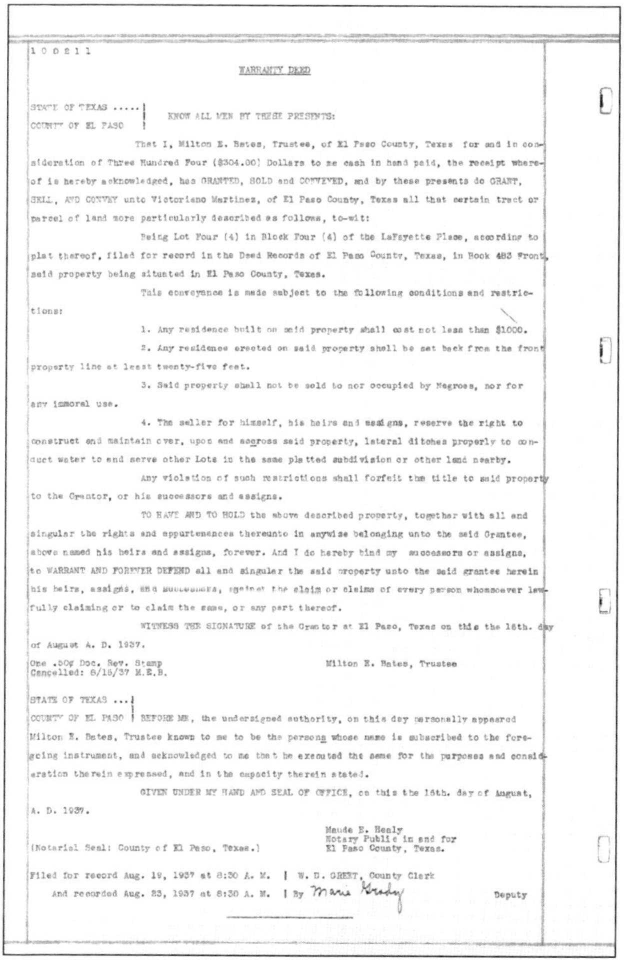

100211

WARRANTY DEED

STATE OF TEXAS .....
COUNTY OF EL PASO
KNOW ALL MEN BY THESE PRESENTS:

That I, Milton E. Bates, Trustee, of El Paso County, Texas for and in consideration of Three Hundred Four ($304.00) Dollars to me cash in hand paid, the receipt whereof is hereby acknowledged, has GRANTED, SOLD and CONVEYED, and by these presents do GRANT, SELL, AND CONVEY unto Victoriano Martinez, of El Paso County, Texas all that certain tract or parcel of land more particularly described as follows, to-wit:

Being Lot Four (4) in Block Four (4) of the LaFayette Place, according to plat thereof, filed for record in the Deed Records of El Paso County, Texas, in Book 483 Front, said property being situated in El Paso County, Texas.

This conveyance is made subject to the following conditions and restrictions:

1. Any residence built on said property shall cost not less than $1000.

2. Any residence erected on said property shall be set back from the front property line at least twenty-five feet.

3. Said property shall not be sold to nor occupied by Negroes, nor for any immoral use.

4. The seller for himself, his heirs and assigns, reserve the right to construct and maintain over, upon and accross said property, lateral ditches properly to conduct water to and serve other Lots in the same platted subdivision or other land nearby.

Any violation of such restrictions shall forfeit the title to said property to the Grantor, or his successors and assigns.

TO HAVE AND TO HOLD the above described property, together with all and singular the rights and appurtenances thereunto in anywise belonging unto the said Grantee, above named his heirs and assigns, forever. And I do hereby bind my successors or assigns, to WARRANT AND FOREVER DEFEND all and singular the said property unto the said grantee herein his heirs, assigns, and successors, against the claim or claims of every person whomsoever lawfully claiming or to claim the same, or any part thereof.

WITNESS THE SIGNATURE of the Grantor at El Paso, Texas on this the 16th. day of August A. D. 1937.

One .50¢ Doc. Rev. Stamp
Cancelled: 8/16/37 M.E.B.

Milton E. Bates, Trustee

STATE OF TEXAS ...
COUNTY OF EL PASO
BEFORE ME, the undersigned authority, on this day personally appeared Milton E. Bates, Trustee known to me to be the persons whose name is subscribed to the foregoing instrument, and acknowledged to me that he executed the same for the purposes and consideration therein expressed, and in the capacity therein stated.

GIVEN UNDER MY HAND AND SEAL OF OFFICE, on this the 16th. day of August, A. D. 1937.

(Notarial Seal: County of El Paso, Texas.)

Maude E. Healy
Notary Public in and for
El Paso County, Texas.

Filed for record Aug. 19, 1937 at 8:30 A. M. | W. D. GREET, County Clerk
And recorded Aug. 23, 1937 at 8:30 A. M. | By Marie Grady Deputy

Mrs. Stull and Lou posed for the camera. (Courtesy of Dr. Maceo Crenshaw Dailey Jr.)

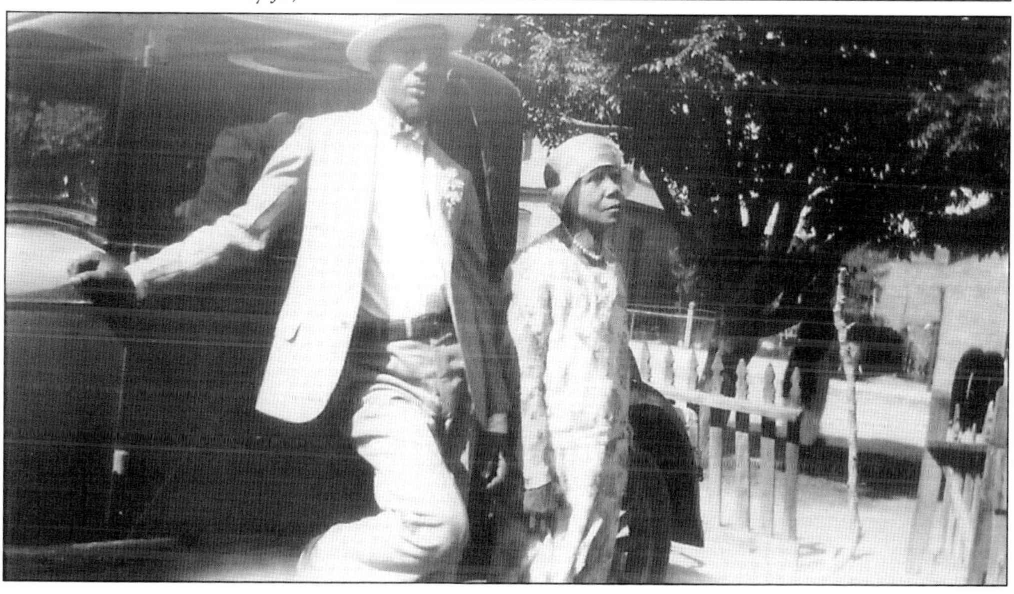

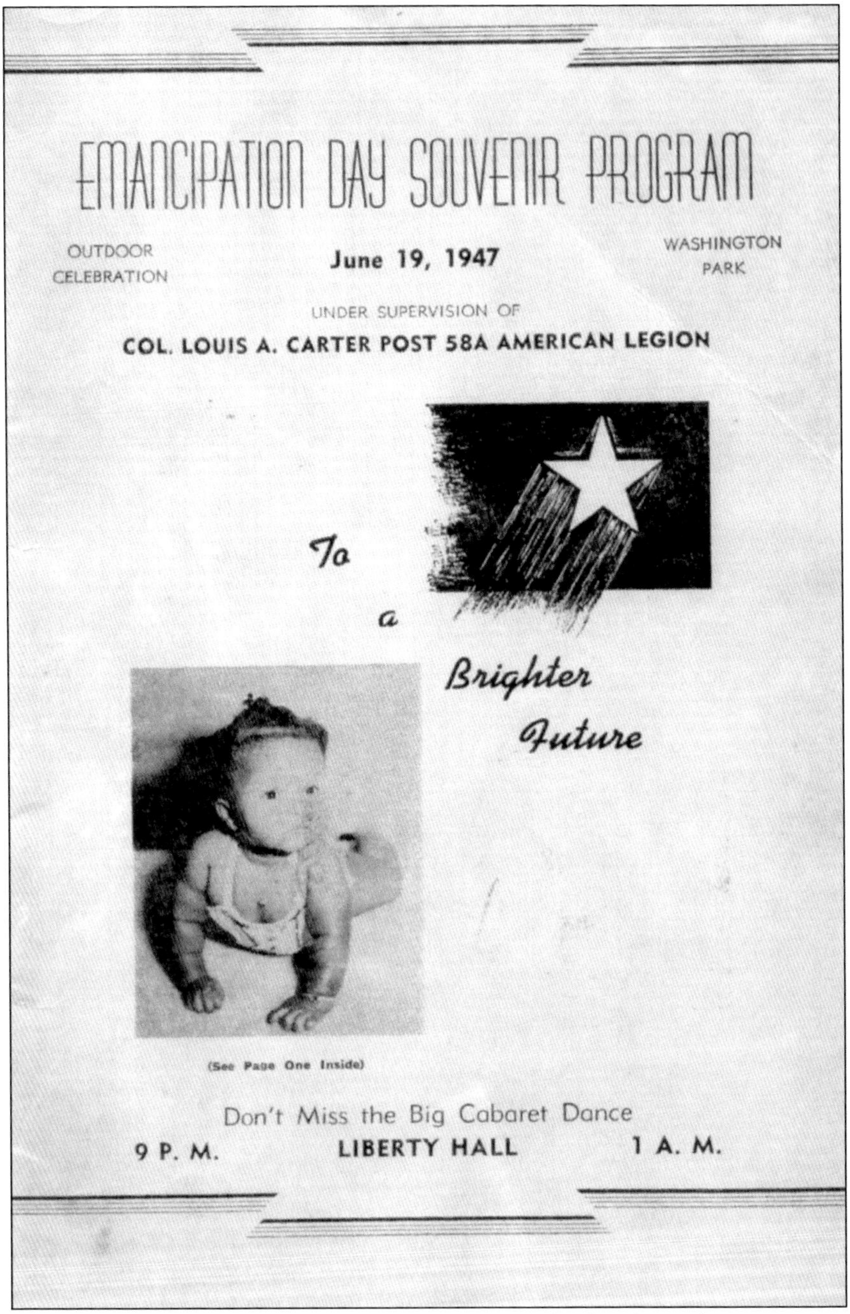

Since June 19, 1865, black Texans have annually celebrated the day that African American slaves were emancipated in the state. Some communities celebrated the occasion as Emancipation Day and others preferred to label it "Juneteenth," which is a combination of June and 19. Whatever the celebration was titled, it was a festive day of activities and events celebrating manumission and progress of black communities throughout the state. In 1979, state representative Al Edwards from Houston secured passage of a bill to make Juneteenth a state holiday. Now, black communities from New England to the West Coast commemorate Juneteenth. This Emancipation Day Souvenir Program is from the celebration in El Paso in 1947. (Courtesy of Dr. Maceo Crenshaw Dailey Jr.)

Four

A Civil Rights Community 1956–1976

African American El Pasoans were attuned to the momentous national change for civil rights in housing, education, and employment. Factors that heightened their interests and involvement in contributing to this change can be attributed to two important developments—the number of black military personnel retiring in El Paso and the Highway Act of 1957, which cut a swath of Interstate 10 through the city's African American community.

Given the fact that black men and women in the military had demonstrated their willingness to make the ultimate sacrifice for their country and that the nation's armed forces were generally ahead of the civilian population in recognizing and accepting the benefits of desegregation, African American Army personnel and retirees became involved in city campaigns for civil rights. The building of superhighway 10 prompted many black El Pasoans to seek housing outside of their traditional residential area of the Second Ward, and this led to integration in formerly all-white communities.

Among the notable accomplishments of black El Pasoans was the formation of an interracial group in the late 1950s to push for civil rights, the passage of an "antidiscrimination ordinance for earth, lodging, and entertainment facilities and services" in 1962, and the stunning and stellar victory of Texas Western College's basketball team with its all-black starting lineup, which defeated the mighty University of Kentucky team in the 1966 NCAA championship. Two African American scholars from Howard University became the first black faculty members at Texas Western College.

Individuals such as Drusilla Nixon, R.E. Washington, and Clint Huling led the reform movement for blacks in El Paso. The black community had a Banneker Literary and Historical Society (formed at Second Baptist Church), whose mission was to discuss local and national racial issues. The city's chapter of the Texas Federation of Women's Clubs contributed to civil rights reform.

Still, all could not be portrayed as progressive, especially in the instance of Dr. Nixon's son-in-law, Dr. McIver, having to move to Albuquerque to begin his medical practice because of a bank's refusal of a business loan in El Paso.

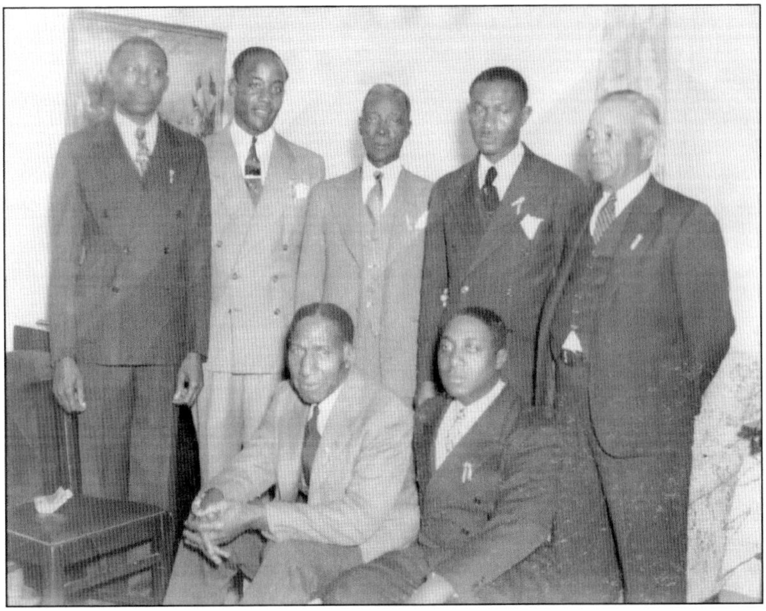

From left to right are (sitting) McDonnell and J. Frazier; (standing) L.A. Turner, H. Gillard, J.W. Prothro, Harris, and Marshall McCall. (Courtesy of the Department of Special Collections and Archives, University of Texas at El Paso Library.)

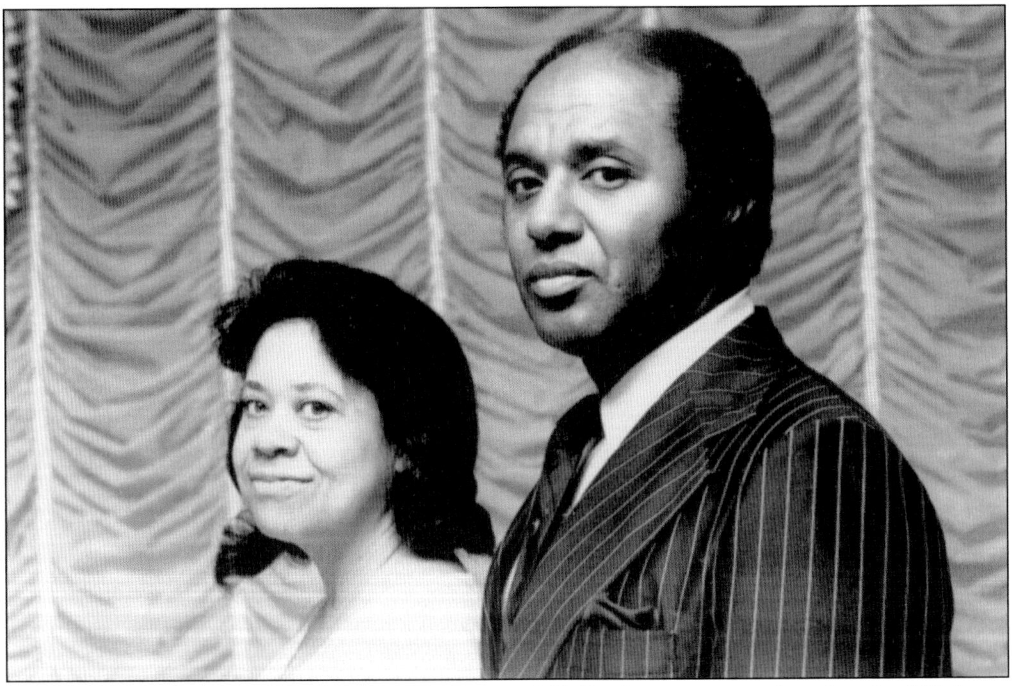

Marjorie and Dr. Juan Lawson came to El Paso in 1965. Dr. Lawson was enlisted in the US Army as a reserve officer and stationed at Fort Bliss. After serving his two-year active duty requirement, the couple decided to make El Paso their home. Marjorie Lawson went on to become the first black professor at the University of Texas at El Paso, while Dr. Lawson became the first African American to hold a doctorate at the University of Texas at El Paso. He was appointed dean of science in 1975. (Courtesy of Dr. Maceo Crenshaw Dailey Jr.)

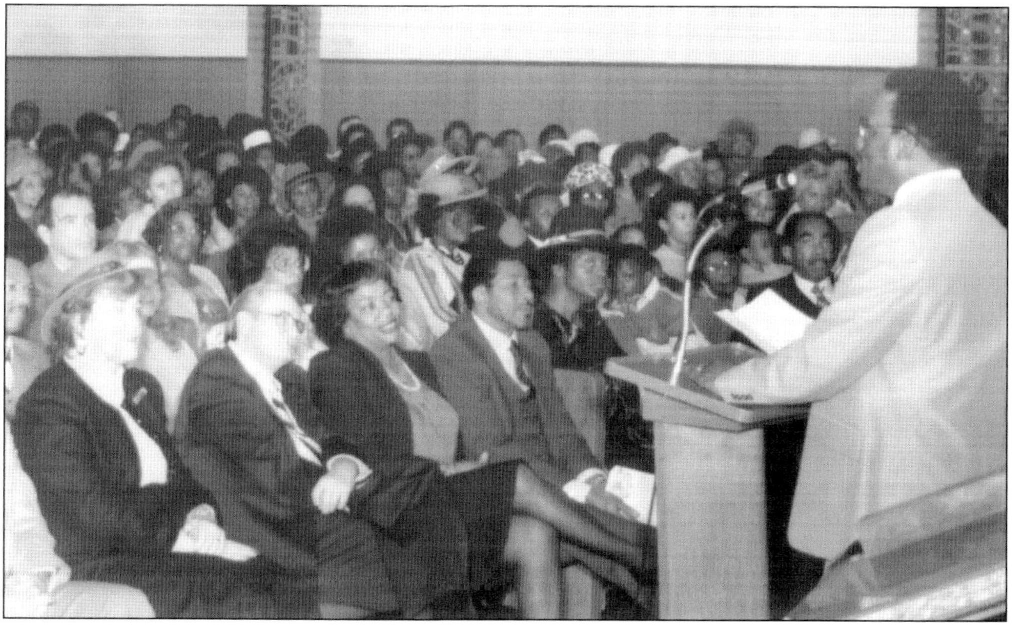

Dusty Rhodes addressed the El Paso branch of the NAACP in 1990. El Paso was the first branch of the NAACP in Texas, beginning in 1914, and initiated three Supreme Court cases along with Dr. Lawrence Nixon to end the white primary in Texas. (Courtesy of Special Collections, University of Texas El Paso.)

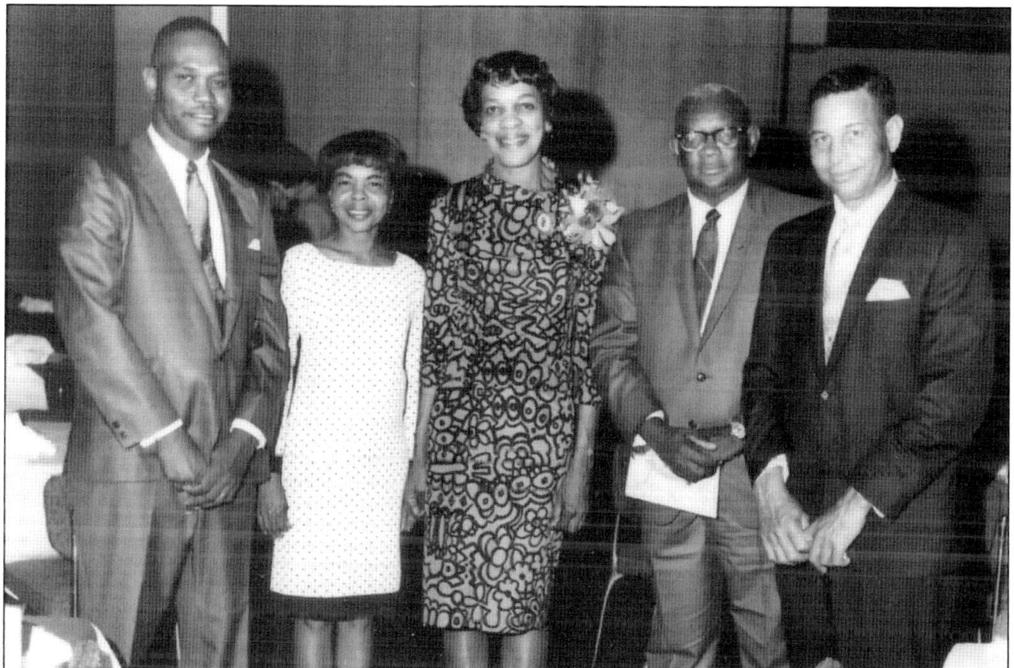

A group of prominent educators at Douglass High School is pictured prior to desegregation. On the back of the photograph, six names are listed: T.W. Franklin, J.H. Calvert, L. Browder, E. Bonkagew, C. DeWitty, and Mangram, but only five are pictured on the front. (Courtesy of Dr. Maceo Crenshaw Dailey Jr.)

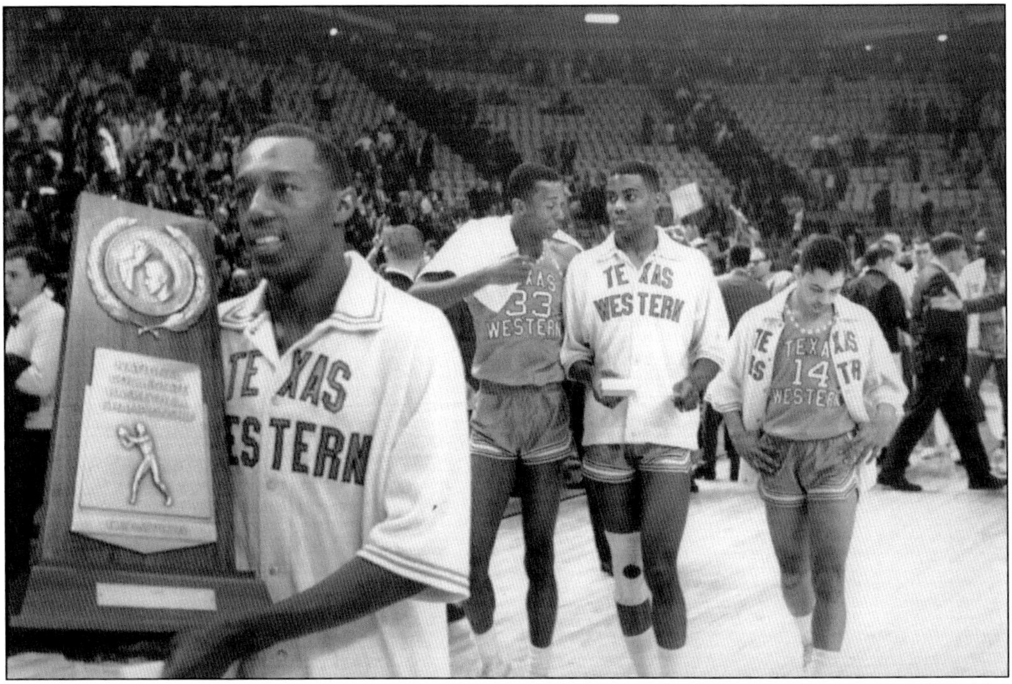

From left to right, Orsten Artis (carrying the trophy), Nevil Shed, Harry Flournoy, and Bobby Joe Hill of Texas Western College walk off the court after their upset win over the powerhouse University of Kentucky team in the 1966 NCAA basketball finals at the University of Maryland's Cole Field House. Texas Western College made an unprecedented move by starting five black players. This prompted other predominately white universities to recruit black athletes. The story of this event is featured in the movie *Glory Road*. (Courtesy of Special Collections, University of Texas El Paso.)

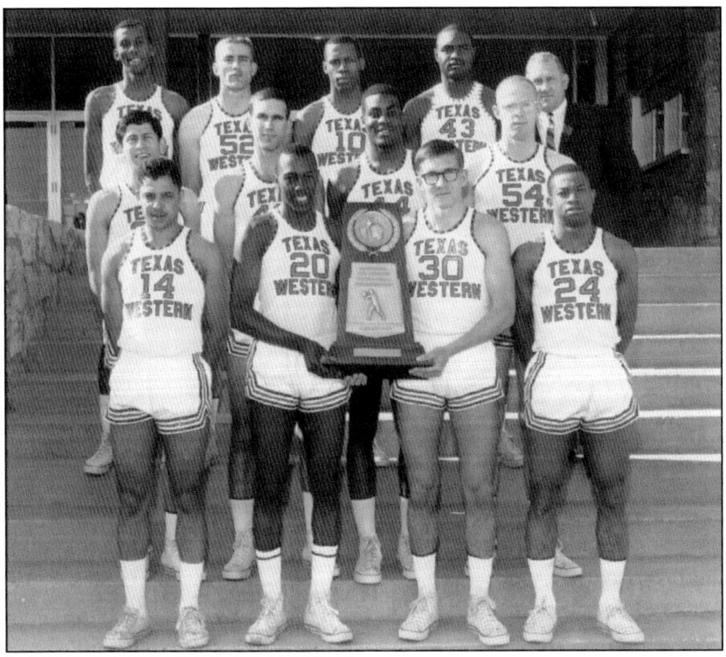

The 1966 Texas Western College championship basketball team posed with their trophy. (Courtesy of Special Collections, University of Texas El Paso.)

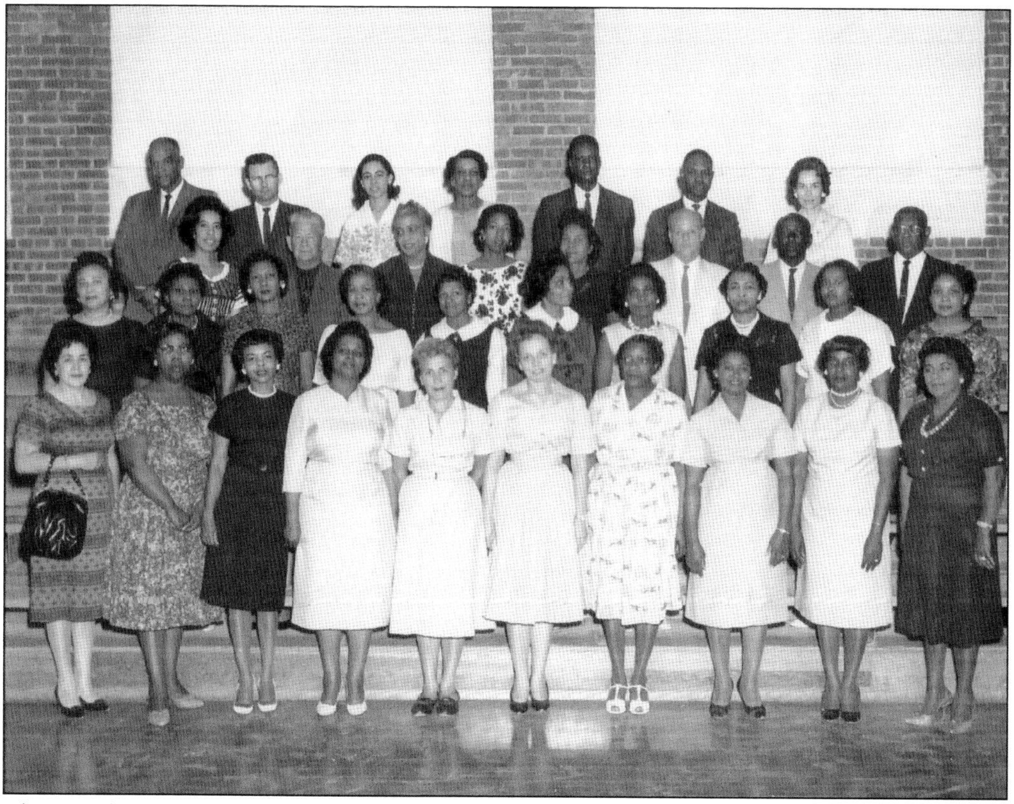

The Douglass School alumni and professors posed for this picture at Douglass School. (Courtesy of the Department of Special Collections and Archives, University of Texas at El Paso Library.)

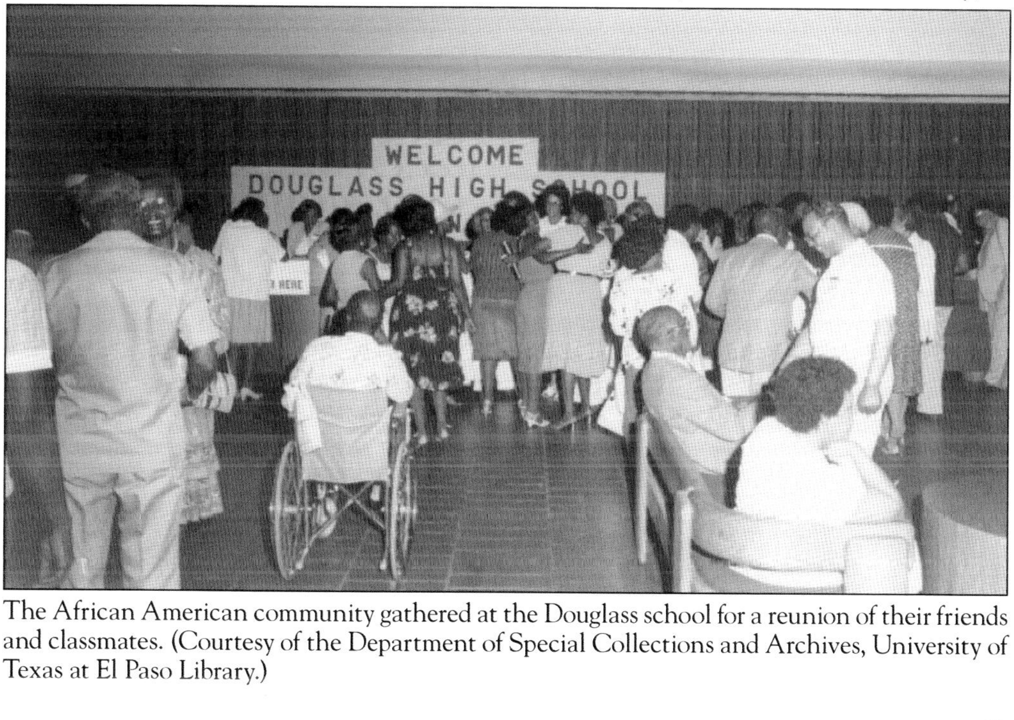

The African American community gathered at the Douglass school for a reunion of their friends and classmates. (Courtesy of the Department of Special Collections and Archives, University of Texas at El Paso Library.)

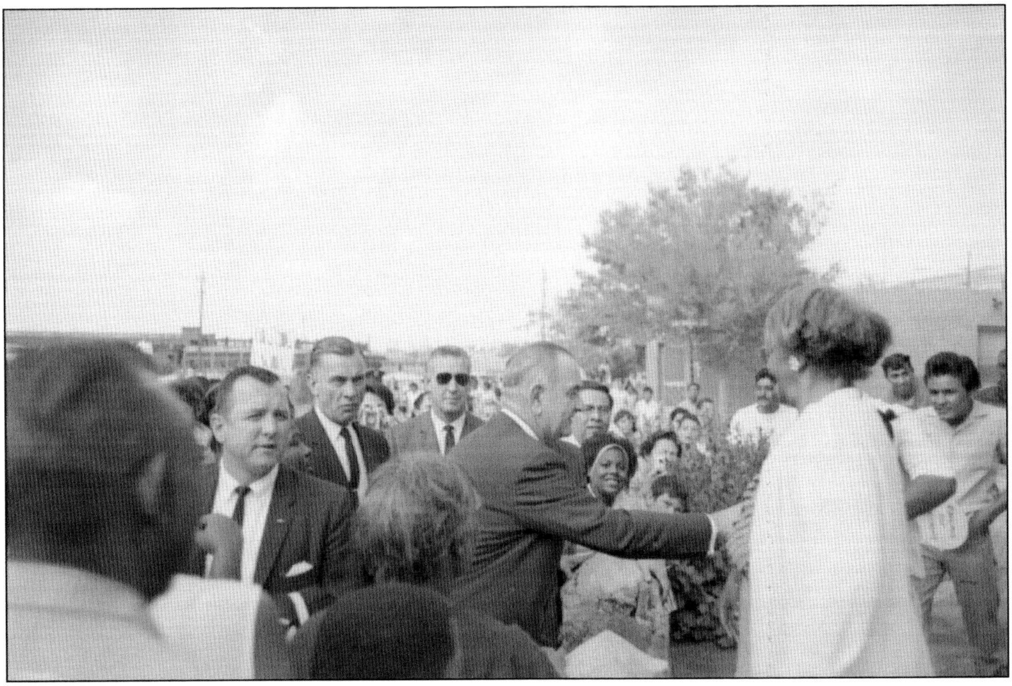

A consummate politician, Pres. Lyndon Johnson halted his motorcade in the El Paso black community to shake hands and greet African Americans. President Johnson was in El Paso in September 1964 to meet with Pres. Lopez Mateos of Mexico to celebrate the Chamizal Treaty. These photographs was taken a little over two months after Johnson signed the historic Civil Rights Act of 1964. (Both, courtesy of *El Paso Times*.)

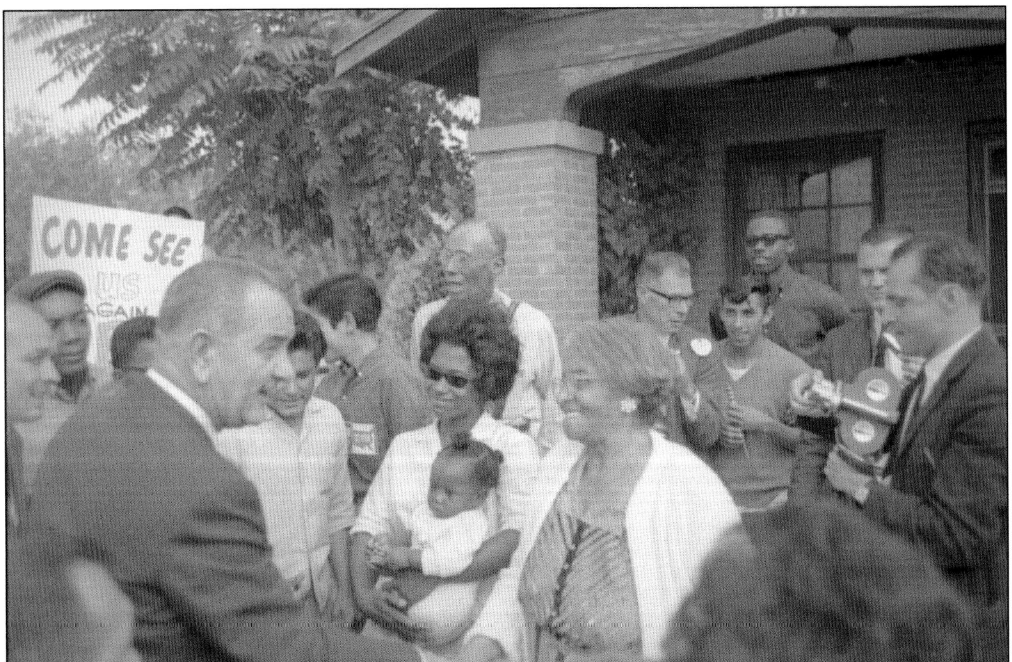

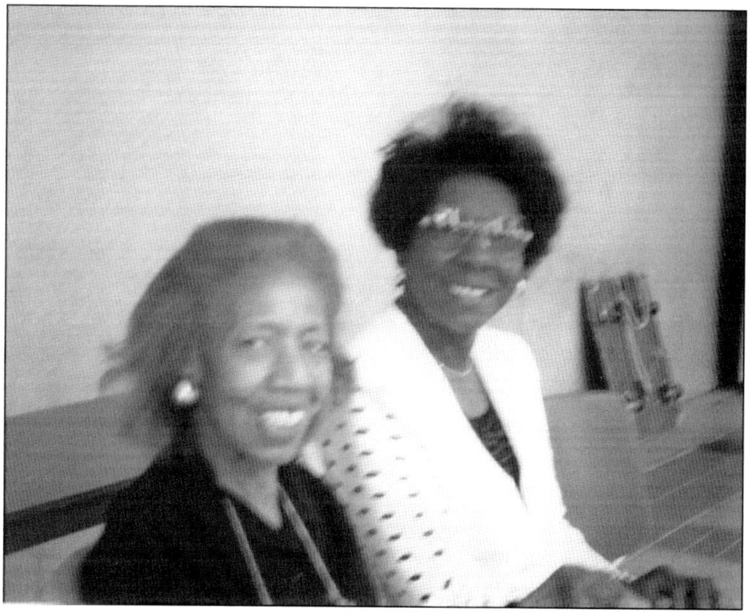

Leona Washington (left), a 1945 graduate of Douglass School, composed the song "The City of El Paso," which the city adopted as its song. Washington also founded the McCall Neighborhood Center. Next to her is Rebecca Rhodes, an active community leader. (Courtesy of Dr. Maceo Crenshaw Dailey Jr.)

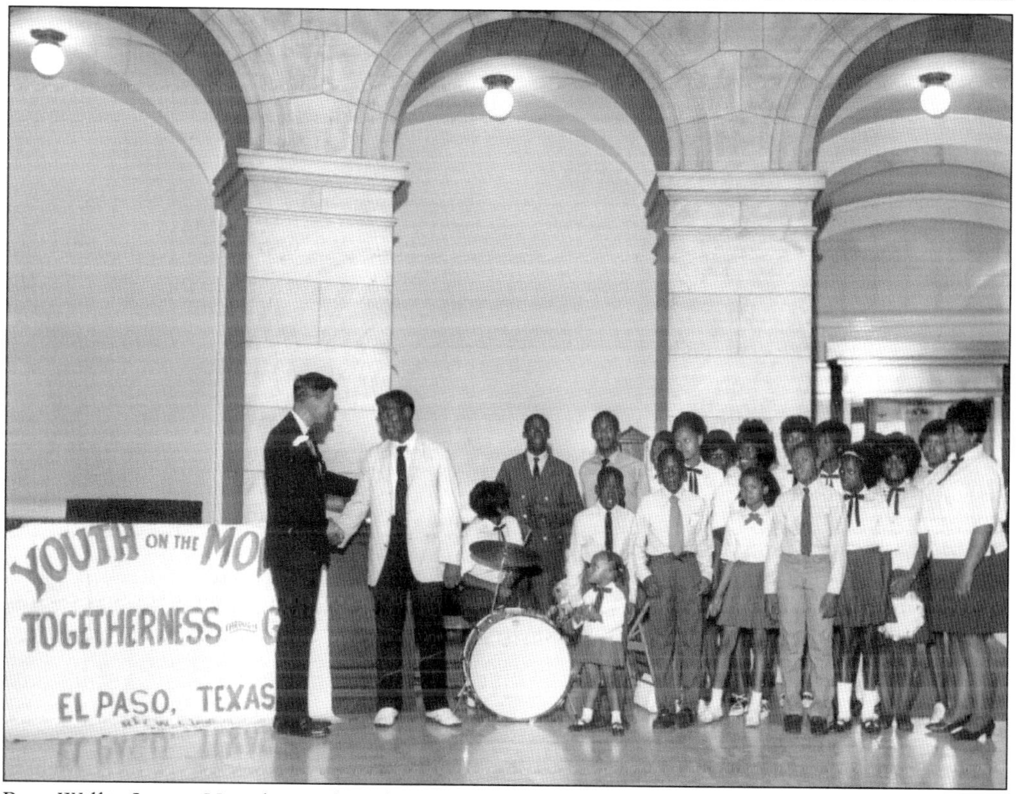

Rev. Willie James Haughton, founder of "Youth on the Move," is pictured with some of the members of his group. Haughton was invited by Pres. Richard Nixon to be a guest at the White House. He was also a guest at the United Nations and was recognized for his work with youth. Haughton promoted "God, education, and work—and more work" to achieve success. (Courtesy of the Department of Special Collections and Archives, University of Texas at El Paso Library.)

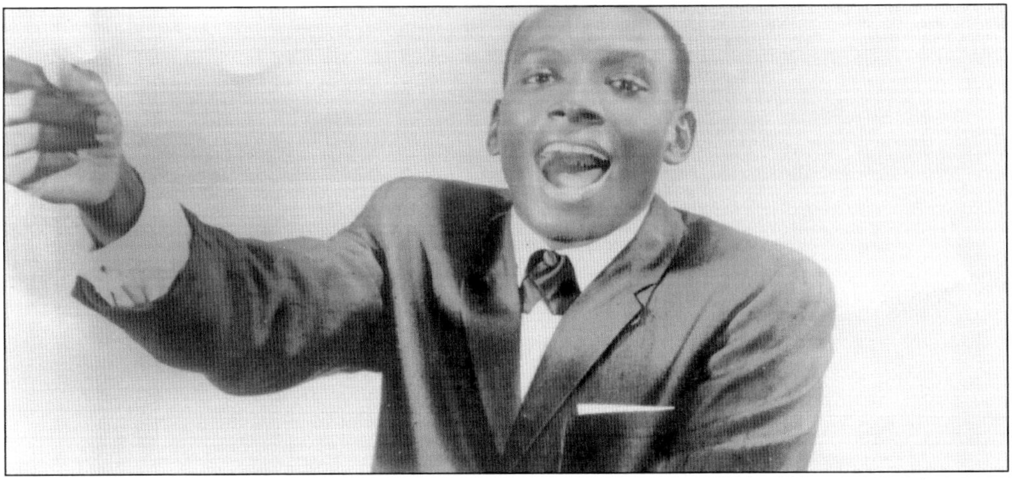

Earl Grant was a vocalist, organist, and popular musician in the 1950s. He came to El Paso as an enlisted serviceman at Fort Bliss. During his time in the military, Grant began performing in clubs across the border in Juarez. He became immensely popular and parlayed his success into a hit career with the release of his million-selling record *The End*. Grant later settled in Los Angeles but maintained a booking agent in El Paso, traveling frequently to perform on both sides of the border. He died in an auto accident in 1970 while driving through Lordsburg, New Mexico, on his way to play a gig in Juarez. (Courtesy of Kathryn Smith-McGlynn.)

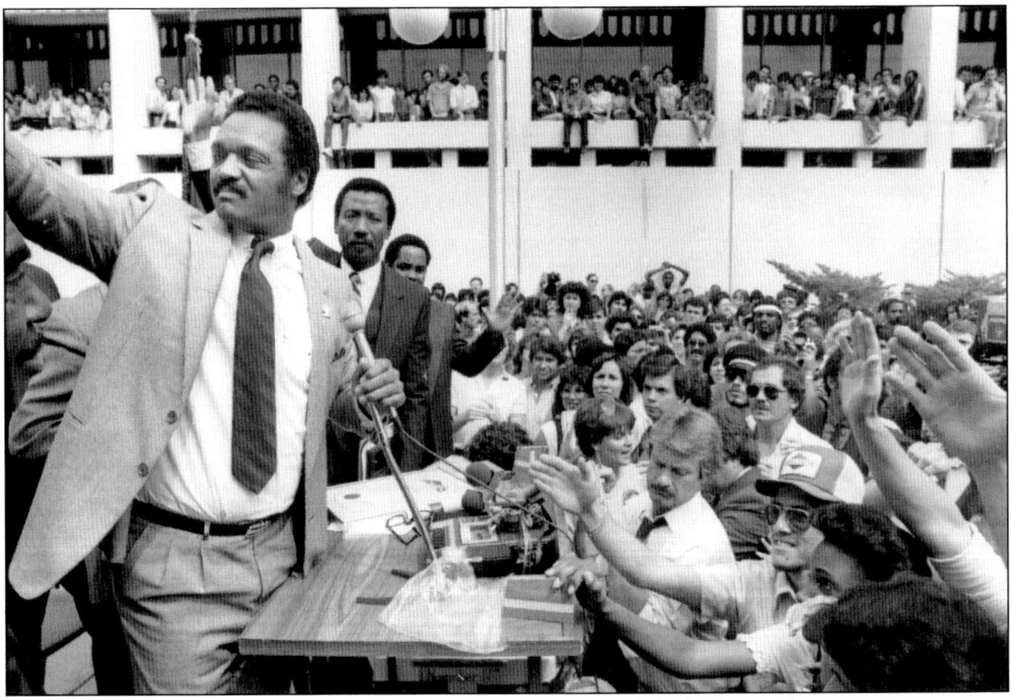

Jesse Jackson and state legislator Al Edwards, who sponsored the bill to make Juneteenth a state holiday, wave to a crowd of more than 2,000 University of Texas at El Paso students on February 15, 1971. Jackson urged the crowd to form a Rainbow Coalition of blacks and Hispanics to vote for the Democratic ticket. (Courtesy of the *El Paso Herald Post*.)

The Murray Theatre was dedicated on February 1, 1948. Located on Mesa Avenue in the heart of downtown, the Murray Theatre was created by George H. Murray as a "place of amusement [to] provide wholesome and helpful entertainment for all the people." The theater was erected at a time when most white-owned theaters would not allow blacks onto the premises to watch films. (Courtesy of Dr. Maceo Crenshaw Dailey Jr.)

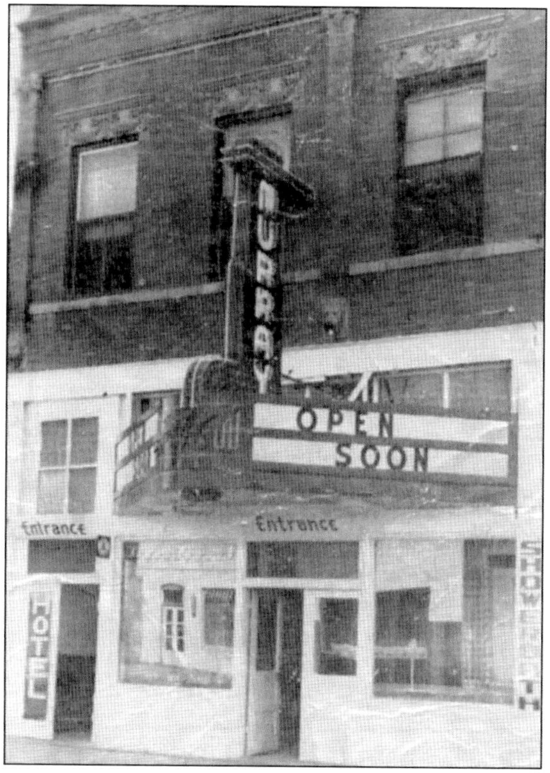

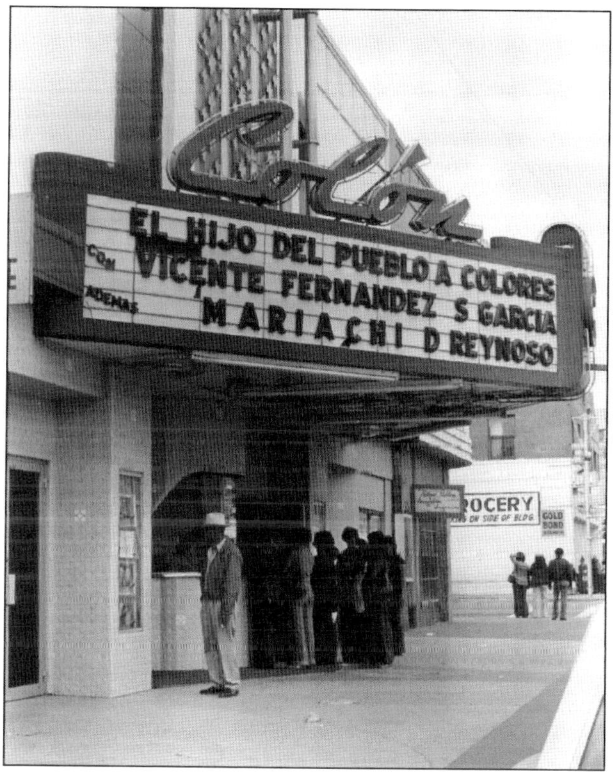

The Colón Theater was built around 1919 and showed Spanish films up until the 1970s. It was one of the few theaters in El Paso that allowed black patrons during the Jim Crow era. (Courtesy of El Paso County Historical Society.)

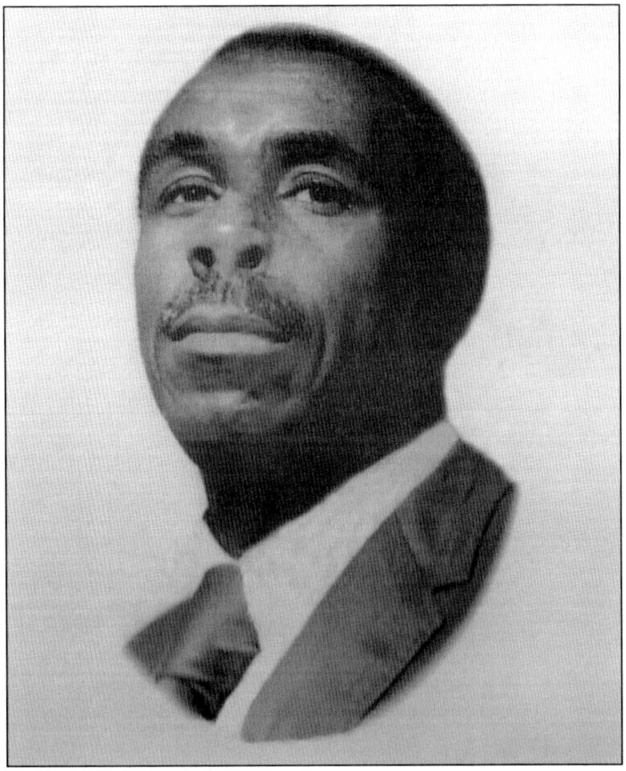

R.E.L. Washington retired from the military as a lieutenant colonel. He was the founder of the Black El Paso Democrats. Washington was also a prominent businessman. (Courtesy of Jim Ball.)

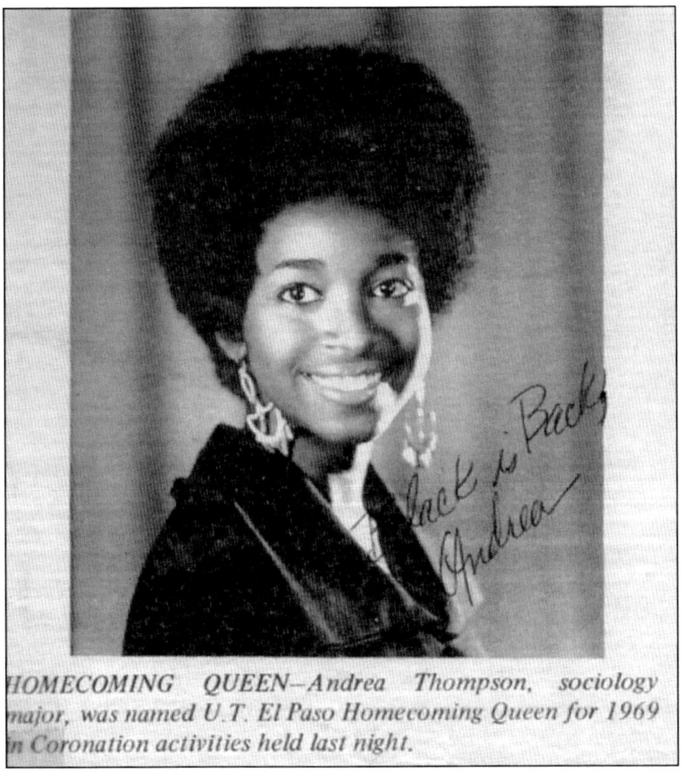

Andrea Johnson was crowned University of Texas at El Paso homecoming queen in 1969. The newspaper clipping featured an announcement of the coronation activities. Johnson autographed her picture, writing "Black is Back." (Courtesy of Leon M. Harden Jr.)

Five

The Conclusion of the 20th Century

1977–Present

African American students at the University of Texas at El Paso (formerly Texas Western College) recall a black renaissance in the talent that came to the campus and El Paso during this era, including Jesse Jackson, Dick Gregory, Richard Pryor, The Temptations, Kool and the Gang, Stevie Wonder, Isacc Hayes, and Sly and the Family Stone, among others.

This era of black talent extended into business as two of the largest African American entrepreneurs emerged in the city with the advent of MACA (now METI—Management and Engineering Technologies International Inc.) and the now Wingo Advertising Company. The founders of these enterprises—the Johnsons and Wingos—have served the city, state, and nation by becoming successful businesspersons and have involved themselves in significant social change and transformation. Robert Wingo's initial efforts and contributions to building the recent Martin Luther King Memorial in Washington, DC, were critical to getting this project off the ground. The Johnsons have funneled money into scholarships for students and supported uplift projects in the black community as well as the larger city.

Black El Pasoans have held many key leadership positions in the city, like commander of Fort Bliss, chief of the police department, head librarian, chief executive officer of the local YWCA (the largest in the nation), and head of the local branch of the FBI, as well as three elected city council members.

Continued interest in uplift endeavors, contributions to the overall positive goals of the city, and promotion of general welfare all remained valued objectives of black leadership in El Paso and the overall African American community. El Paso Black Chamber of Commerce, McCall Neighborhood Center, Pan-Hellenic Council, NAACP, Thelma White Network, and Interdenominational Ministerial Alliance remain at the forefront of growth and development. The formulation of the University of Texas at El Paso African American Studies Program led to a resurgence of interest, research, and celebration of black history.

If there was one person who was the voice and conscience of the African American El Paso community, it would be Leona Washington, former teacher and founder of the McCall Neighborhood Center. She kept the black community grounded and focused on the cause of citizenship, education, and community development at large.

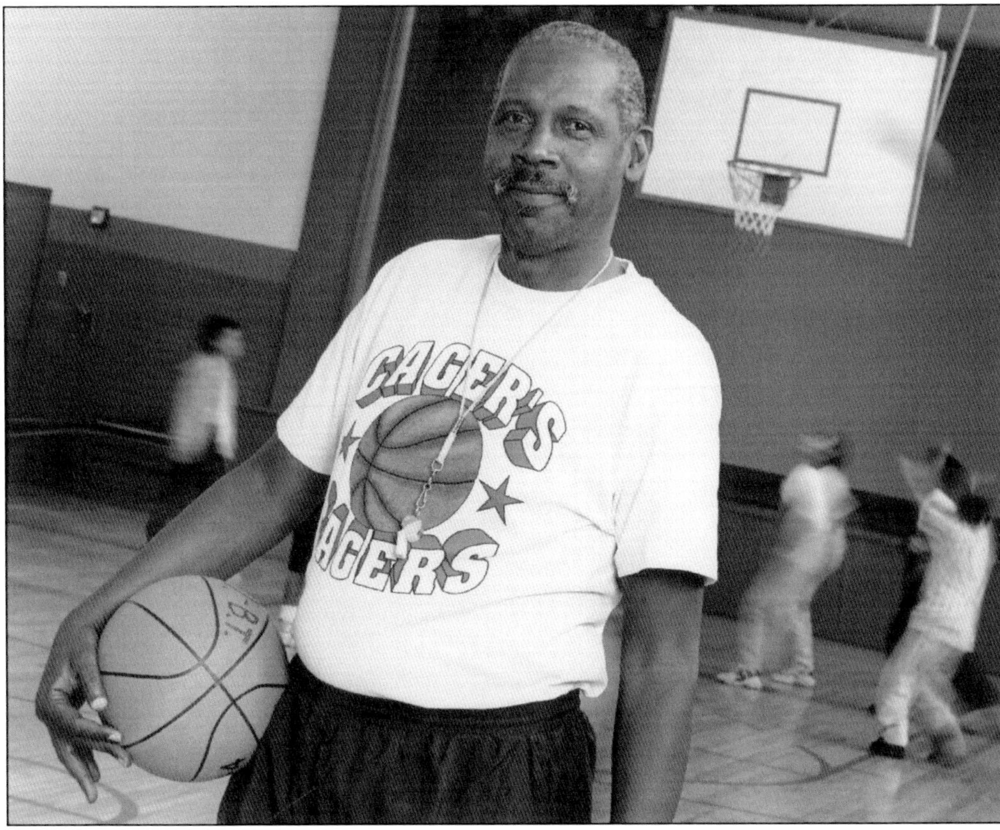

Willie Cager played forward on the celebrated 1966 Texas Western basketball team that was inducted into Naismith Memorial Basketball Hall of Fame in 2007 as the first team in history to win an NCAA championship with five African American players in the starting lineup. Originally from the Bronx, New York, Willie made El Paso his home and became an integral part of the community, making a tremendous impact on the lives of children throughout the region through the Willie Cager Foundation. (Courtesy of the African American Studies Program, University of Texas at El Paso.)

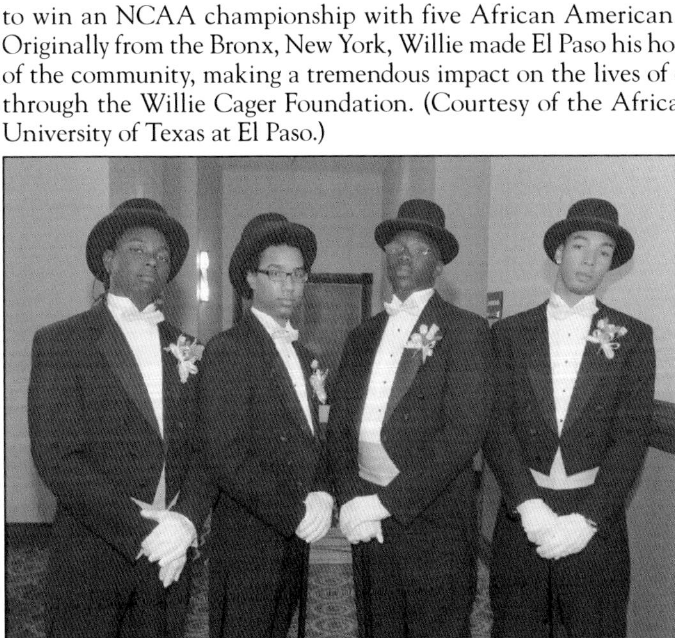

Young black men are pictured participating in the annual botillion held by Alpha Kappa Alpha, the oldest black sorority, which was founded at Howard University in 1908. The botillion is a rite of passage, celebrating the transition from boyhood to manhood. (Courtesy of *El Paso Times*.)

Dr. Raymond O. Lundy, a graduate of Morehouse College and Meharry Medical School, is a specialist with over 46 years of experience in the fields of hematology and oncology. He has served on numerous boards and received high acclaim for his support of progressive developments within the community. Most notably, Dr. Lundy was a mover and shaker in keeping the McCall Neighborhood Center afloat with his general contributions and good advice as vice chair of the board. (Courtesy of *El Paso Times*.)

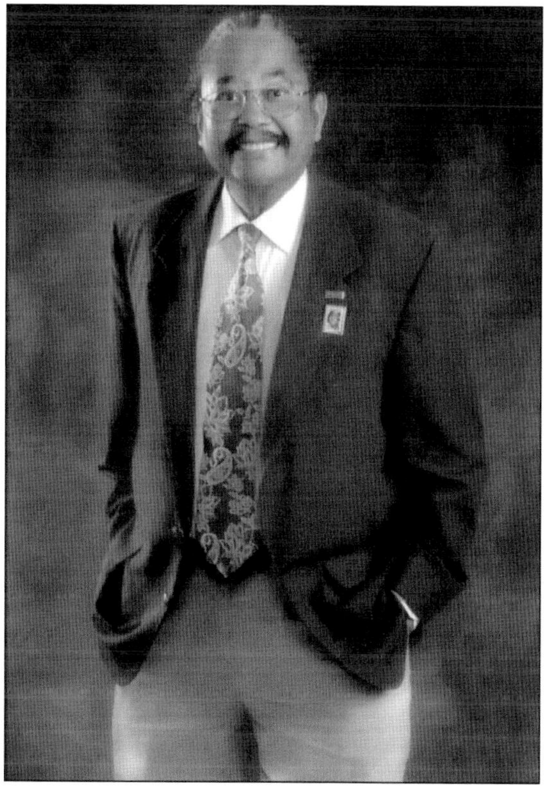

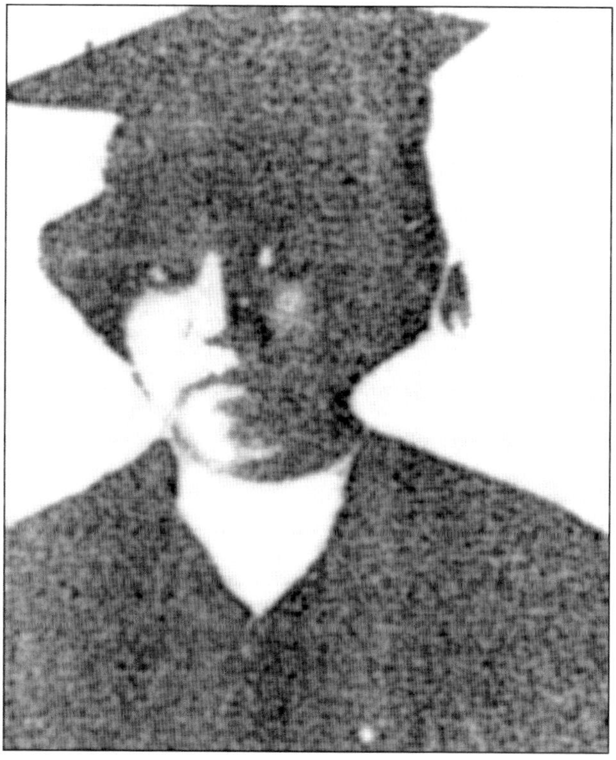

Native El Pasoan Zephyr Chisom Carter was a founding member of the Delta Sigma Theta sorority at Howard University, where she was active in the collegiate chapter of the NAACP. She kept busy in the El Paso community, giving her time and effort to those in need. While in Delta Sigma Theta, she became the Alpha Chapter's first reporter. (Courtesy of Delta Sigma Theta Sorority Inc.)

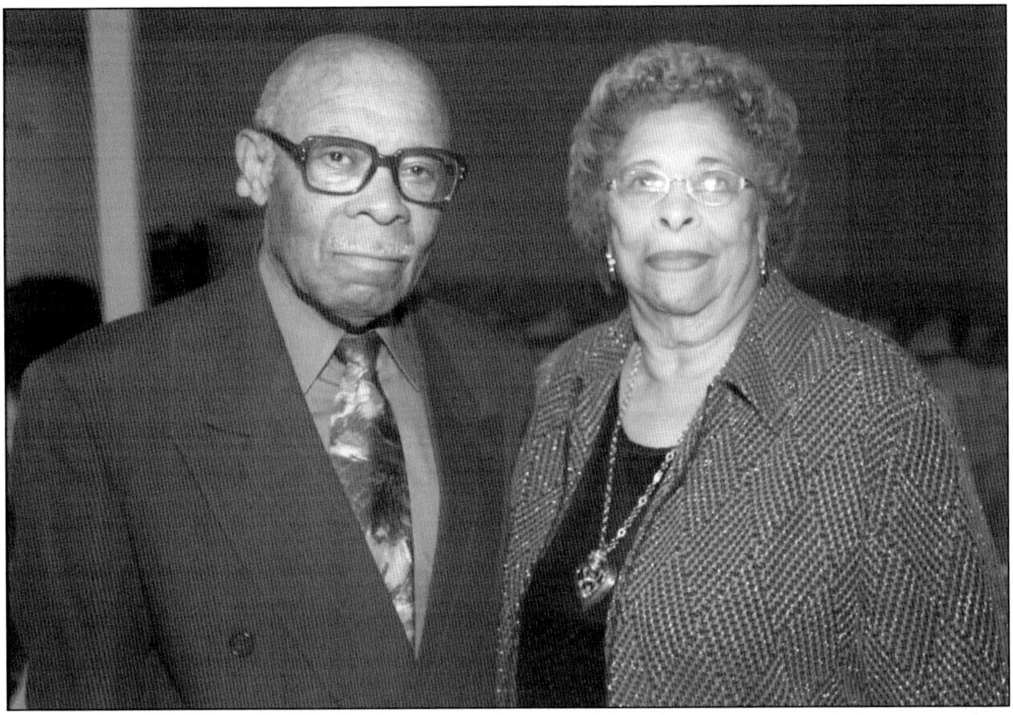

Leo and Avice Pleasants were two longtime educators in El Paso; he was a principal, she was teacher. Through their membership in various organizations, they donated financially and intellectually to progress in the black community and larger city of El Paso. (Courtesy of *El Paso Times*.)

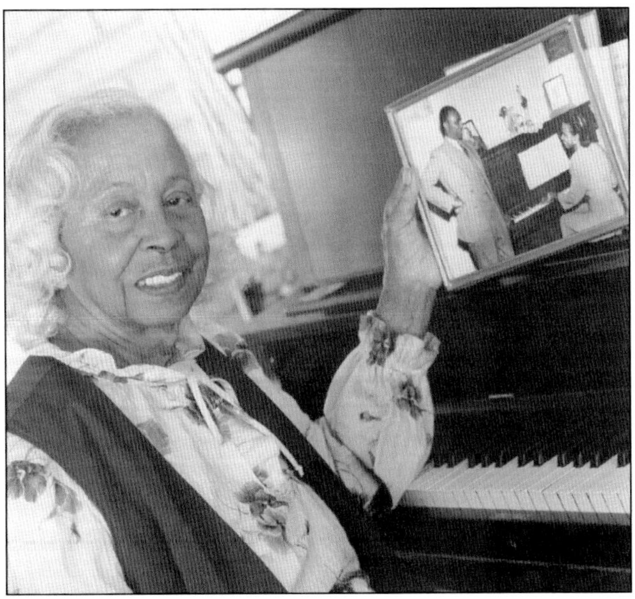

Lula Traylor was born on November 26, 1911, in Faker, Texas, later moving to El Paso. She once recounted a story regarding Texas segregation laws that were sometimes ignored in El Paso. On an excursion to a drugstore fountain to buy ice cream, she was prepared to make her purchase and leave since blacks were not served at most restaurants. To her surprise, the store clerk showed her to a seat, gave her a menu, and commenced to serve her once she ordered her ice cream, which she enjoyed without incident. (Courtesy of the African American Studies Program, University of Texas at El Paso.)

Mrs. Pratt was born in 1925 and retired as a teacher from El Paso Independent School District (EPISD). She was honored with the EPISD's Excellence in Teaching Award in 1989. Mrs. Pratt has been active with the American Heart Association, the Irvin High School Band Boosters, the Parent-Teacher and Parent-Teacher-Student Associations, and the American Association of University Women's Expanding Your Horizons Conference at the University of Texas at El Paso. She continued to volunteer in the public schools in El Paso and participates in the University of Texas at El Paso's Center for Lifelong Learning. When asked about her attitude on aging, she proclaimed that it "has become an amazing journey full of surprises, endurances, and learning through adversity." (Courtesy of the African American Studies Program, University of Texas at El Paso.)

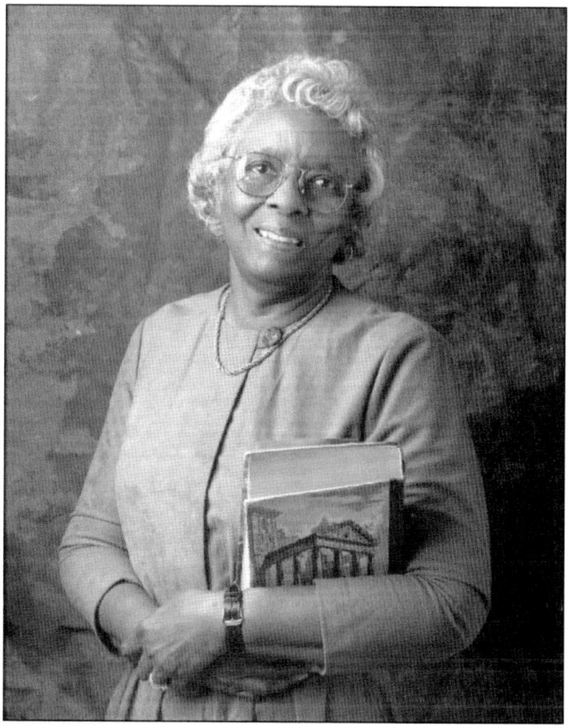

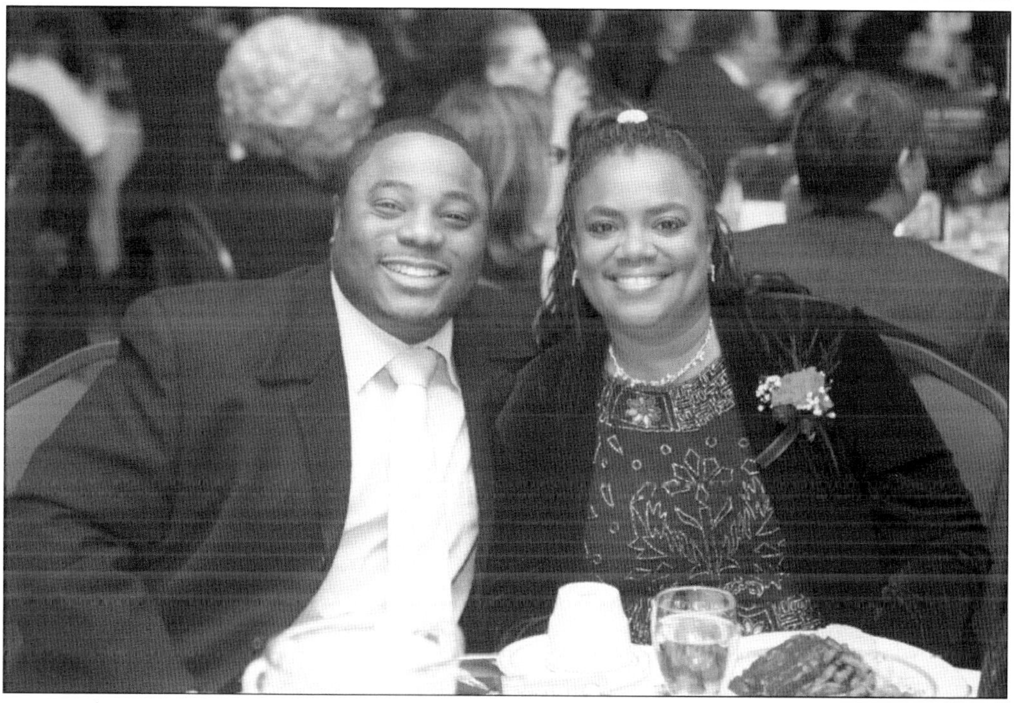

Dr. Sandra Braham is the chief executive officer of the nation's largest YWCA, with a yearly operating budget of $32 million, 500 employees, 51 after-school programs, and 13 preschool programs. She is a member of Mount Zion Church, married to Eric Braham (seated beside her), and has four children. (Courtesy of *El Paso Times*.)

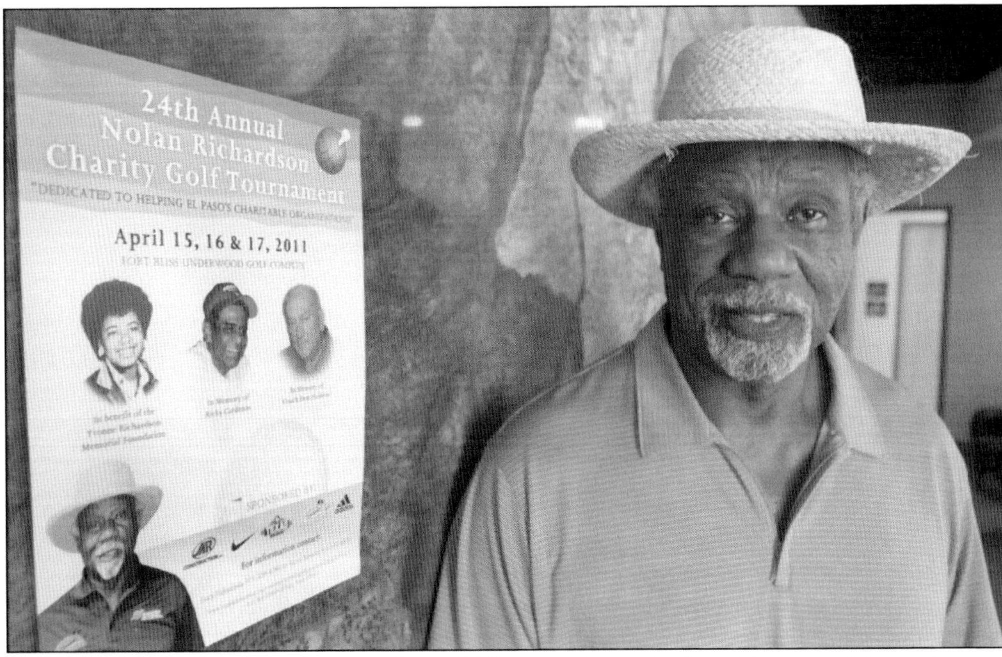

Coach Nolan Richardson, a native-born El Pasoan fluent in Spanish, made his mark as an exceptional athlete in the city. He played for legendary Hall-of-Fame coach Don Haskins at the University of Texas at El Paso. Coach Richardson won an NCAA basketball championship as head coach at the University of Arkansas in 1994, and, prior to this, the National Invitation Tournament and junior college basketball championships, becoming the only coach to win at the three different levels. Coach Richardson sponsors an annual golf tournament in El Paso to raise money for the many deserving charities in the city. (Courtesy of *El Paso Times*.)

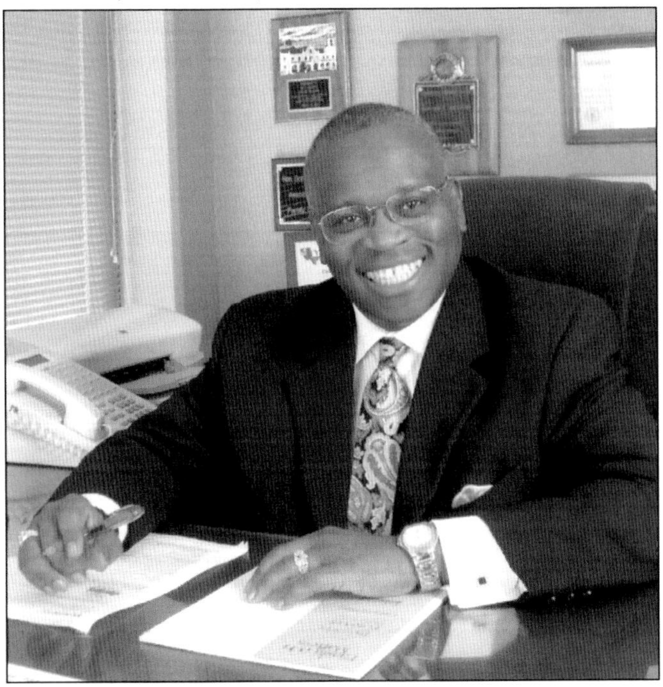

Donald Williams has a long and distinguished career as a public servant and supporter of development in the African American community. An alumnus of the University of Texas El Paso, he was the first African American to become president of the Student Government Association. After receiving his law degree from the University of Texas in Austin, Williams returned to live and practice law in El Paso. He became the first African American to be appointed to a judgeship in El Paso with his installation as associate Family Court judge. He currently serves as president of the El Paso Black Democrats. (Courtesy of Donald Williams.)

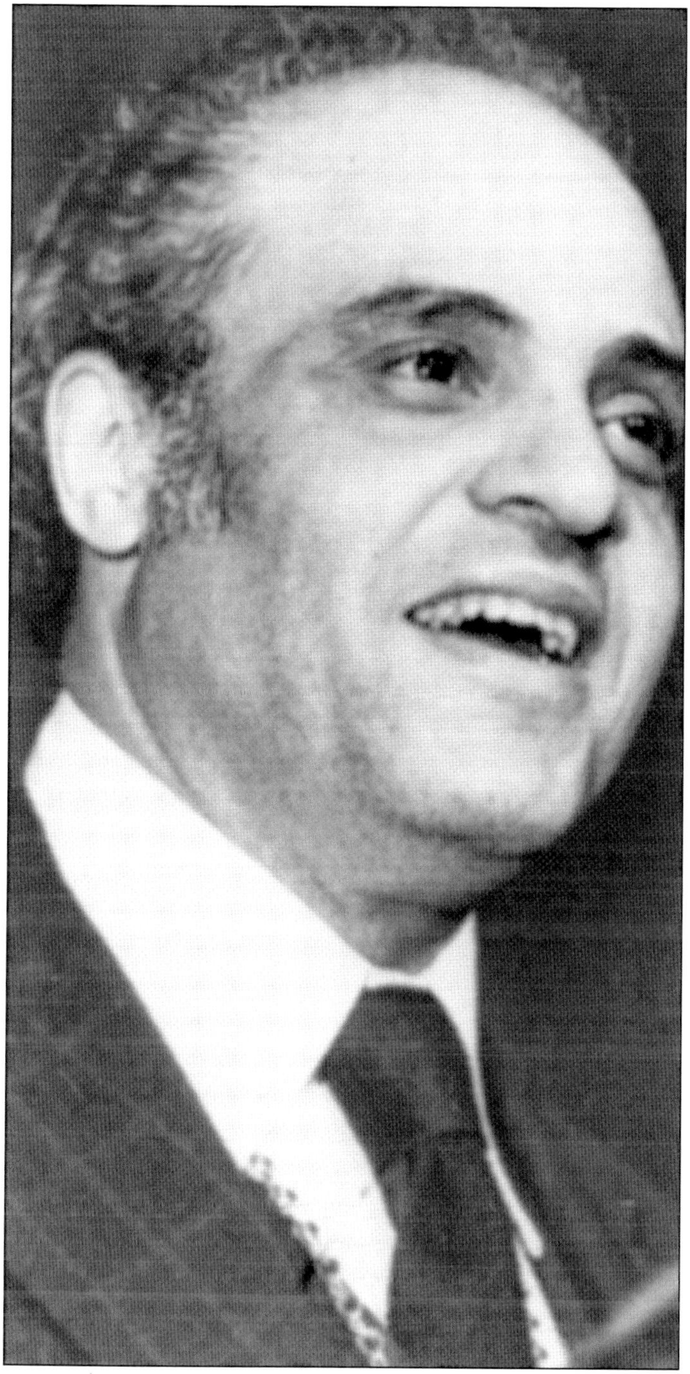

On February 9, 1979, the executive director of the NAACP, Benjamin Hooks, spoke at the University of Texas at El Paso for Black History Month. El Paso mayor Ray Salazar presented Hooks with the key to the city. Hooks told the crowd he remembered coming through El Paso when he was in the service and having to move to the front of the train. He asked the crowd to support the NAACP and become active members of the "oldest and most significant civil rights organization." (Courtesy of *El Paso Times*.)

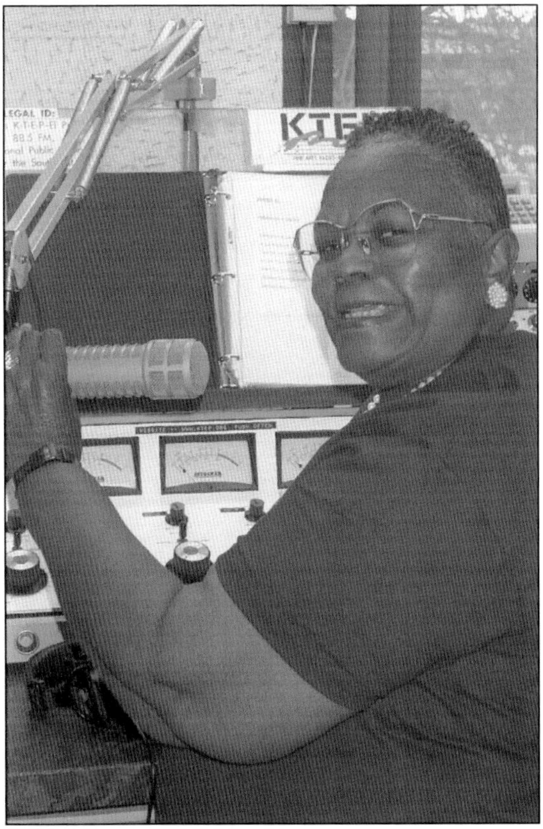

Betty A. Robinson is legendary in El Paso as the DJ of the *The Best of Gospel* show, which airs on NPR affiliate and University of Texas at El Paso–based radio station KTEP. Her program takes place each Sunday morning from 5:00 to 9:00 a.m. Robinson's first broadcast was in 1980, and since then, it has been a "must listen" for those interested in good gospel music, the schedule of events (mostly religious services and activities), and news of sacred and secular speakers in the city. A musician, Robinson has received numerous awards and citations in recognition of her good work. (Courtesy of KTEP-FM.)

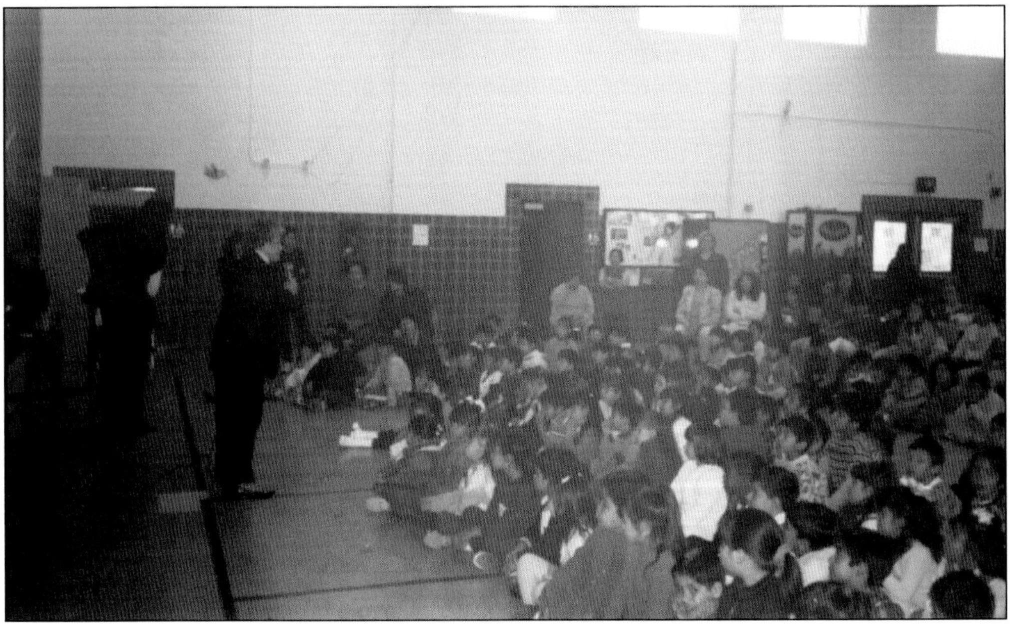

Booker T. Washington's granddaughter Margaret Clifford is pictured speaking, at the request of Principal Dr. Robert Hemphill, to a group of elementary students in El Paso's Segundo Barrio on the occasion of Black History Month in 1998. (Courtesy of Dr. Maceo Crenshaw Dailey Jr.)

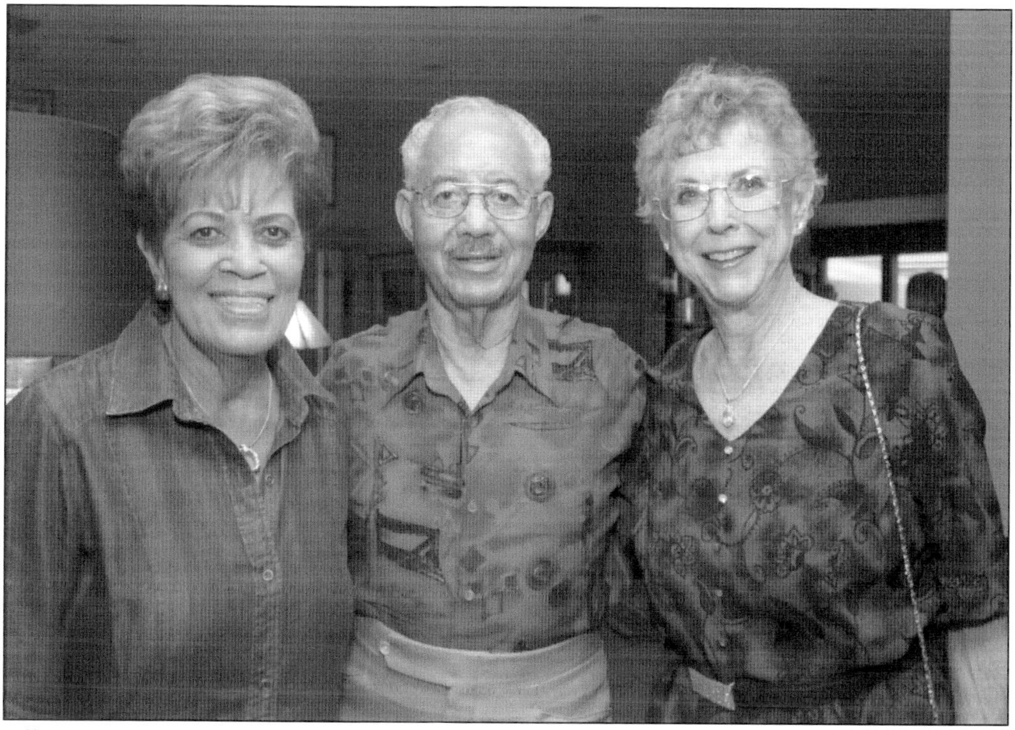

Lillian Crouch retired from El Paso Independent School District, where she held various positions including elementary teacher, junior high school principal, and executive director of human resources. She graduated in 1972 from the University of Texas at El Paso with a master's of education. In 2012, she was honored as a distinguished University of Texas at El Paso alum. She is a stalwart of the El Paso community, serving on several community boards, and is the recipient of several community awards. Crouch is pictured here at left with her husband, Jim Crouch, and Gerry Porter at an El Paso County Historical Society event. (Courtesy of El Paso Inc.)

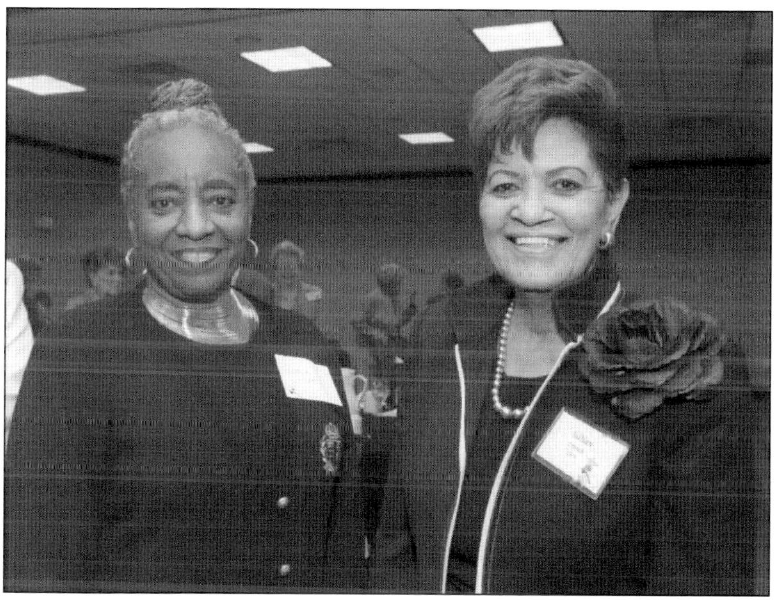

Lillian Crouch (left) is pictured at the Women's Department of the Greater El Paso Chamber of Commerce annual installation luncheon with Bettie Carter. Crouch also ran for political office. (Courtesy of El Paso Inc.)

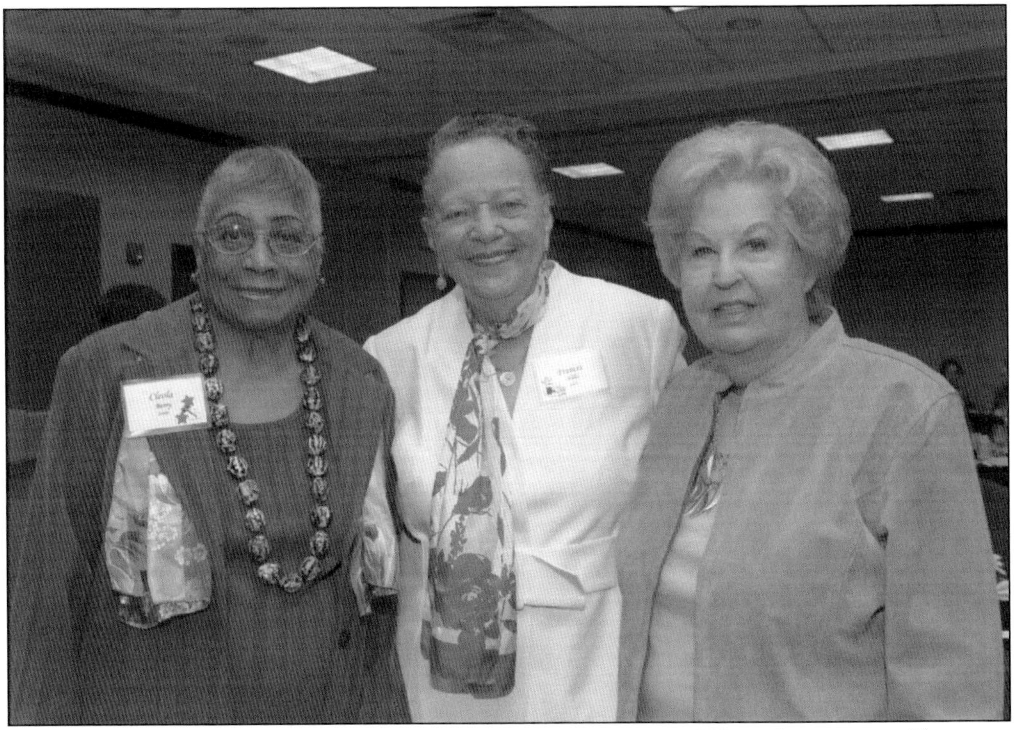

Cleola Berry (left) moved to El Paso in the 1940s from Houston. When she recounted her time in El Paso, she noted that African Americans were treated better than in the rest of the United States. There were exceptions, of course. She has stated that El Paso theaters were segregated and that African Americans would venture to Mexico to see American pictures shown in theaters there. She is pictured at the Women's Department of the Greater El Paso Chamber of Commerce annual installation luncheon with Frances Grundy Hills (center) and Barbara Brown. (Courtesy of El Paso Inc.)

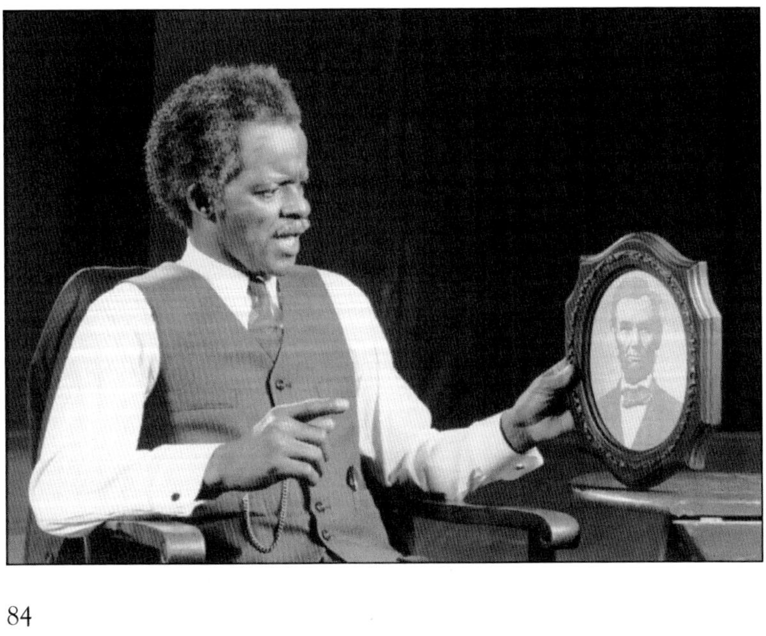

Bob Snead, actor, artist, historian, and recipient of three Purple Hearts (41 medals overall) for his heroism during the Vietnam War and over 30 years of military service, is seen performing his highly acclaimed one-person drama of Lt. Henry O. Flipper, the first African American graduate of West Point Military Academy. (Courtesy of *El Paso Times*.)

Archie Waters was a distinguished journalist, chess expert, and author of two books. He was also a mentor to famed chess wizard Bobby Fisher. Waters was best known in El Paso for his columns in the *El Paso Times*, in which he addressed questions related to the black community and overall contributions to American society. (Courtesy of *El Paso Times*.)

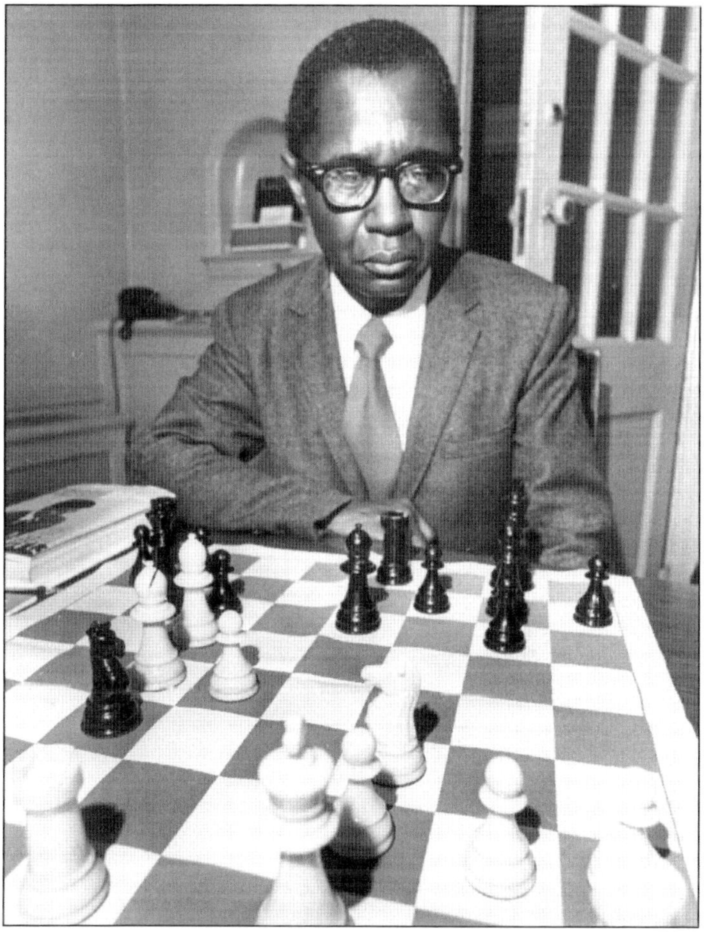

Below, El Paso's African American youth exercise their political power, attending an event hosted by the Black El Paso Democrats. (Courtesy of Joyce Stahmer.)

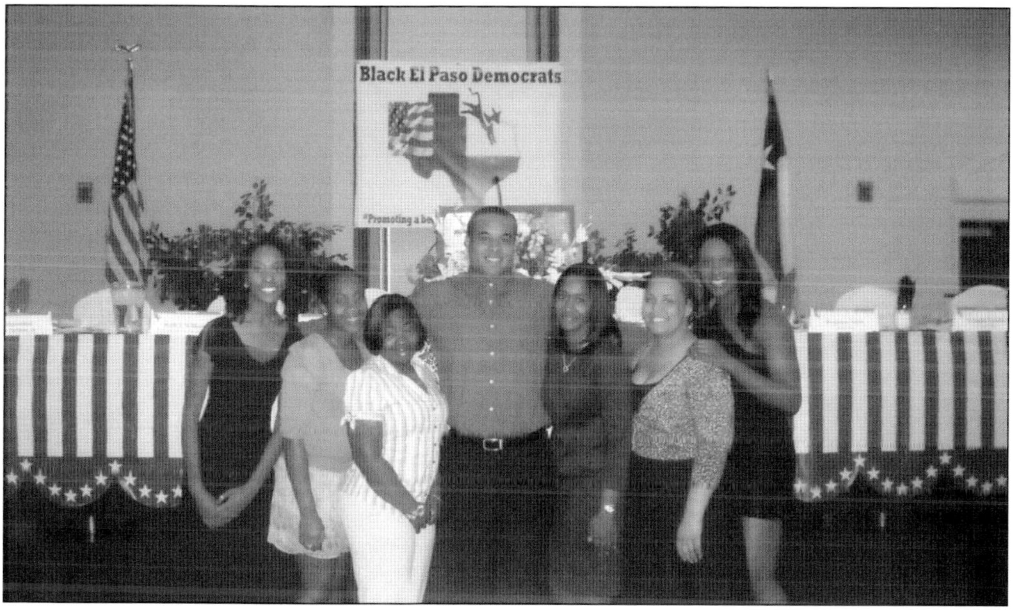

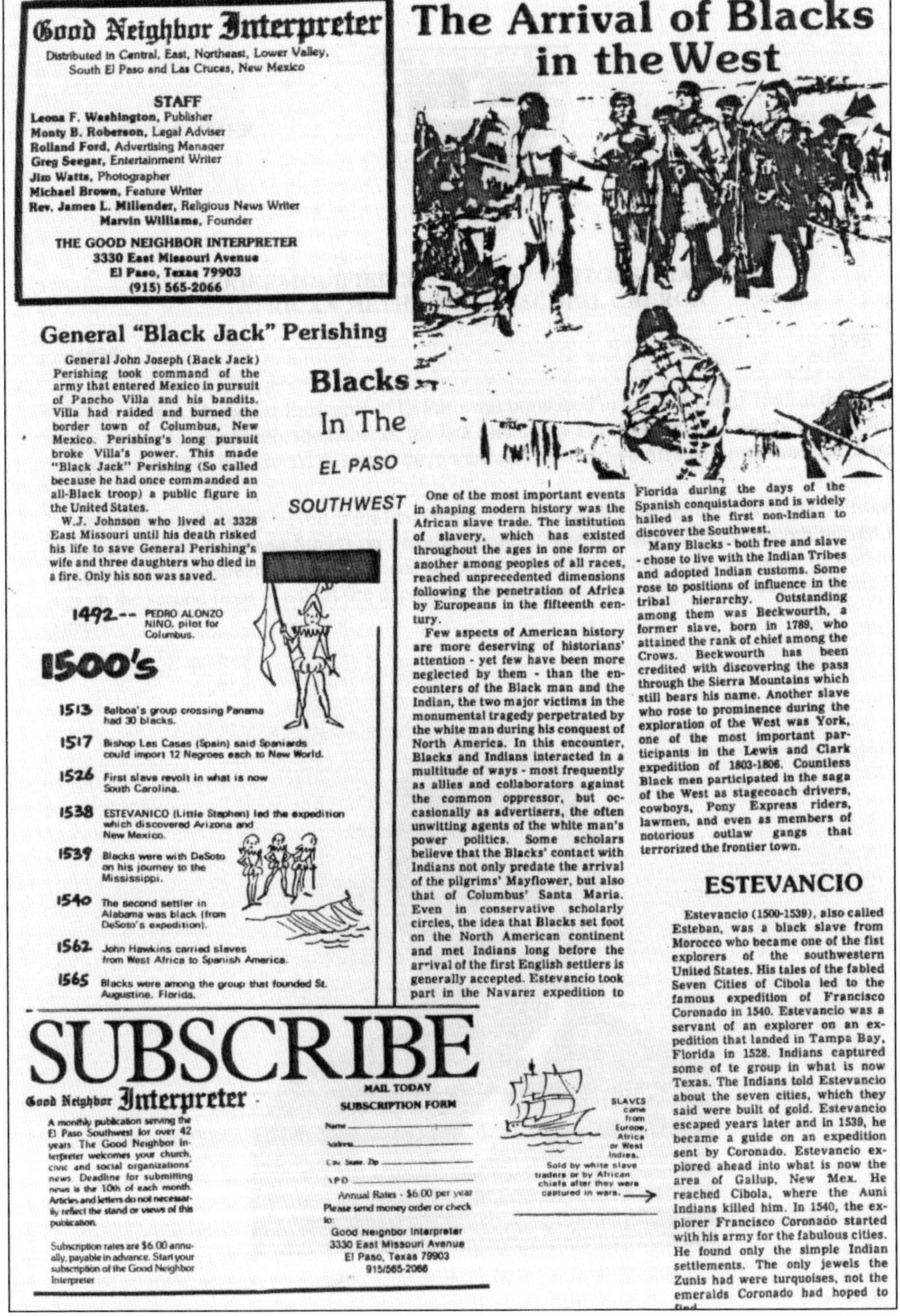

Page 2 Good Neighbor Interpreter 4 Centuries '81 Edition - July, 1981

Good Neighbor Interpreter

Distributed in Central, East, Northeast, Lower Valley, South El Paso and Las Cruces, New Mexico

STAFF

Leona F. Washington, Publisher
Monty B. Roberson, Legal Adviser
Rolland Ford, Advertising Manager
Greg Seegar, Entertainment Writer
Jim Watts, Photographer
Michael Brown, Feature Writer
Rev. James L. Millender, Religious News Writer
Marvin Williams, Founder

THE GOOD NEIGHBOR INTERPRETER
3330 East Missouri Avenue
El Paso, Texas 79903
(915) 565-2066

The Arrival of Blacks in the West

General "Black Jack" Perishing

General John Joseph (Back Jack) Perishing took command of the army that entered Mexico in pursuit of Pancho Villa and his bandits. Villa had raided and burned the border town of Columbus, New Mexico. Perishing's long pursuit broke Villa's power. This made "Black Jack" Perishing (So called because he had once commanded an all-Black troop) a public figure in the United States.

W.J. Johnson who lived at 3328 East Missouri until his death risked his life to save General Perishing's wife and three daughters who died in a fire. Only his son was saved.

Blacks In The EL PASO SOUTHWEST

1492-- PEDRO ALONZO NINO, pilot for Columbus.

1500's

1513 Balboa's group crossing Panama had 30 blacks.

1517 Bishop Las Casas (Spain) said Spaniards could import 12 Negroes each to New World.

1526 First slave revolt in what is now South Carolina.

1538 ESTEVANICO (Little Stephen) led the expedition which discovered Arizona and New Mexico.

1539 Blacks were with DeSoto on his journey to the Mississippi.

1540 The second settler in Alabama was black (from DeSoto's expedition).

1562 John Hawkins carried slaves from West Africa to Spanish America.

1565 Blacks were among the group that founded St. Augustine, Florida.

One of the most important events in shaping modern history was the African slave trade. The institution of slavery, which has existed throughout the ages in one form or another among peoples of all races, reached unprecedented dimensions following the penetration of Africa by Europeans in the fifteenth century.

Few aspects of American history are more deserving of historians' attention - yet few have been more neglected by them - than the encounters of the Black man and the Indian, the two major victims in the monumental tragedy perpetrated by the white man during his conquest of North America. In this encounter, Blacks and Indians interacted in a multitude of ways - most frequently as allies and collaborators against the common oppressor, but occasionally as advertisers, the often unwitting agents of the white man's power politics. Some scholars believe that the Blacks' contact with Indians not only predate the arrival of the pilgrims' Mayflower, but also that of Columbus' Santa Maria. Even in conservative scholarly circles, the idea that Blacks set foot on the North American continent and met Indians long before the arrival of the first English settlers is generally accepted. Estevancio took part in the Navarez expedition to Florida during the days of the Spanish conquistadors and is widely hailed as the first non-Indian to discover the Southwest.

Many Blacks - both free and slave - chose to live with the Indian Tribes and adopted Indian customs. Some rose to positions of influence in the tribal hierarchy. Outstanding among them was Beckwourth, a former slave, born in 1789, who attained the rank of chief among the Crows. Beckwourth has been credited with discovering the pass through the Sierra Mountains which still bears his name. Another slave who rose to prominence during the exploration of the West was York, one of the most important participants in the Lewis and Clark expedition of 1803-1806. Countless Black men participated in the saga of the West as stagecoach drivers, cowboys, Pony Express riders, lawmen, and even as members of notorious outlaw gangs that terrorized the frontier town.

ESTEVANCIO

Estevancio (1500-1539), also called Esteban, was a black slave from Morocco who became one of the fist explorers of the southwestern United States. His tales of the fabled Seven Cities of Cibola led to the famous expedition of Francisco Coronado in 1540. Estevancio was a servant of an explorer on an expedition that landed in Tampa Bay, Florida in 1528. Indians captured some of te group in what is now Texas. The Indians told Estevancio about the seven cities, which they said were built of gold. Estevancio escaped years later and in 1539, he became a guide on an expedition sent by Coronado. Estevancio explored ahead into what is now the area of Gallup, New Mex. He reached Cibola, where the Auni Indians killed him. In 1540, the explorer Francisco Coronado started with his army for the fabulous cities. He found only the simple Indian settlements. The only jewels the Zunis had were turquoises, not the emeralds Coronado had hoped to find.

SLAVES came from Europe, Africa or West Indies. Sold by white slave traders or by African chiefs after they were captured in wars.

SUBSCRIBE

Good Neighbor Interpreter

A monthly publication serving the El Paso Southwest for over 42 years. The Good Neighbor Interpreter welcomes your church, civic and social organizations' news. Deadline for submitting news is the 10th of each month. Articles and letters do not necessarily reflect the stand or views of this publication.

Subscription rates are $6.00 annually, payable in advance. Start your subscription of the Good Neighbor Interpreter

MAIL TODAY
SUBSCRIPTION FORM

Name ____
Address ____
City, State, Zip ____
\PO ____

Annual Rates - $6.00 per year
Please send money order or check to:
Good Neighbor Interpreter
3330 East Missouri Avenue
El Paso, Texas 79903
915/565-2066

The *Good Neighbor Interpreter*, subsequently produced by publisher and owner Leona Washington, evolved out of the *Southwest Torch* newspaper, founded by Marvin E. Williams. The paper was established to inform the African American El Paso community of events and issues pertinent to its welfare. (Courtesy of McCall Neighborhood Center.)

Thelma White graduated valedictorian from El Paso's Douglass High School and applied for enrollment in the city's Texas Western College in 1954. Denied entry, she drew on resources from the local and state chapters of the NAACP to bring a lawsuit against the college. Though she never attended Texas Western College, her lawsuit led to the integration of the college in 1955, when 12 black students enrolled. (Courtesy of *El Paso Times*.)

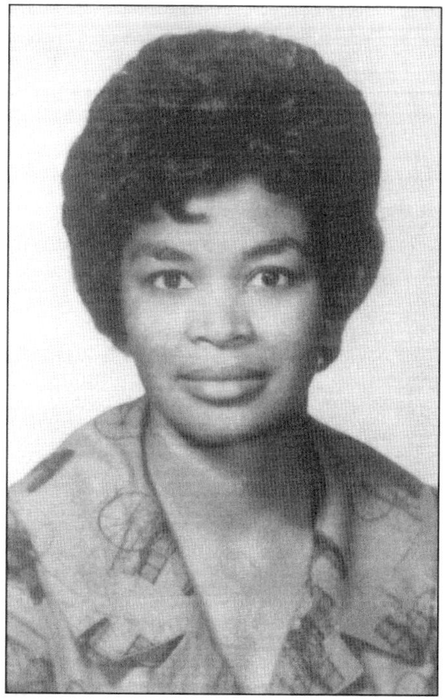

Alvin T. and Louise E. Johnson founded the Management Assistance Corporation of America, a multimillion-dollar company, which, at its peak, employed more than 325. The Johnsons are retired now and spend their time between their home in El Paso and one in the Caribbean. Their children have followed in their footsteps as entrepreneurs. Their son Renaud is owner and chief executive officer of his own company in El Paso and has received much recognition as a young businessman. (Courtesy of Alvin T. Johnson.)

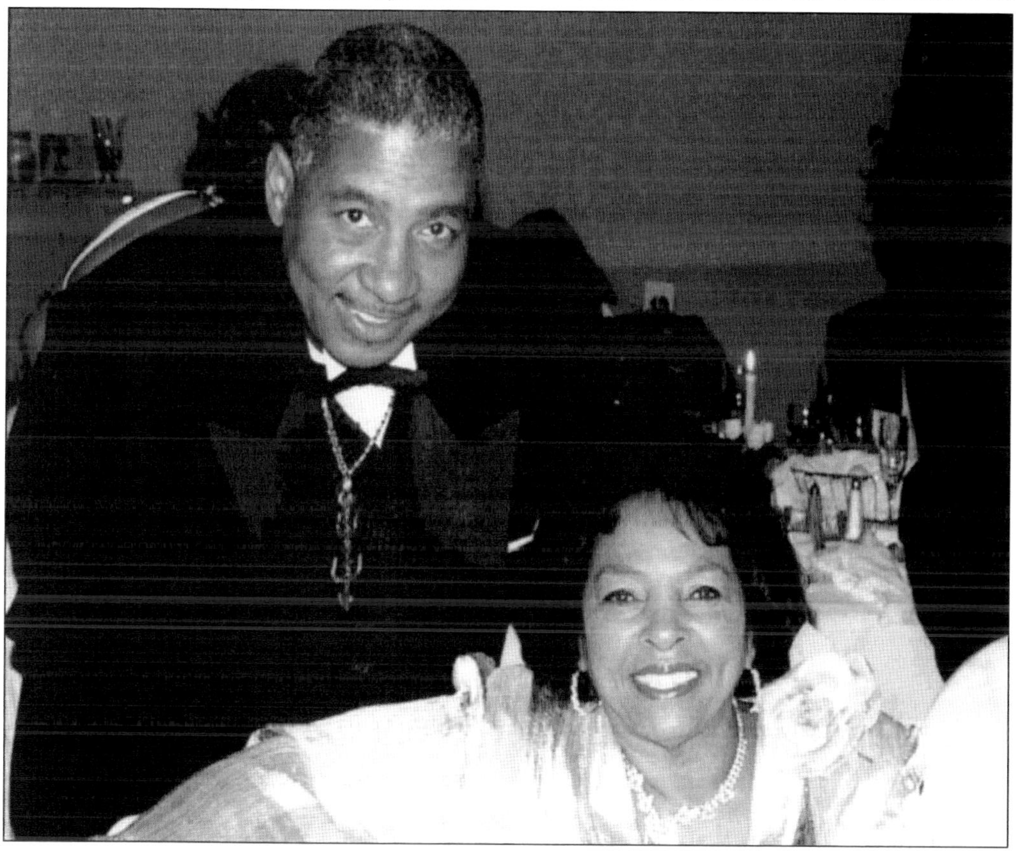

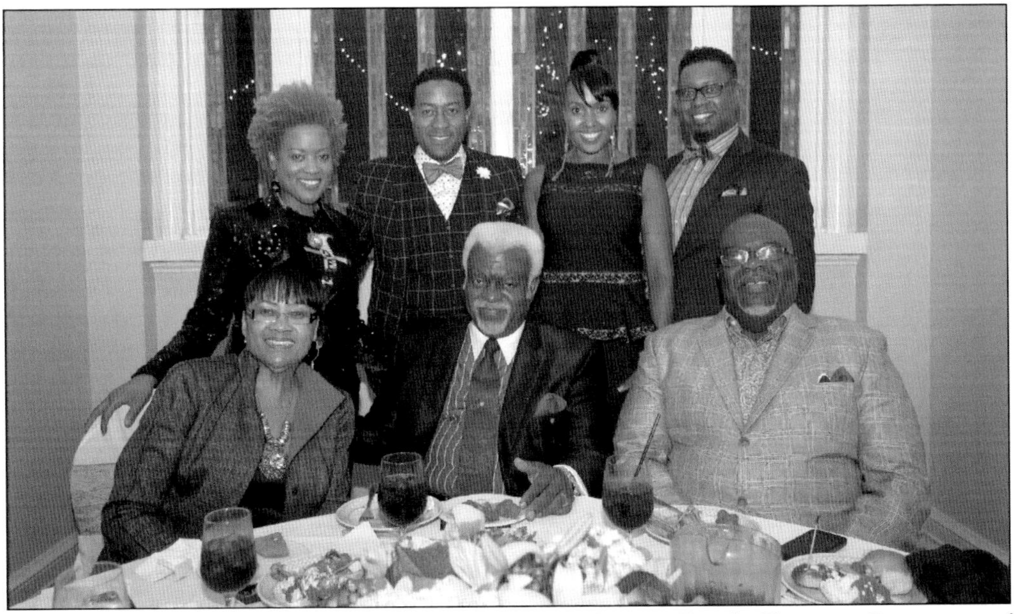

Bishop Richard L. and Pastor Adele Johnson minister to Destiny Family Christian Center, one of the largest churches in El Paso at which worshippers are predominately black, but represent the many other communities in the city. The church has a community outreach focus to strengthen families and help youth navigate the road of life. Food drives for the needy and blood drives for the sick are but some of the church's activities through the Omega Vision Community Development organization founded by Bishop and Pastor Johnson. In this photograph, they are pictured in El Paso with two of their three children (a doctor, lawyer, and minister) with the iconic T.D. Jakes. (Courtesy of Destiny Family Christian Center.)

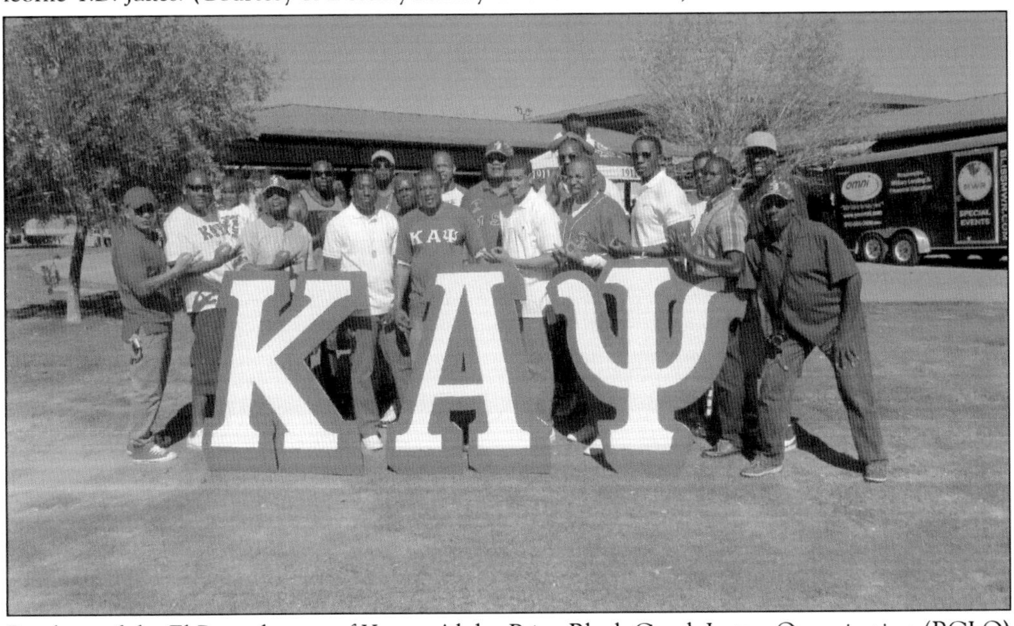

Brothers of the El Paso chapter of Kappa Alpha Psi, a Black Greek Letter Organization (BGLO) are pictured here. The fraternity is part of the "Divine Nine," a group of nine BGLOs, many of which were established at Howard University in Washington, DC. (Courtesy of James Ball.)

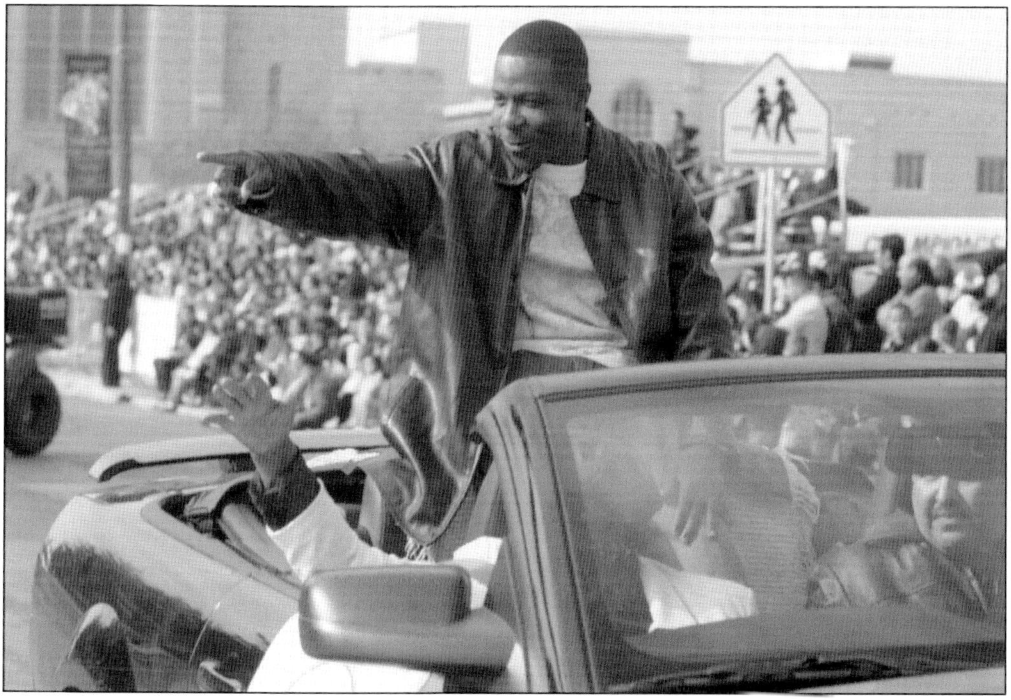

Ray Mickens is a retired National Football League cornerback for the New York Jets, Cleveland Browns, and New England Patriots. He grew up in El Paso and was All-State at Andress High. Because of his illustrious athletic career, Ray has been inducted into the El Paso Athletic Hall of Fame. (Courtesy of the African American Studies Program, University of Texas at El Paso.)

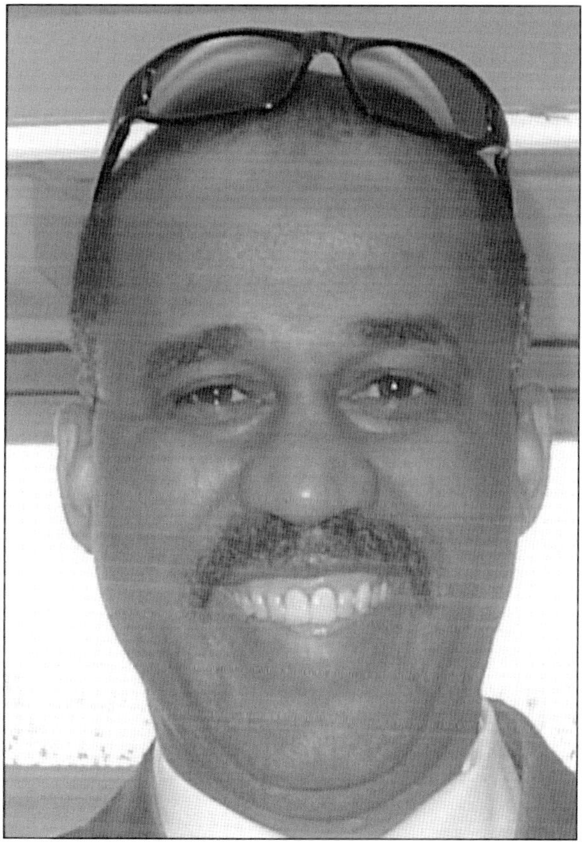

Wayne Thornton is a public relations officer with El Paso Department of Parks and Recreation. He is also a columnist for the *El Paso Times*. His essays frequently cover sports activities, icons, and recreational history and events in El Paso. (Courtesy of *El Paso Times*.)

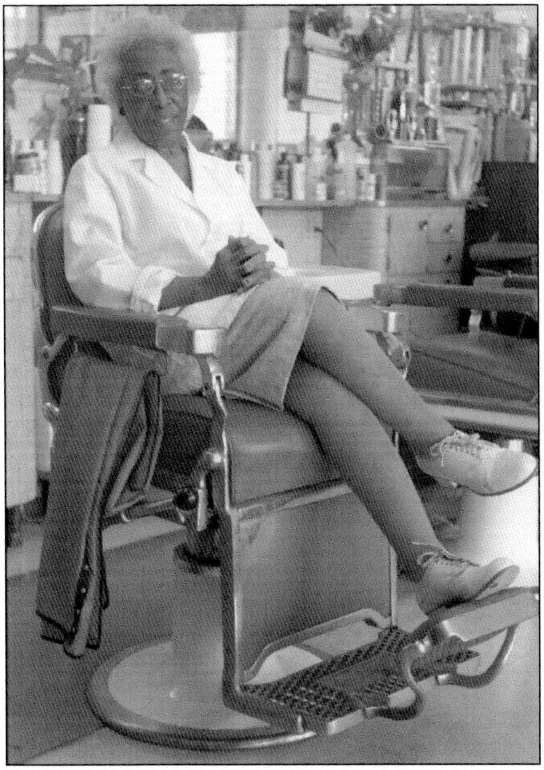

Estine Davis is an entrepreneur and civil leader. Estine's Barbershop is the place where many El Pasoans go to get a haircut and discuss the latest events. Davis annually and almost singlehandedly builds a float for the city's Thanksgiving parade. She was president of the Donnie W. Brown Buffalo Soldiers Chapter; each year, it is one of the major organizers of the Miss Black El Paso Pageant. (Courtesy of Estine Davis.)

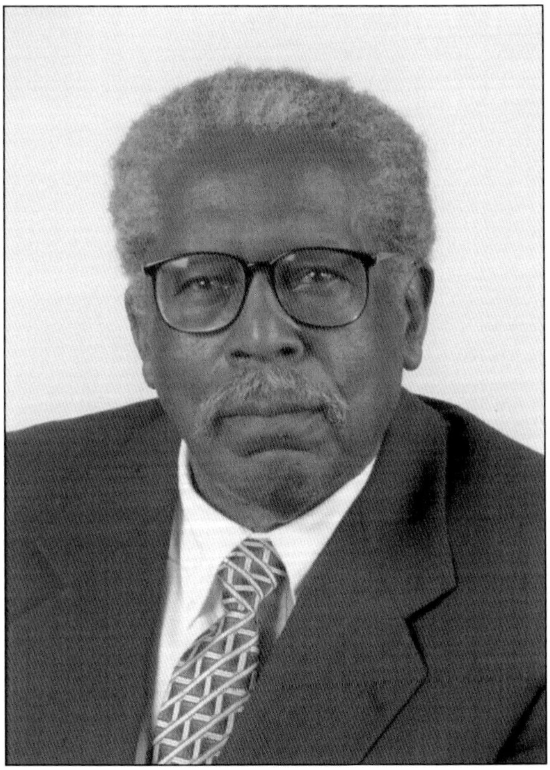

Algie A. Felder is owner of El Paso–based radio station KPAS-FM 103.1, which plays inspirational and gospel music and the news. Programming is done in English and Spanish and the station has listeners in Fabens, El Paso County, Hudspeth, and other border areas extending into Mexico. (Courtesy of the African American Studies Program, University of Texas at El Paso.)

Raymond Cartwright retired as chief warrant officer from the military and took up residency in El Paso. He is a senior instructor at Park College and is known for his good work in the Pan-Hellenic Council and McCall Neighborhood Center. Cartwright is also a licensed private pilot. (Courtesy of *El Paso Times.*)

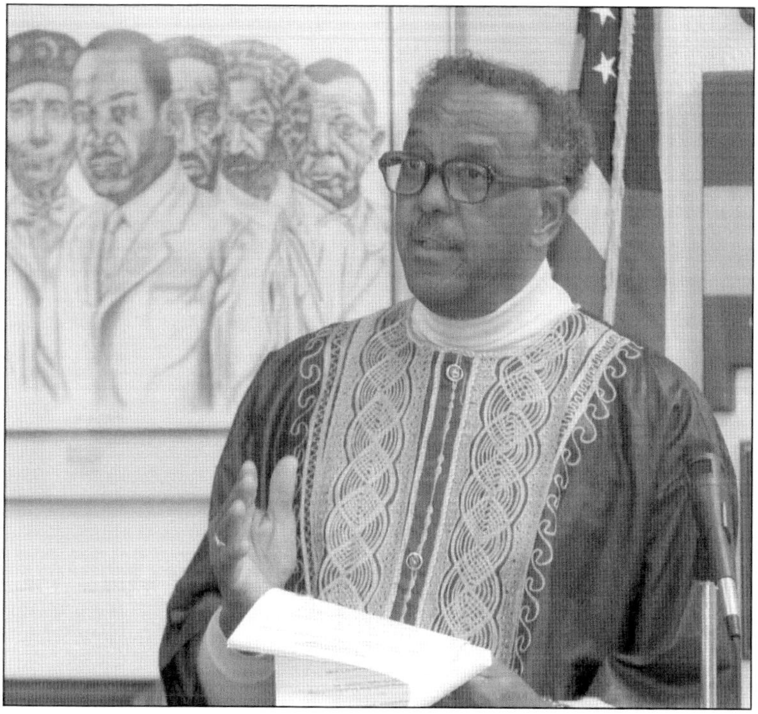

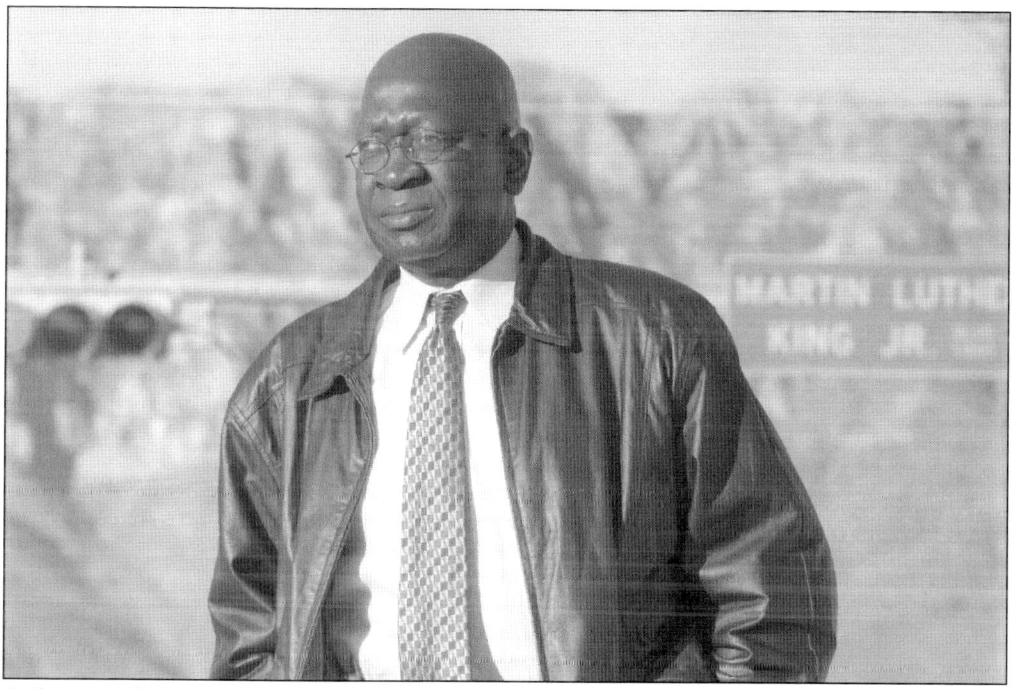

A decorated Vietnam veteran, Carl Robinson is the third African American elected to El Paso City Council. He has been very active in serving the larger city of El Paso and takes a keen interest in organizing events for Juneteenth and Black History Month. He serves as chairman of the annual Dr. Martin Luther King Food Drive committee. He is the recipient of many awards for his civic-minded activities to uplift the community. (Courtesy of *El Paso Times.*)

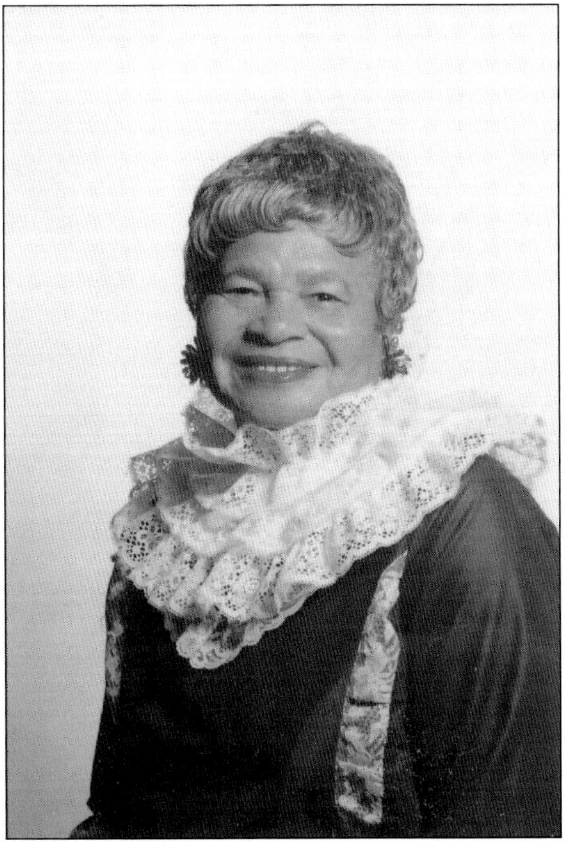

In 1997, Hermie Brown was honored as Fashionable Woman of the Southwest. She was always dressed impeccably in fashion befitting the occasion, especially the Black History Month and Juneteenth celebrations. She was a member of the Zeta Sorority and Shiloh Church. She mentored and connected people to work together for progress. The Donnie W. Brown Buffalo Soldiers Chapter of El Paso was named after her husband. (Courtesy of Dr. Maceo Crenshaw Dailey Jr.)

Raymond and Julie Hart are participating in a Kwanzaa celebration at the McCall Neighborhood Center. (Courtesy of *El Paso Times*.)

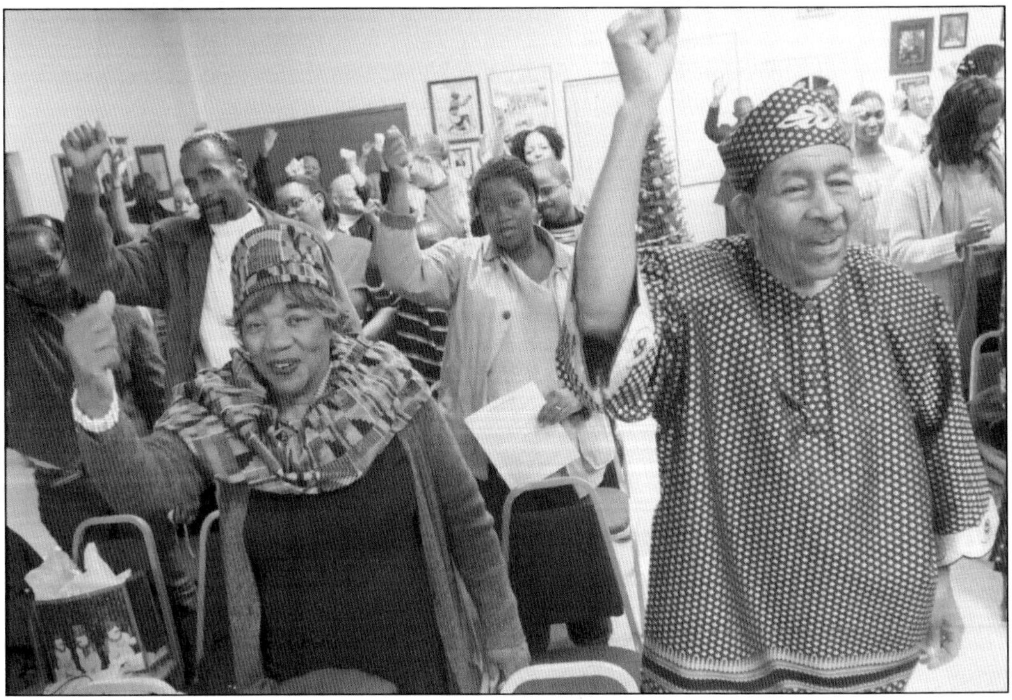

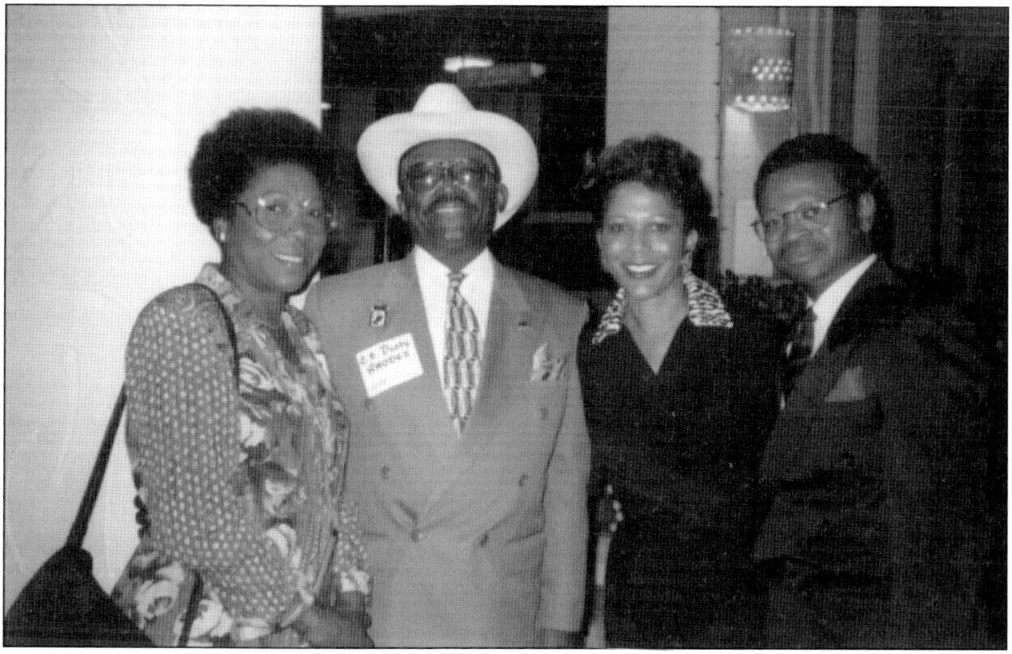

Dusty and Rebecca Rhodes and Michael and Ethel Kindred are pictured on the occasion of a University of Texas at El Paso reception to announce the formation of the African American Studies Program and the naming of its director, Dr. Maceo Crenshaw Dailey Jr. (Courtesy of Dr. Maceo Crenshaw Dailey Jr.)

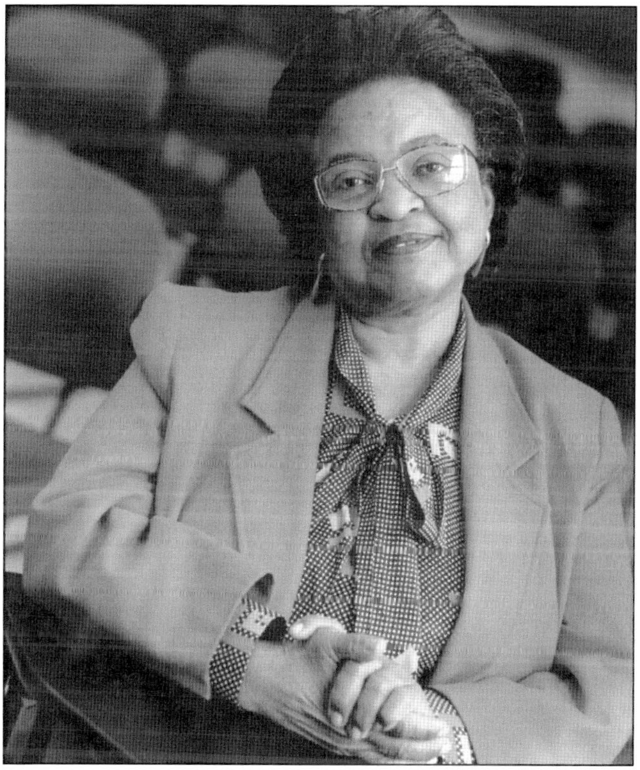

Born in 1932, Sarah Watley-Beal was the first black Douglass School graduate to become a professor at the University of Texas at El Paso in 1972, where she was an instructor in sociology. She earned both her bachelor's and master's degrees at Texas Tech University. Watley-Beal, pictured in 1997, was 71 years old when she died in 2004. (Courtesy of the African American Studies Program, University of Texas at El Paso.)

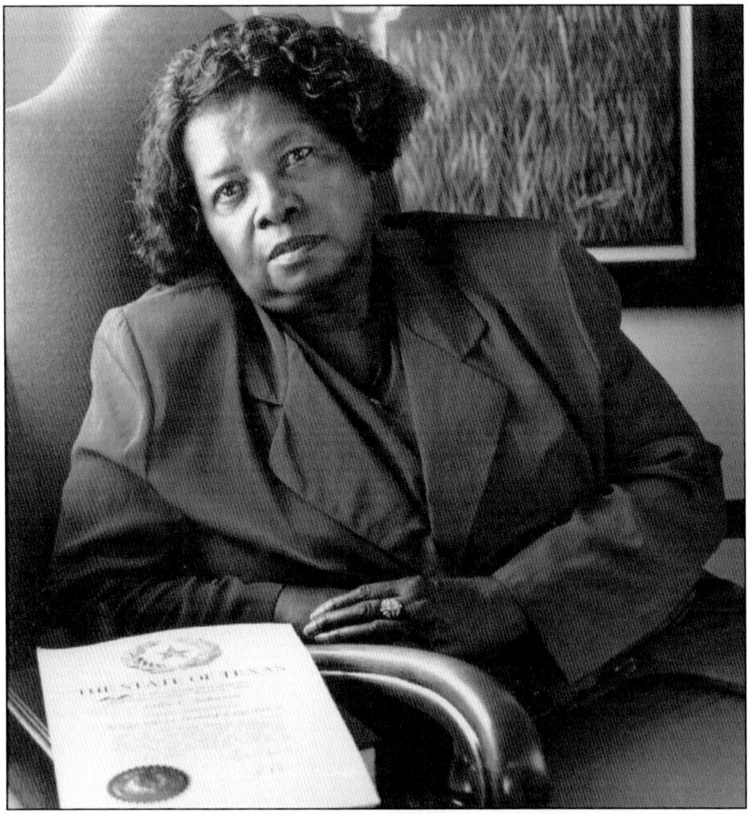

Sallie Johnson was a 1944 graduate of Douglass High School. She later attended Dillard University and Memorial Hospital School of Nursing and spent her career as a nurse manager at El Paso City-County Health Department. She served on the El Paso Area Agency on Aging board and was appointed by Pres. George W. Bush to the Texas Silver-Haired Legislature. (Courtesy of the African American Studies Program, University of Texas at El Paso.)

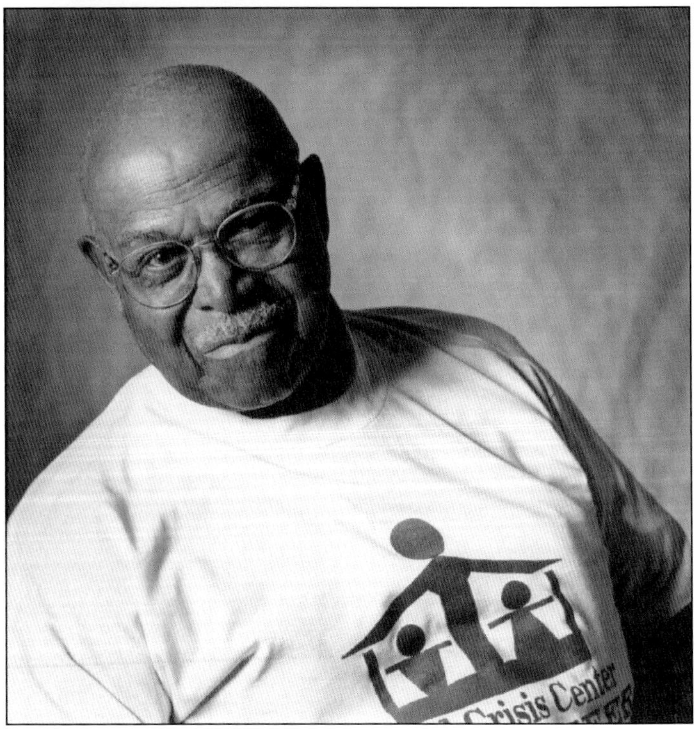

Tommie Lee Bell moved to El Paso in the 1930s and lived here for 60 years with his wife, Lenora, and their two children. He began his career at the Plaza Hotel as a hotel operator and, eventually, moved on to Beaumont Army Medical Center, where he was one of the first three blacks to work as a civilian. After 25 years of service, Bell retired from Beaumont Army Medical Center. (Courtesy of the African American Studies Program, University of Texas at El Paso.)

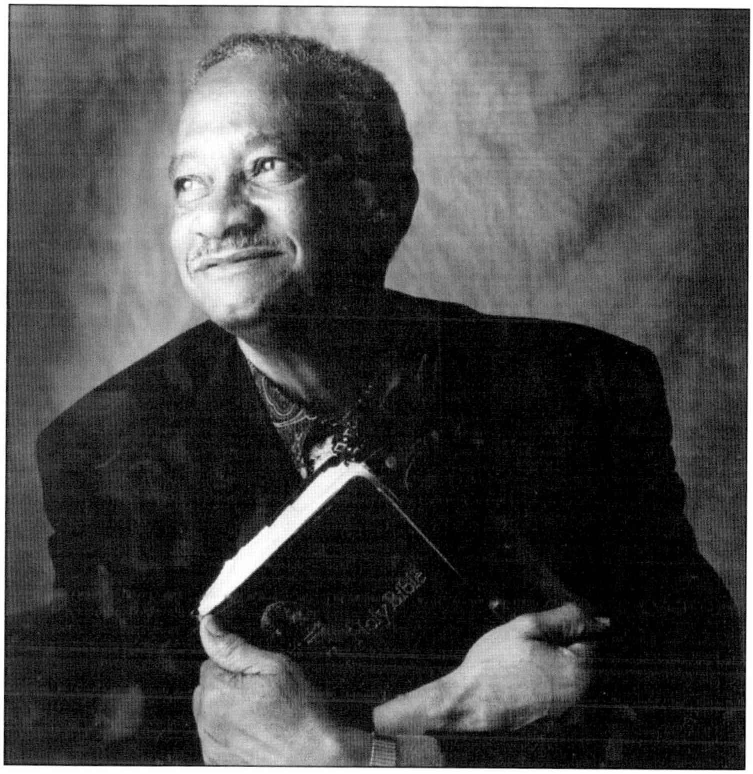

Sr. District Elder Clayton Carr and his wife, Carmi, migrated to El Paso from Albuquerque, New Mexico. Carr was pastor and founder of Bethlehem Temple located at 4131 East Yandell Drive in El Paso. (Courtesy of the African American Studies Program, University of Texas at El Paso.)

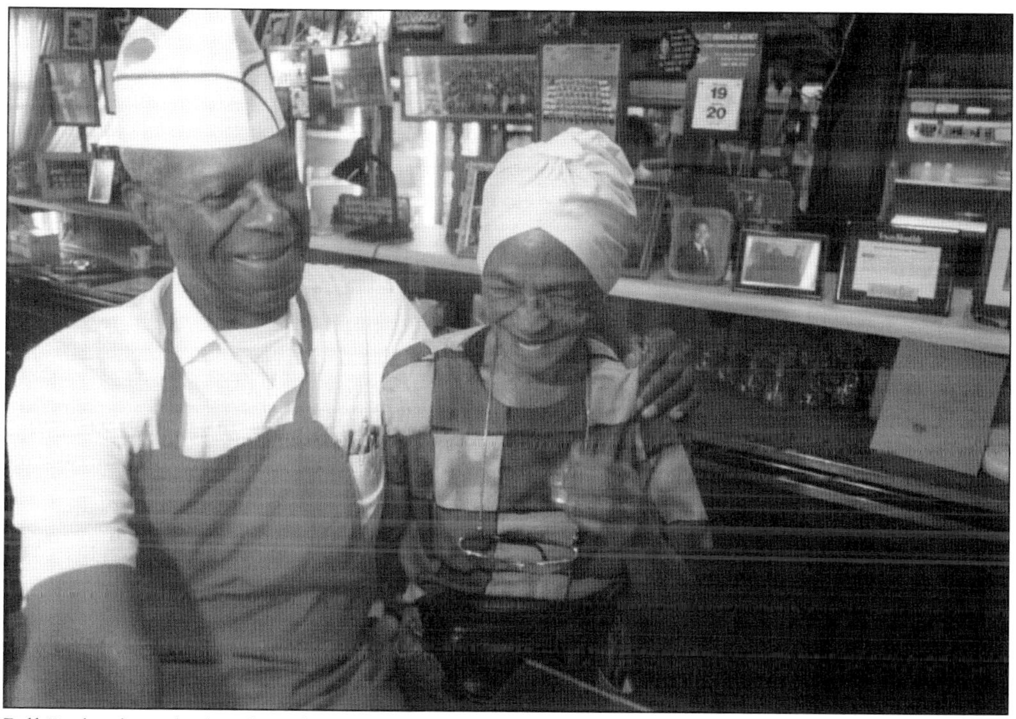

Bill Parks shared a laugh with a friend in his dining establishment in El Paso which was known for great barbecue. (Courtesy of *El Paso Times*.)

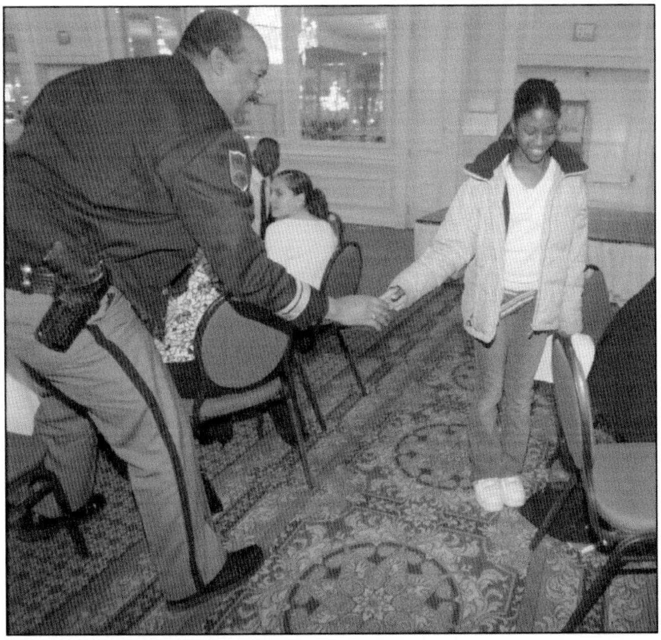

Paul E. Cross currently works for the El Paso County Sheriff's Department and was formerly an officer in the El Paso Police Department. Among his awards are El Paso Police Department Executive of the Year in 2006 and the Adelante Con Ganas Award from state senator Eliot Shapleigh in 2005. Officer Cross is one of the foremost investigators in crimes of homicide, robbery, and sexual assaults. He is also an expert in counter terrorism and teaches courses in this subject at the University of Texas at El Paso. (Courtesy of *El Paso Times*.)

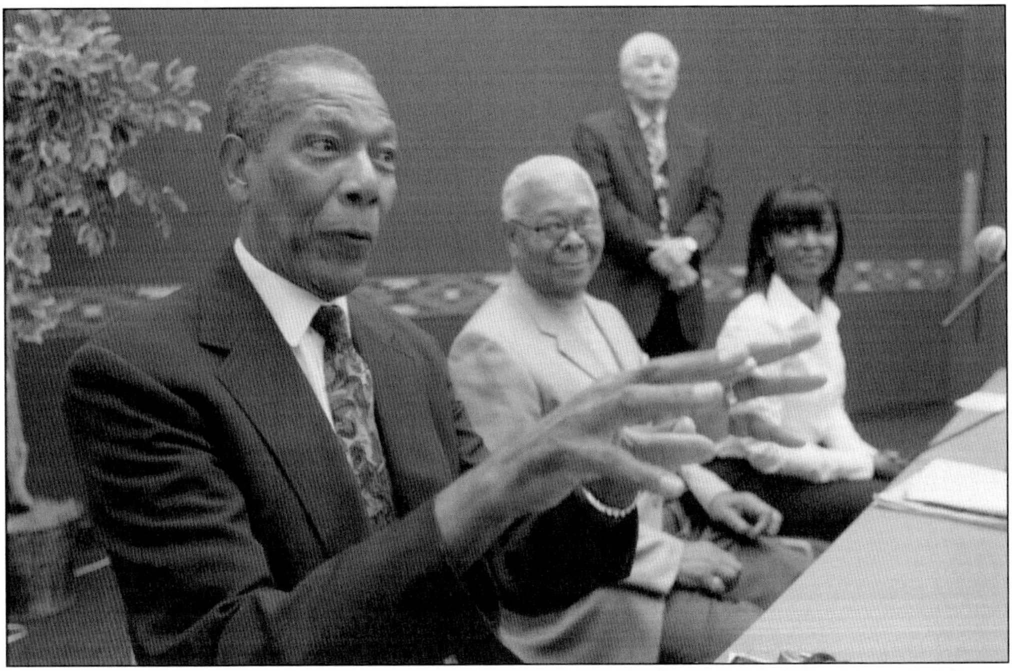

Dr. Maceo Crenshaw Dailey Jr. (standing) is pictured overlooking two of the original African American students, Joe Atkins (seated, left) and Marcellus Fullmore (seated, center), who attended the University of Texas at El Paso. Both spoke at the 50-year celebration for integration of the university. Joe Atkins was refused admission because of his race at now University of North Texas, so he came to the University of Texas at El Paso. His father and the NAACP filed a lawsuit against University of North Texas and won, but by the time of the verdict, Atkins had found a home at the University of Texas at El Paso. Seated at right is Chantre Camack, daughter of Thelma White. (Courtesy of *El Paso Times*.)

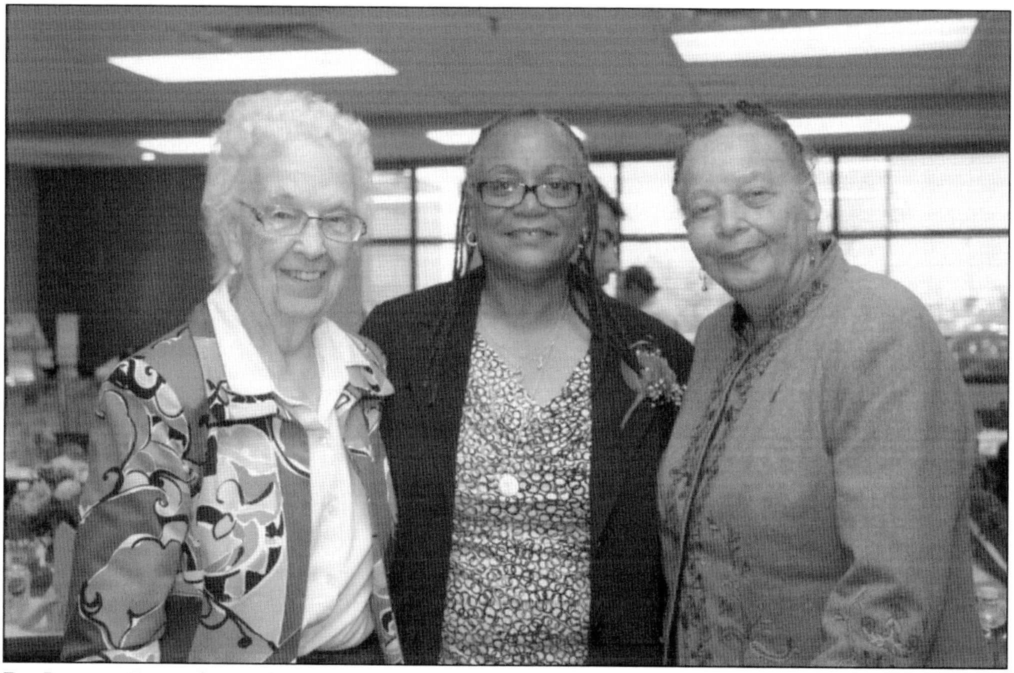

Dr. Patricia Davis (center) is a member of the Hills family, who have resided in El Paso for several generations. Dr. Davis is an OB/GYN. She is pictured with Edith Reaves (left) and her mother, Frances Grundy Hills (right), at a Doctors Day celebration at Del Sol Hospital. (Courtesy of El Paso Inc.)

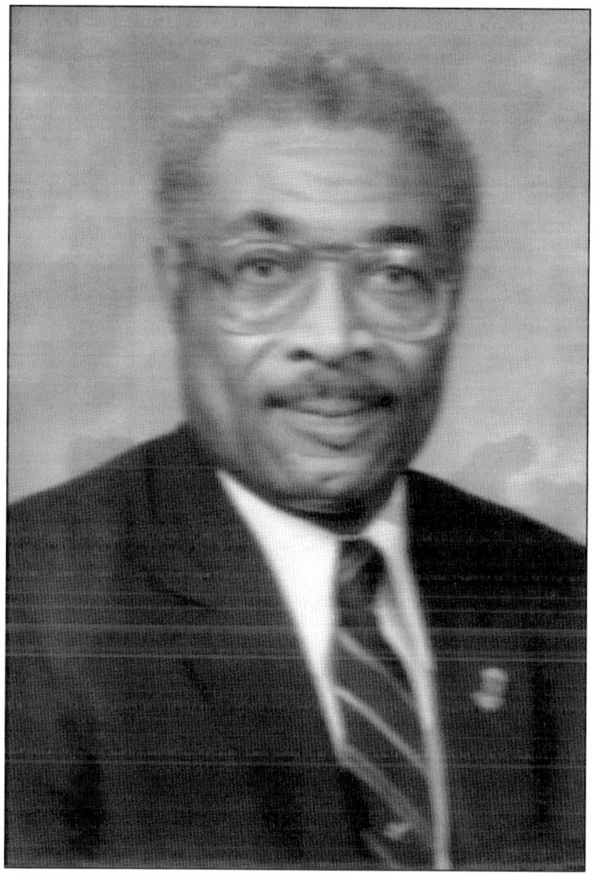

Jethro Lee Hills Sr. was El Paso's first African American city representative, elected in 1987. Born in Chicago Heights, Illinois, in 1927, Hills served in the armed forces from 1946 until 1955. He married El Pasoan Frances Marie Grundy in 1949 and worked at White Sands Missile Range for 21 years. He later retired as the chief of the review and analysis branch of the comptroller's office. Hills served on many volunteer boards and commissions, remaining active in the community until his death in 2003. (Courtesy of the Hills family.)

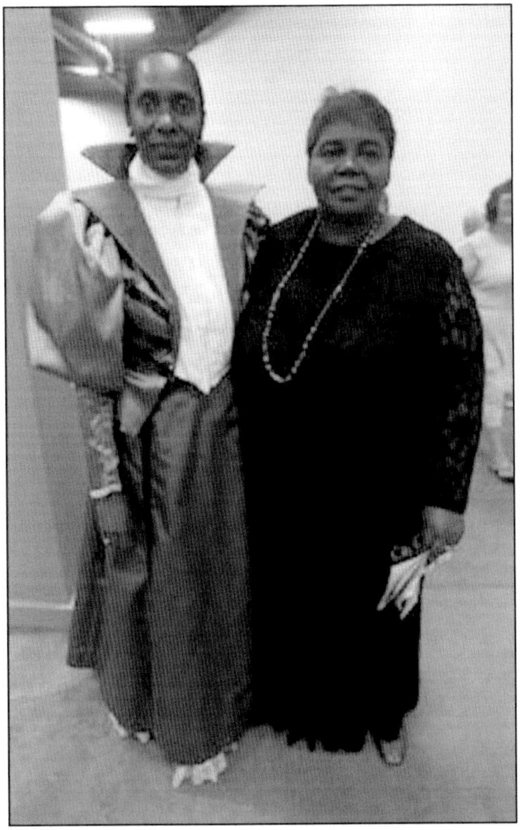

Pastor Carolyne Redic (right) stands with an unidentified person. Carolyne and John Redic launched the Victory Warriors Drill and Dance Academy in 1995 as part of their ministry to strengthen children and their families. In addition to learning through dance and drill instructions, the children, ranging in ages from 6 to 17, are provided with instructions for educational development and cultural programs. Pres. George W. Bush recognized Pastor Redic's work with the Victory Warriors, and she receives the support of a number of agencies and institutions for her work with youngsters. (Courtesy of the African American Studies Program, University of Texas at El Paso.)

The Victory Warriors Drill and Dance Academy performs at the McCall Neighborhood Center for a Juneteenth celebration. (Courtesy of *El Paso Times*.)

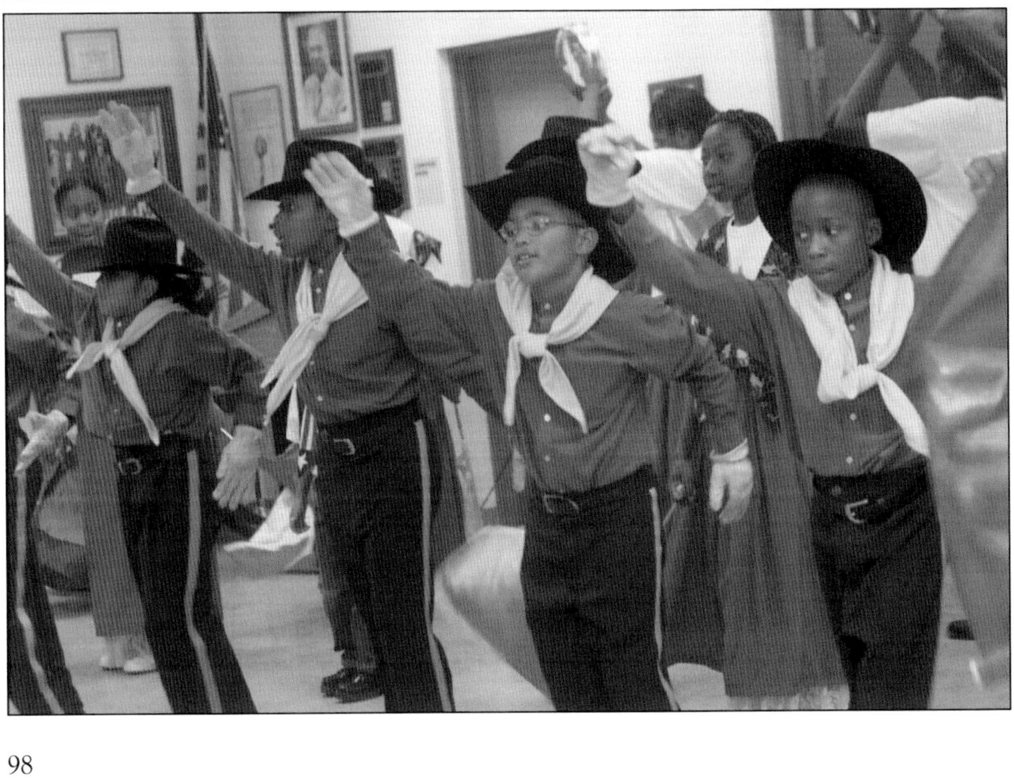

Bob and Paulette Wingo have made a tremendous difference in the quality of life in El Paso by their accomplishments in entrepreneurship and education. Bob Wingo is president and chief executive officer of Sanders and Wingo, a national advertising company with prominent clients like State Farm, AT&T, Chevrolet, the US Postal Service, and Peter Piper Pizza. He was a significant factor in the fundraising and erecting of the Washington, DC, memorial for Martin Luther King Jr. Paulette Wingo is a former schoolteacher who has published a prize-winning book, *Learning Doesn't Have to Be Complicated: A Parent's Survival Guide for the School Years.* (Courtesy of *El Paso Times.*)

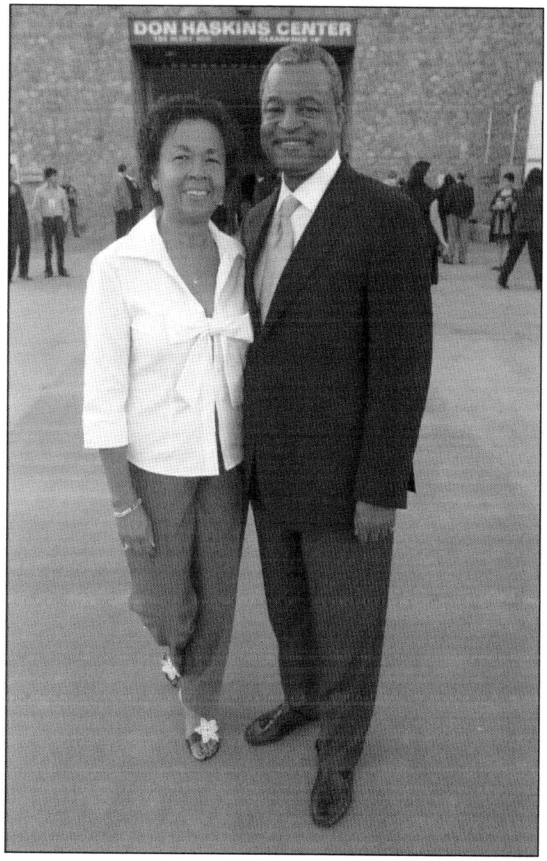

African American historian Dr. Quintard Taylor (left) and Dr. Brown (right), pastor of Shiloh Baptist Church, are enjoying their breakfast before Taylor addressed a crowd for the Juneteenth celebration at the McCall Neighborhood Center on June 16, 2006. (Courtesy of *El Paso Times.*)

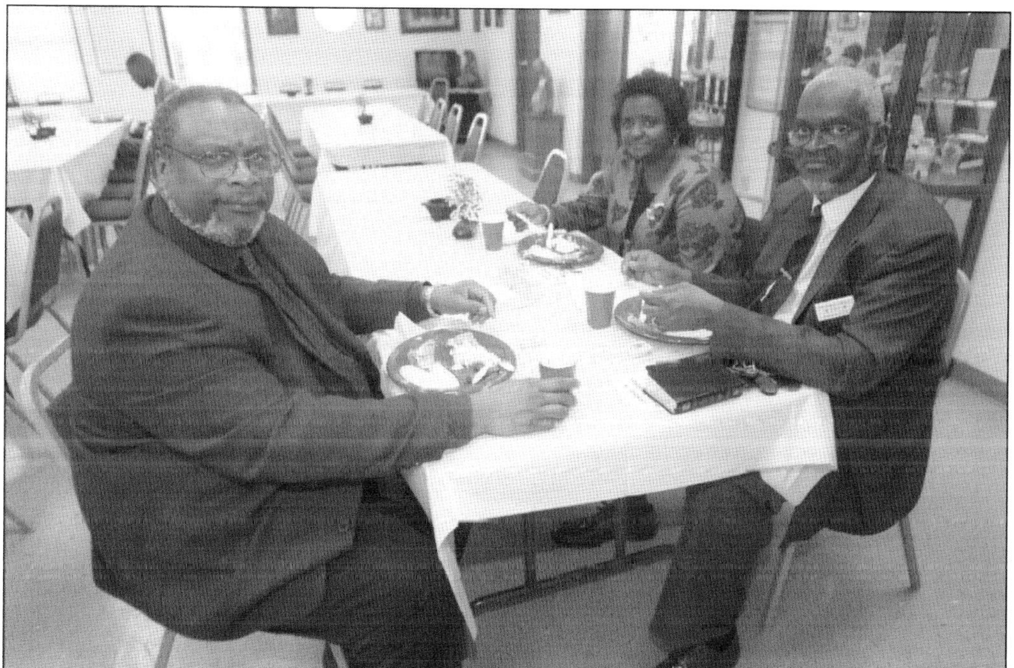

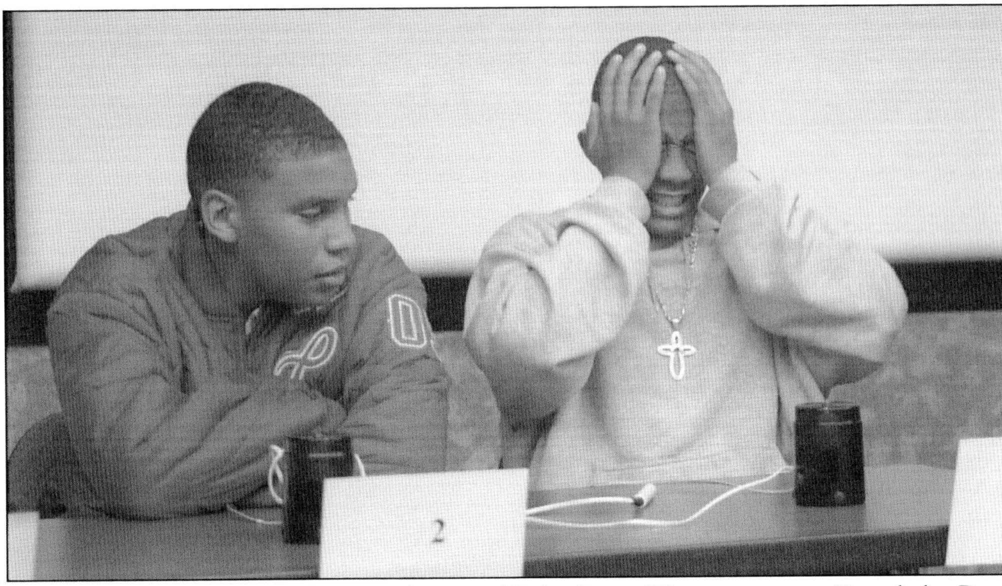

Every February, the El Paso alumnae chapter of Delta Sigma Theta sponsors a Knowledge Bowl to educate and celebrate the history of African Americans. Teams from various schools and churches participate, and they are tested on global, national, and local history pertaining to African Americans. (Courtesy of *El Paso Times.*)

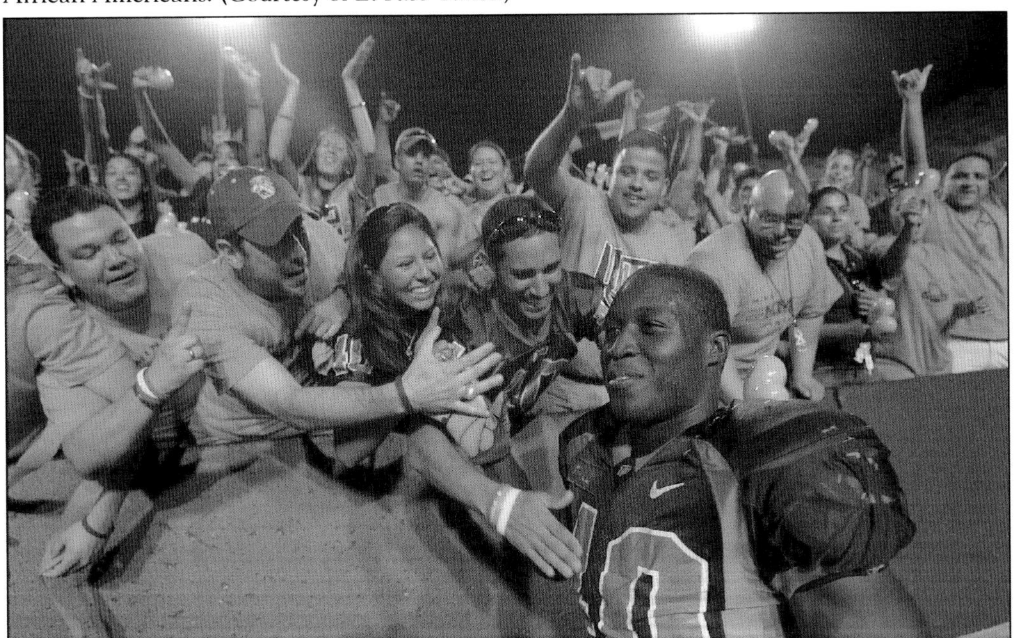

Thomas Howard played with the University of Texas at El Paso Miners, and in 2006, he was drafted by the Oakland Raiders and played linebacker for them until 2011. In 2012, he played for the Cincinnati Bengals. Howard initiated the Thomas Howard Foundation in 2012 for University of Texas at El Paso athletes and hosted an inaugural Athletic & Academic Awards Reception at Coronodo Country Club. Howard died in a car crash on November 18, 2013, at the age of 30. (Courtesy of *El Paso Times.*)

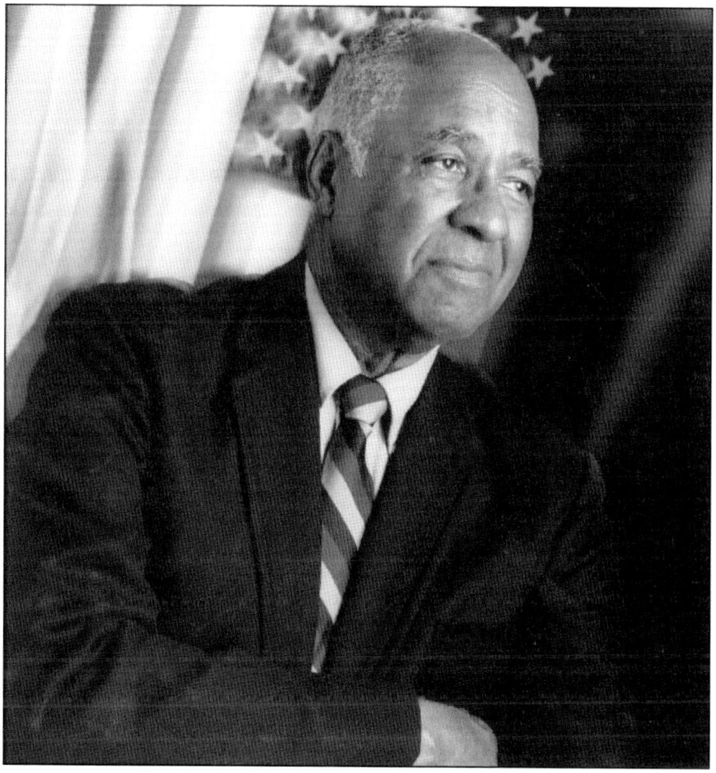

Maj. Gen. Edward Greer chose El Paso as his home after a distinguished career in the US Army that spanned over three decades. He has been awarded the Distinguished Service Medal, one of the military's highest honors. In 2013, General Greer served as chairman of the El Paso Retiree Council and was inducted into the Fort Bliss Hall of Fame. (Courtesy of the African American Studies Program, University of Texas at El Paso.)

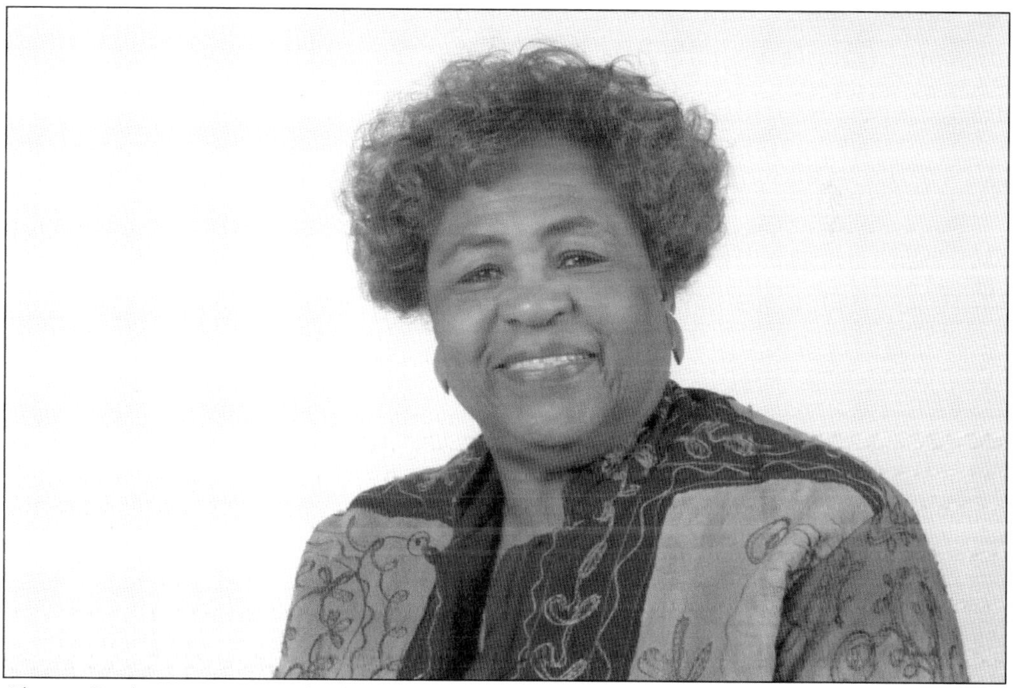

Cherrie Buchanon is a retired schoolteacher and former principal living in El Paso. She has been a stellar force in promoting education and community progress through her activities in several organizations and groups. (Courtesy of *El Paso Times*.)

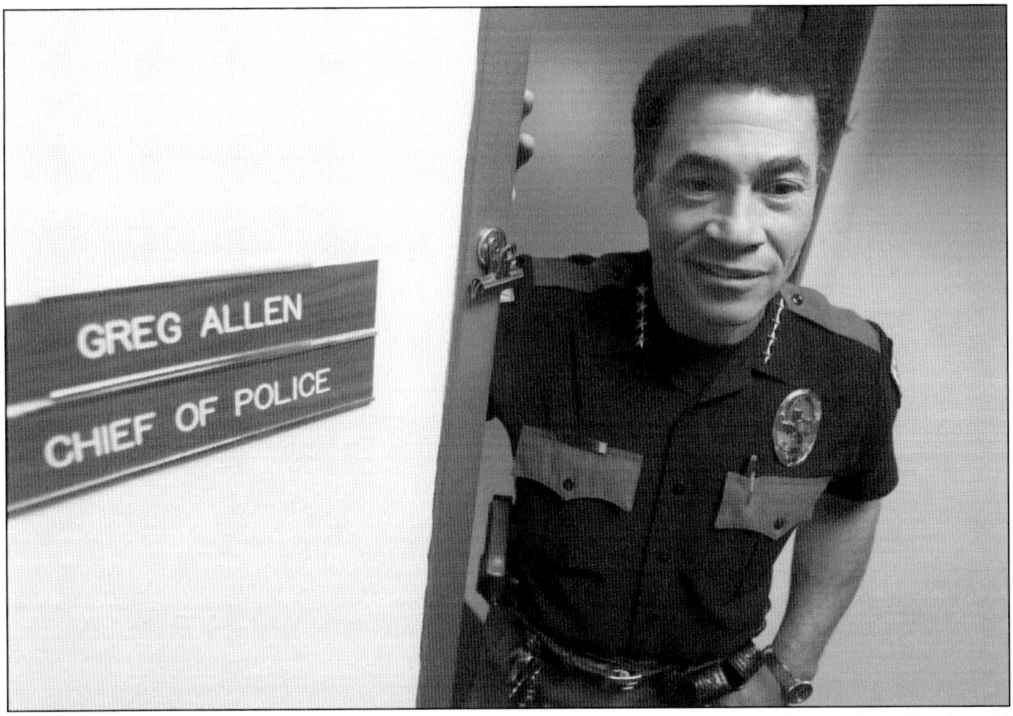

In 2008, Greg Allen became the first African American to be appointed as police chief in El Paso. He is a 33-year veteran of the El Paso Police Department and worked his way up through the ranks. Chief Allen graduated from the University of Texas at El Paso with a sociology degree in 1975. He is a martial arts expert. On his watch, El Paso has been named one of the safest cities in America. (Both, courtesy of *El Paso Times*.)

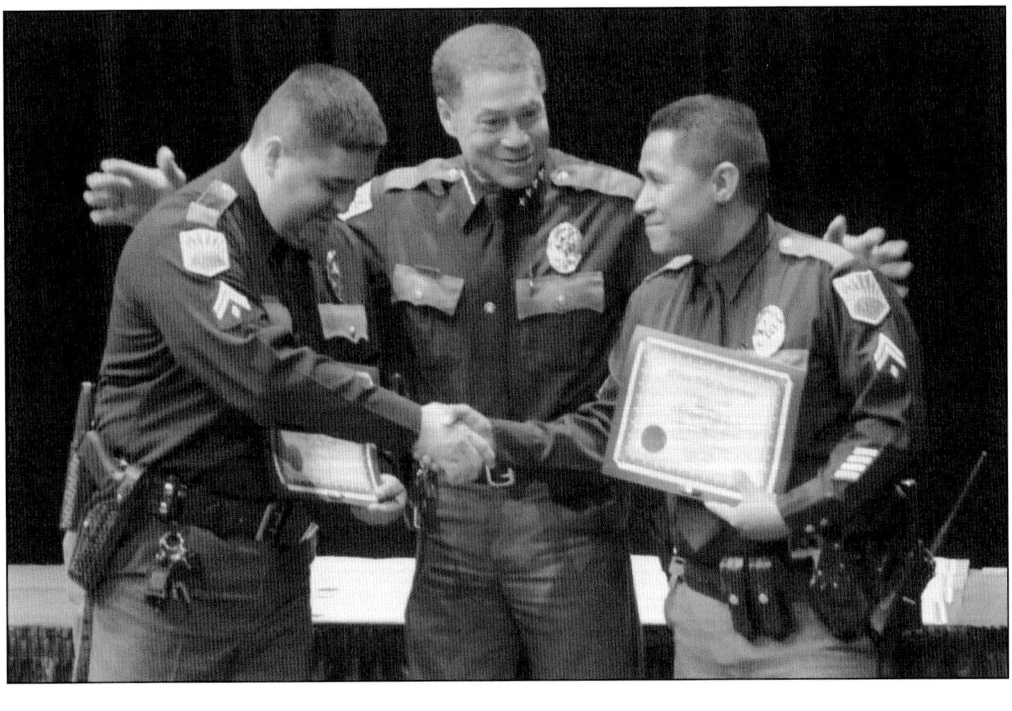

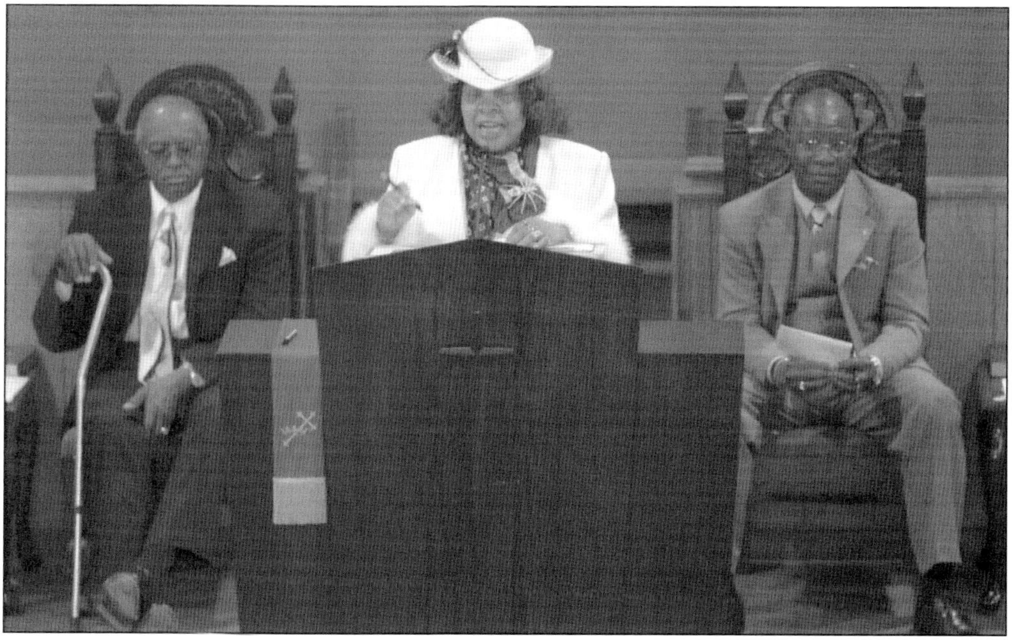

Bishop Johnnie Marion Washington of Full Gospel Evangelistic Temple of El Paso was president of the local chapter of the NAACP for 22 years. A participant in civil rights marches and sit-ins for jobs and equality during the 1950s and 1960s, Bishop Washington promoted similar change in El Paso. Her secular and ministerial leadership has led to significant and positive growth and development in El Paso. (Courtesy of *El Paso Times*.)

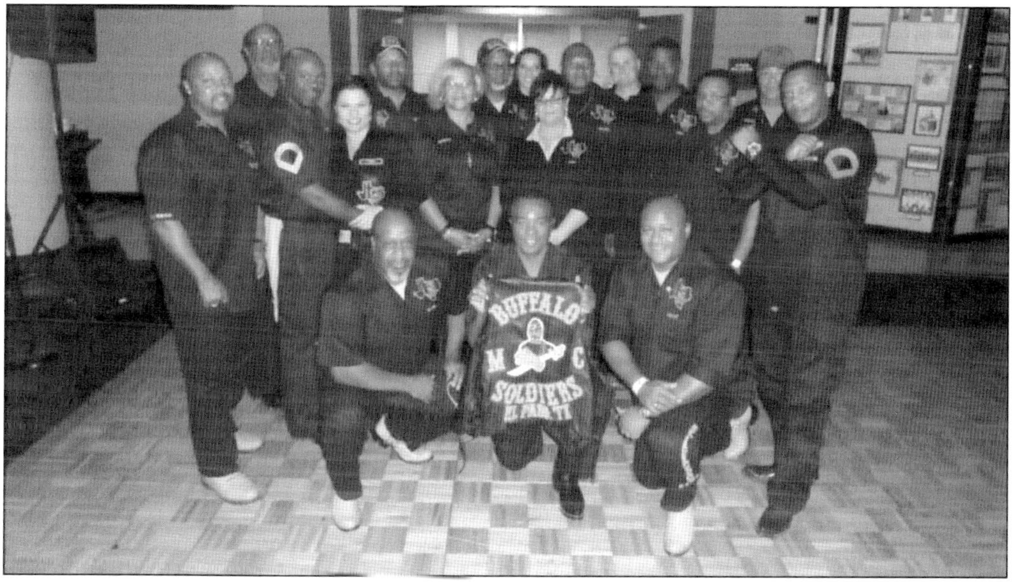

The Buffalo Soldiers Motorcycle Club of El Paso has a distinguished record of community service and charitable giving. Comprised mostly of former military men, this club singlehandedly led the campaign to erect headstones for unidentified Buffalo Soldiers buried in El Paso's Concordia Cemetery. The club has made significant contributions to El Paso Child Crisis Center, McCall Neighborhood Center, and Indian reservations in New Mexico and Arizona. (Courtesy of *El Paso Times*.)

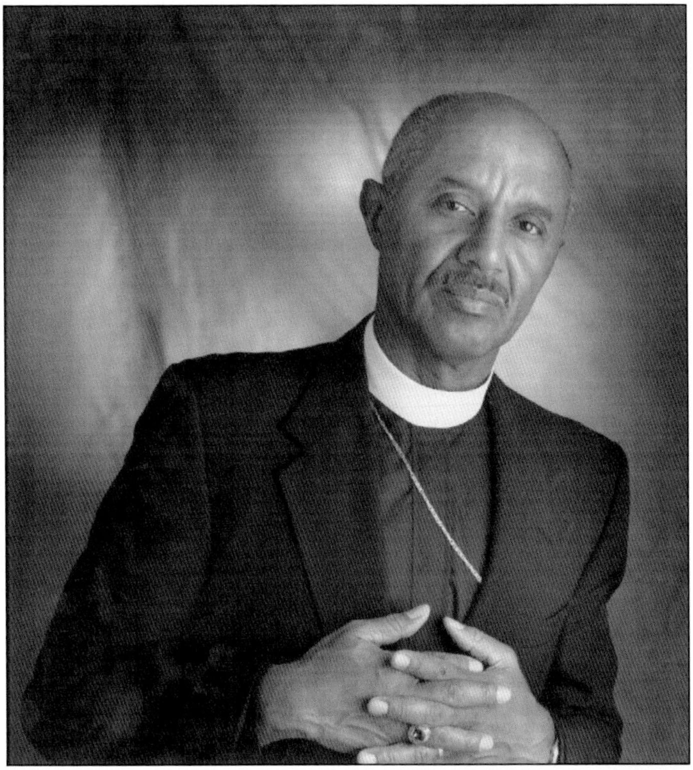

Bishop Lawson is a professor emeritus of physics at the University of Texas at El Paso and a widely published scientist. In 1967, he became the first African American with a doctorate to teach at the university. He was installed as bishop of the Texas Western Jurisdiction of the Church of God in Christ, and serves as pastor of Holy Light Church of God in Christ in El Paso. His civic endeavors include projects benefitting both the El Paso and Juarez communities. (Courtesy of the African American Studies Program, University of Texas at El Paso.)

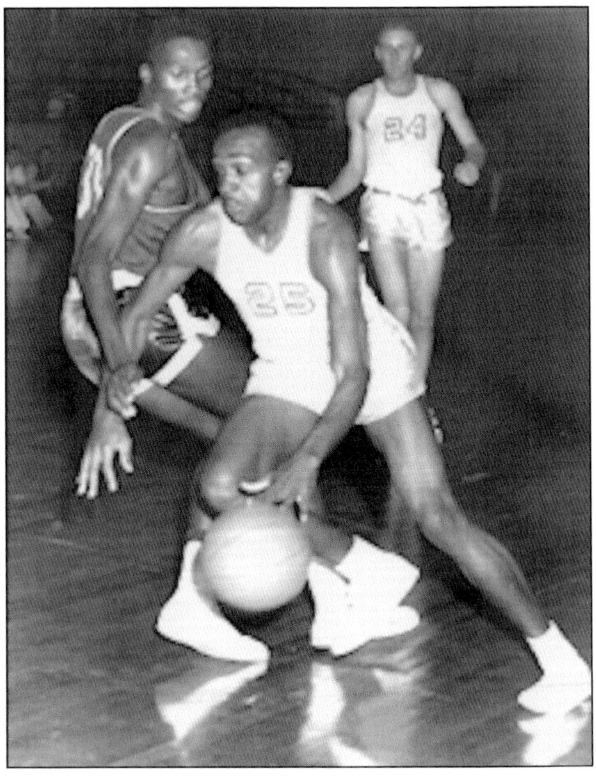

Charles Brown was the first African American student-athlete to attend Texas Western College in 1956. His performance both in the classroom and on the basketball court raised the bar considerably and led to the recruitment of other African American student-athletes. He led the Texas Western College team in scoring and rebounding during the three years he played. Brown subsequently moved to California, where he taught school and served as a top-level administrator until his retirement. (Courtesy of *El Paso Times*.)

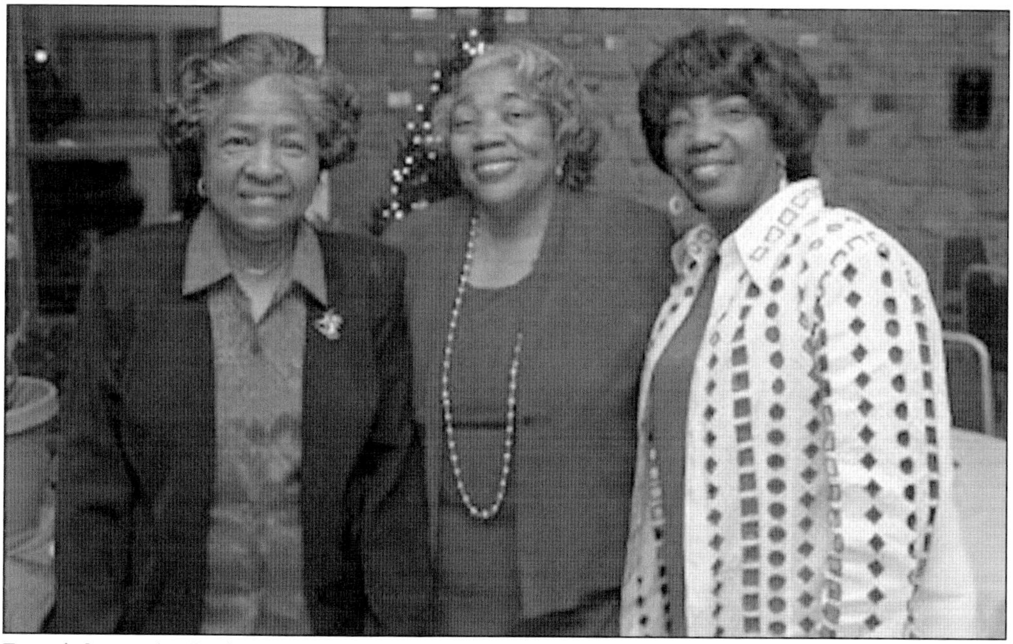

From left to right, Barbara J. Byrd, Juliet M. Hart, and Anna Howell posed at the 25th anniversary celebration for the McCall Neighborhood Center. These women donate their time to the operations of the McCall center, which is a gathering place for the African American community. (Courtesy of *El Paso Times*.)

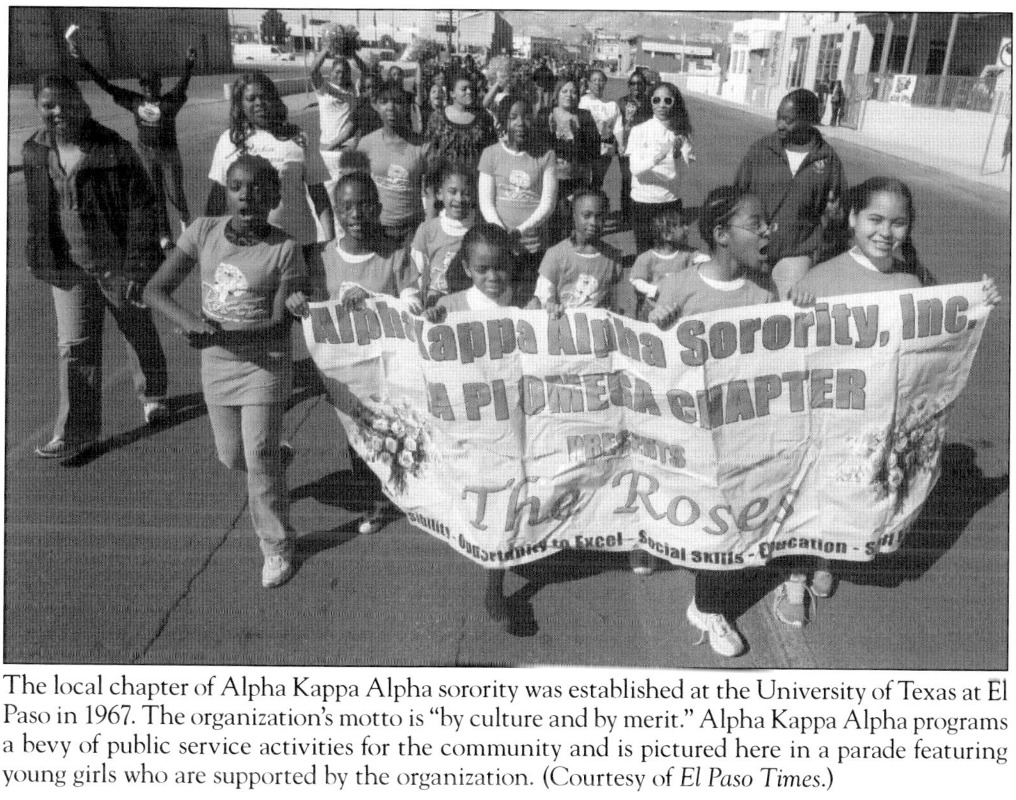

The local chapter of Alpha Kappa Alpha sorority was established at the University of Texas at El Paso in 1967. The organization's motto is "by culture and by merit." Alpha Kappa Alpha programs a bevy of public service activities for the community and is pictured here in a parade featuring young girls who are supported by the organization. (Courtesy of *El Paso Times*.)

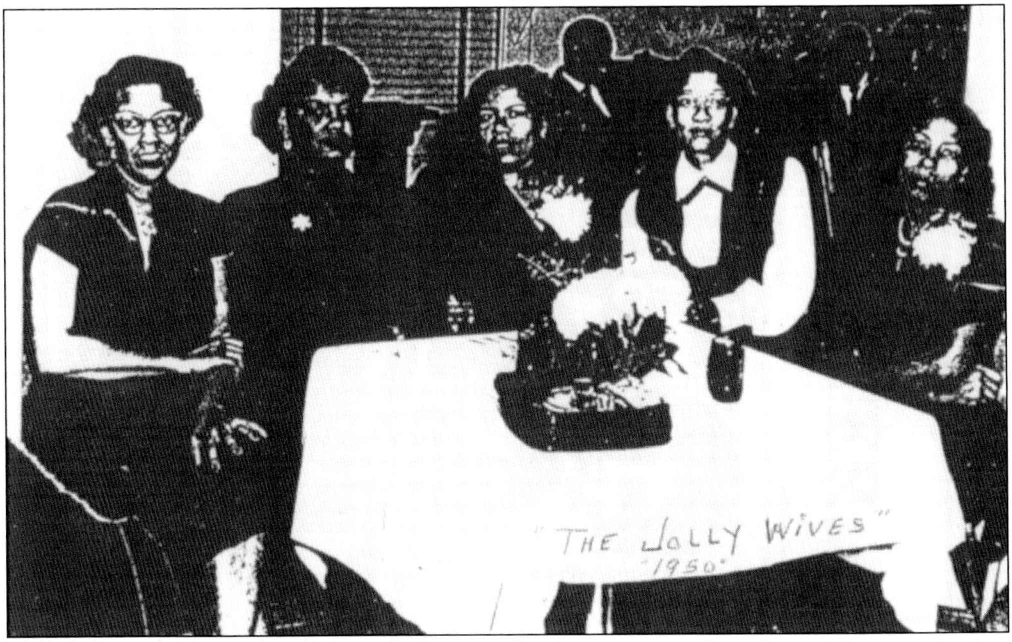

The Jolly Wives of El Paso consisted of wives of military men and civilians. The organization provided logistical and infrastructure support and planning for civic activities and major banquets in the black community. The antecedent of this organization was the Colored Women Club, led by Mrs. Edward Sampson, which had previously participated in the campaign to obtain the vote for women in the early 20th century. (Courtesy of *El Paso Times*.)

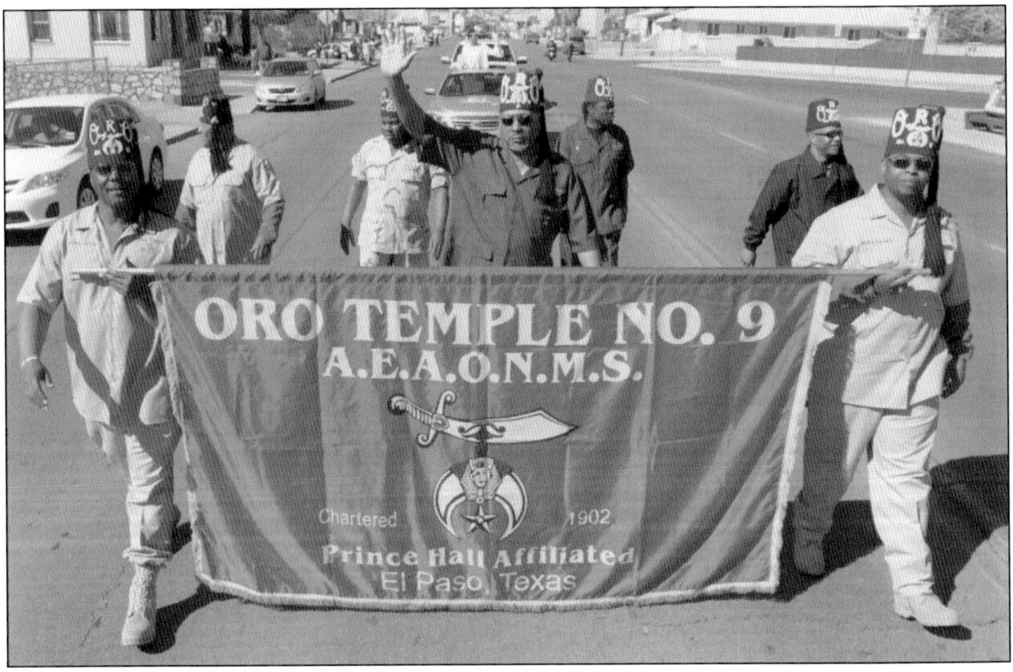

Oro Temple No. 9 is a benevolent fraternal organization, committed to service to the El Paso community. These members of the organization are marching in the Black History Parade. (Courtesy of *El Paso Times*.)

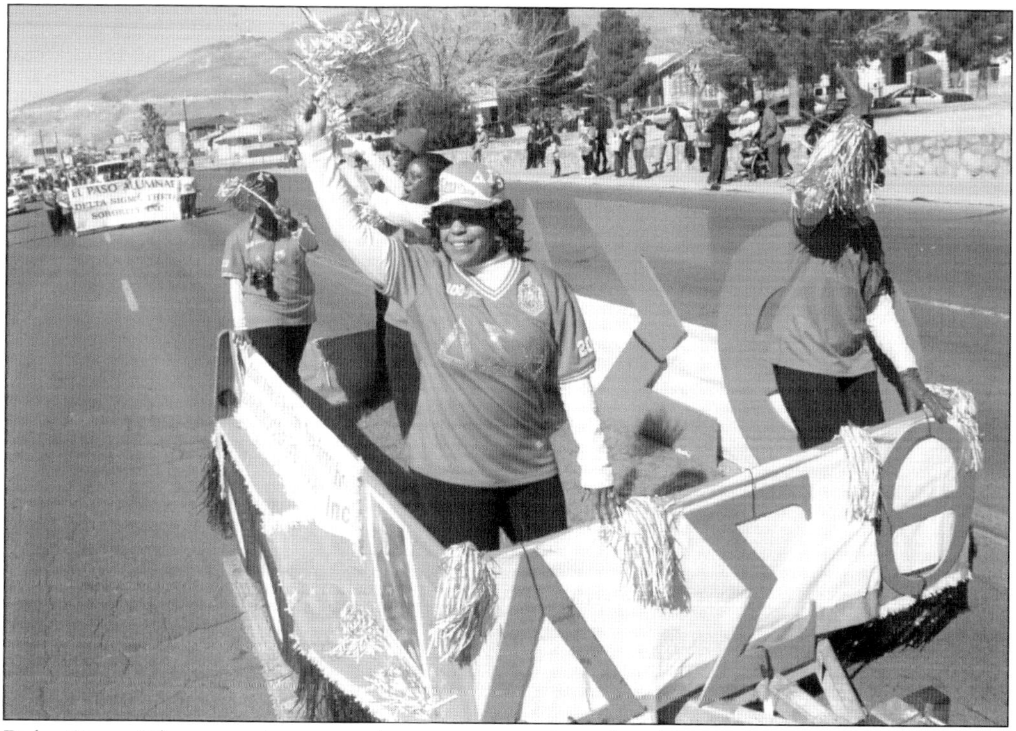

Delta Sigma Theta sorority serves the community through public service programming such as mentoring youth. It was the first predominately African American sorority chartered in the El Paso area. Some of its members wave to the crowd during the Black History Parade. (Courtesy of *El Paso Times*.)

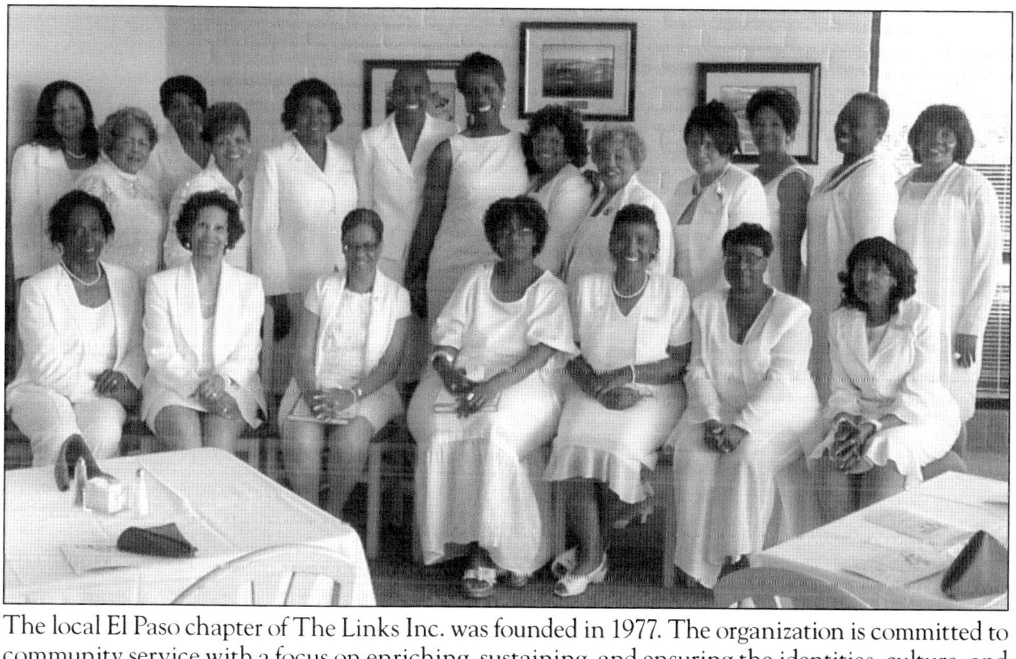

The local El Paso chapter of The Links Inc. was founded in 1977. The organization is committed to community service with a focus on enriching, sustaining, and ensuring the identities, culture, and economic survival of African Americans and persons of color. (Courtesy of The Links Inc.)

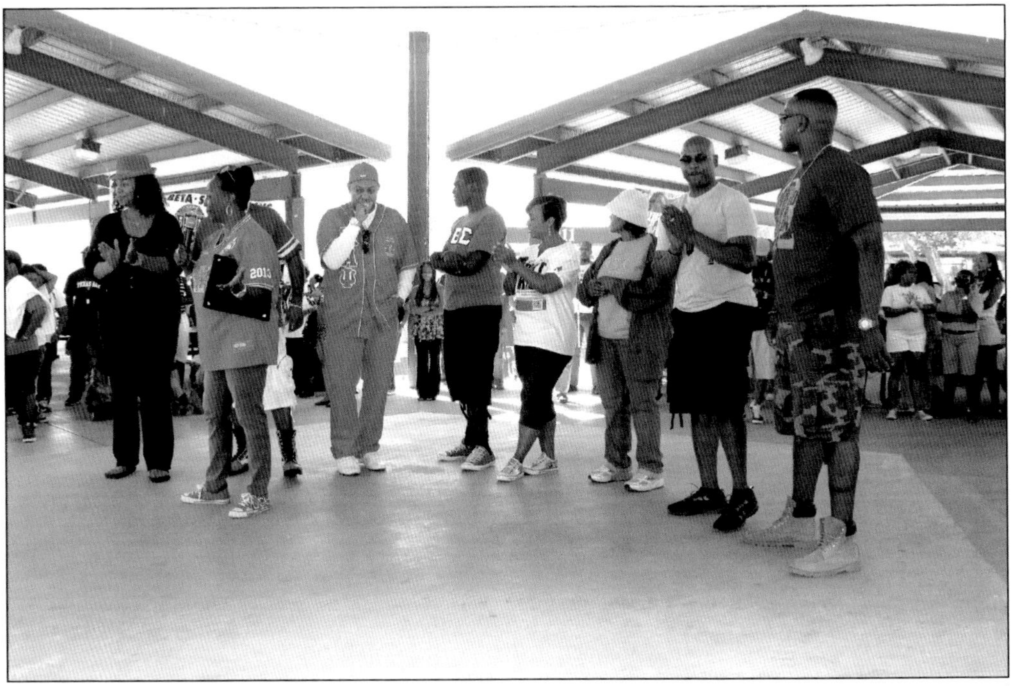

The Pan-Hellenic Council of El Paso is a confederation of the Divine Nine black fraternities and sororities. The council pools its member organizations' financial resources and talent to contribute to larger efforts in education and civil improvement. The council also works to keep the history and heritage of the African American community alive in El Paso. (Courtesy of James Ball.)

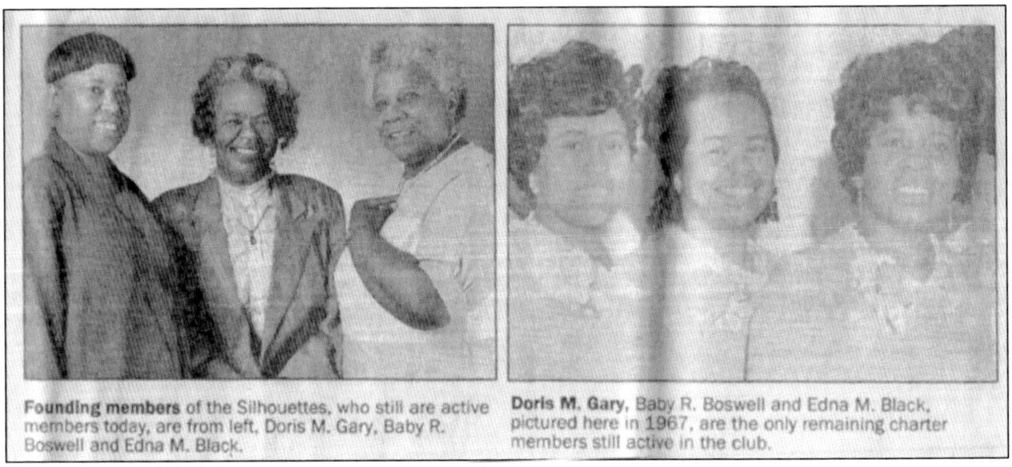

Founding members of the Silhouettes, who still are active members today, are from left, Doris M. Gary, Baby R. Boswell and Edna M. Black.

Doris M. Gary, Baby R. Boswell and Edna M. Black, pictured here in 1967, are the only remaining charter members still active in the club.

The Silhouettes Social and Civic Club was formed in El Paso in 1965 to promote interest in African American history and to help the aged. (Courtesy of *El Paso Times*.)

Bob Snead was president of the El Paso Black Chamber of Commerce. During his tenure, he organized seminars and sundry meetings to encourage and train black El Pasoans to establish their own businesses. (Courtesy of *El Paso Times*.)

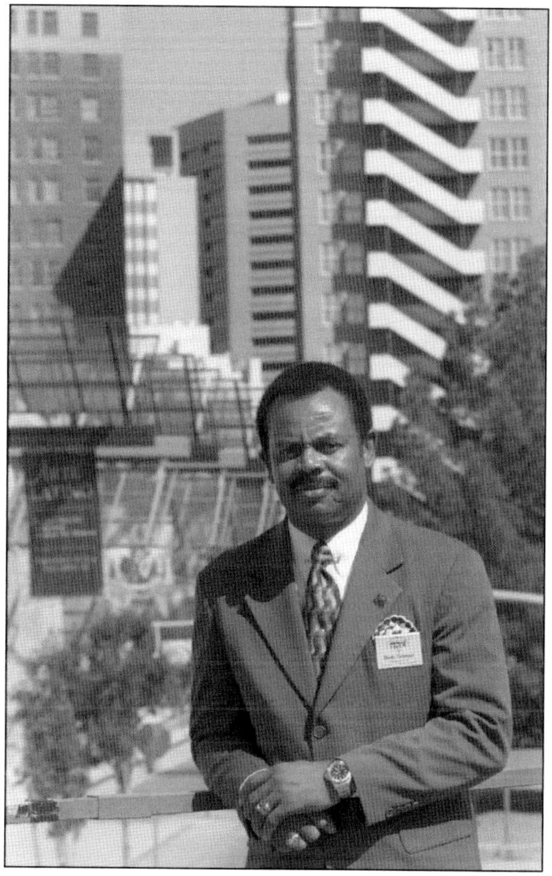

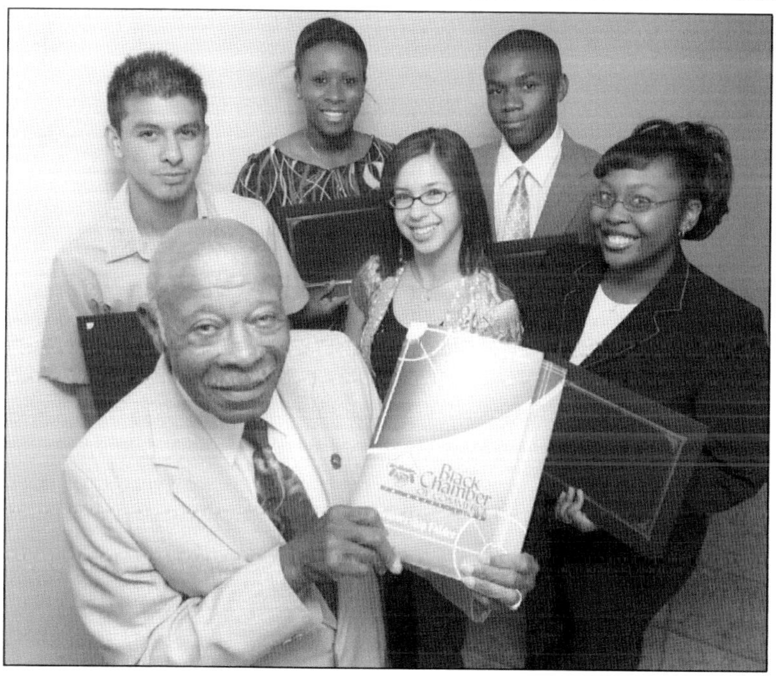

Leo Pleasants handed out scholarship awards on behalf of the El Paso Black Chamber of Commerce. (Courtesy of *El Paso Times*.)

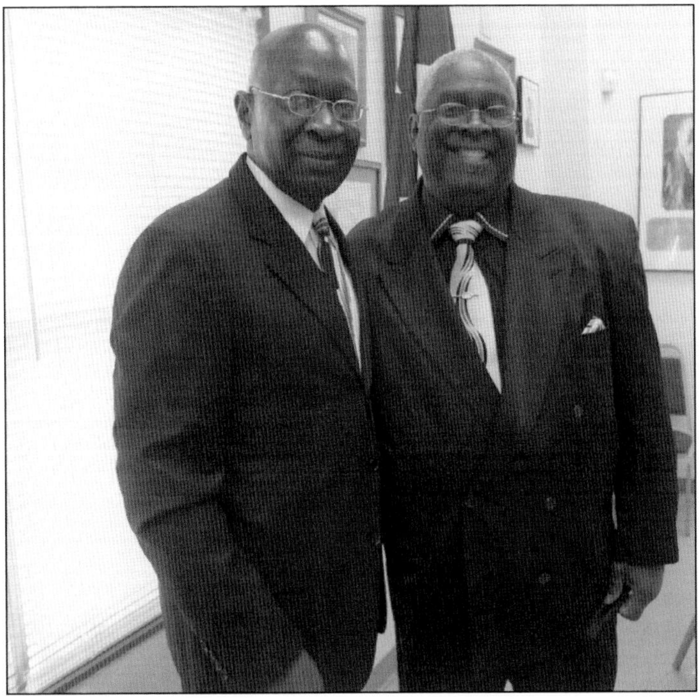

Councilman Carl Robinson and Mount Zion Church's Pastor Larry Williams are pictured here. (Courtesy of *El Paso Times*.)

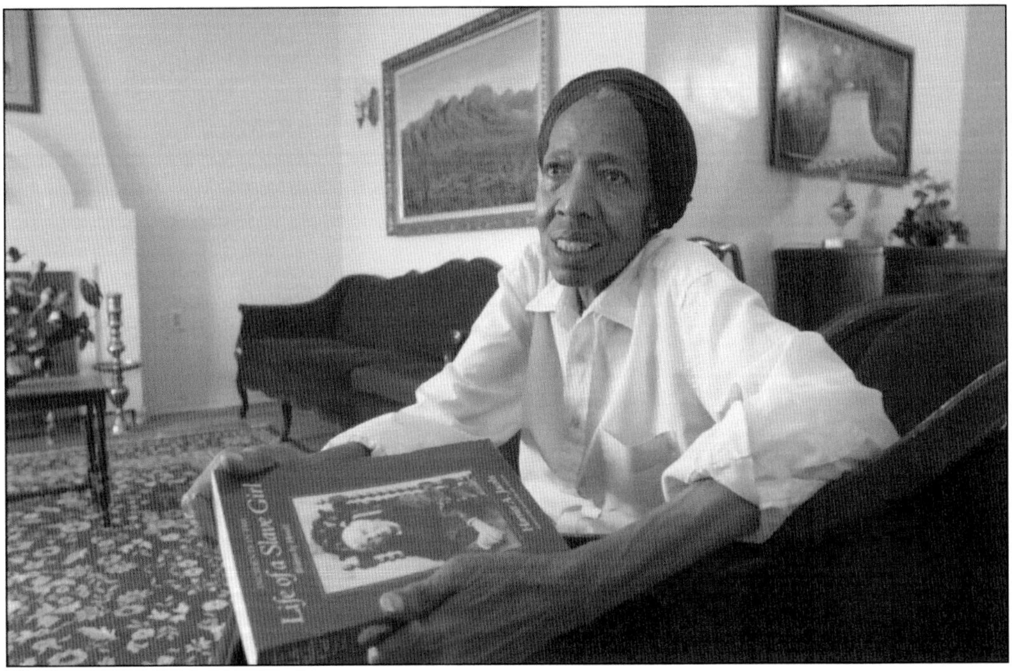

Native El Pasoan, alumna of Prairie View College, and bilingual Leona Washington was a teacher in the public schools, mentor, motivator, community organizer/activist, bibliophile, newspaper publisher, musician, and founder and executive director of the McCall Neighborhood Center. It is estimated that Washington raised close to $1 million to keep the McCall Neighborhood Center operating. She received numerous civic awards and could be counted on to provide good advice and instruction to anyone in El Paso, from the mayor on down. (Courtesy of *El Paso Times*.)

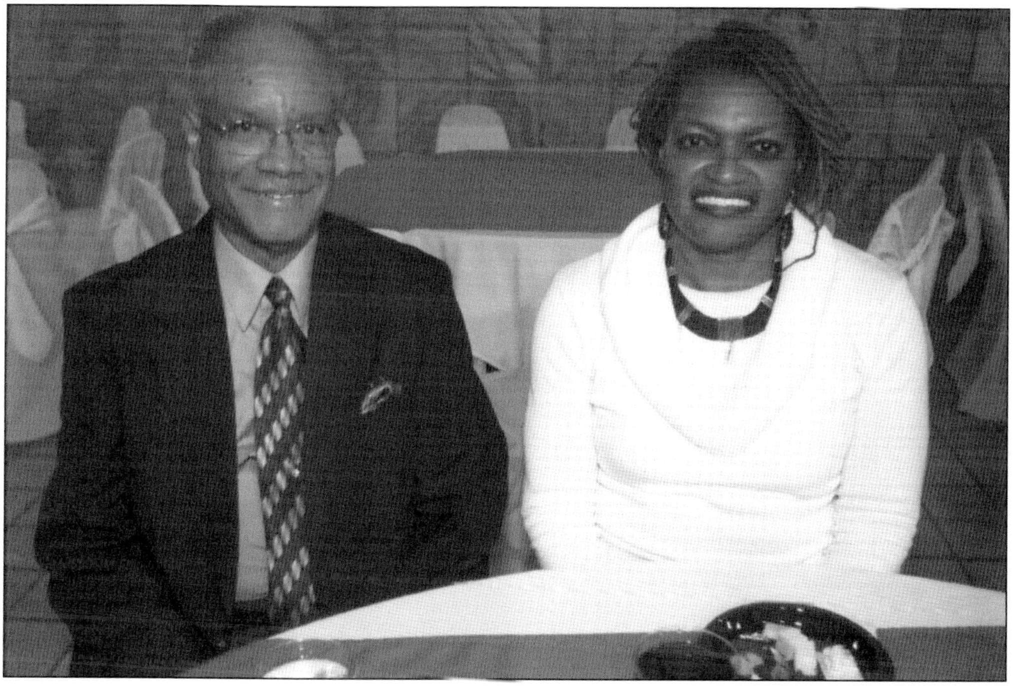

James Ball is seated with friend Carolyn Mackey at a local event. (Courtesy of *El Paso Times*.)

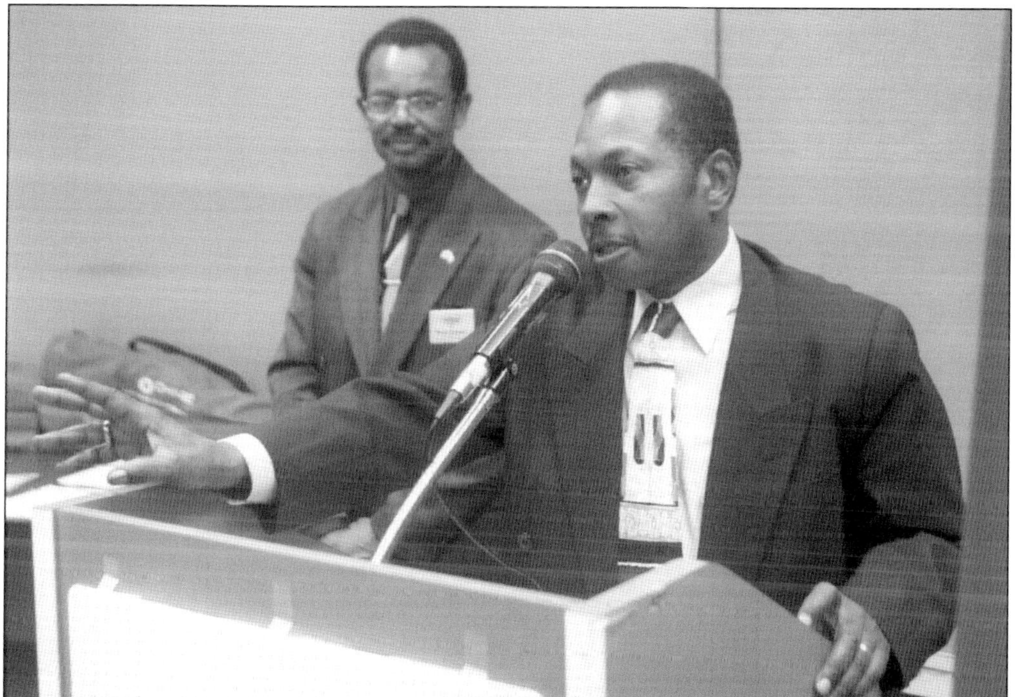

Otis Hopkins (foreground) and Bob Snead (background) both contributed to the work of the El Paso Black Chamber of Congress. A top executive at Raytheon, Otis Hopkins brought his vast expertise to foster black entrepreneurship in El Paso, and Bob Snead, president of the Black Chamber of Congress, helped in networking and identifying resources. (Courtesy of *El Paso Times*.)

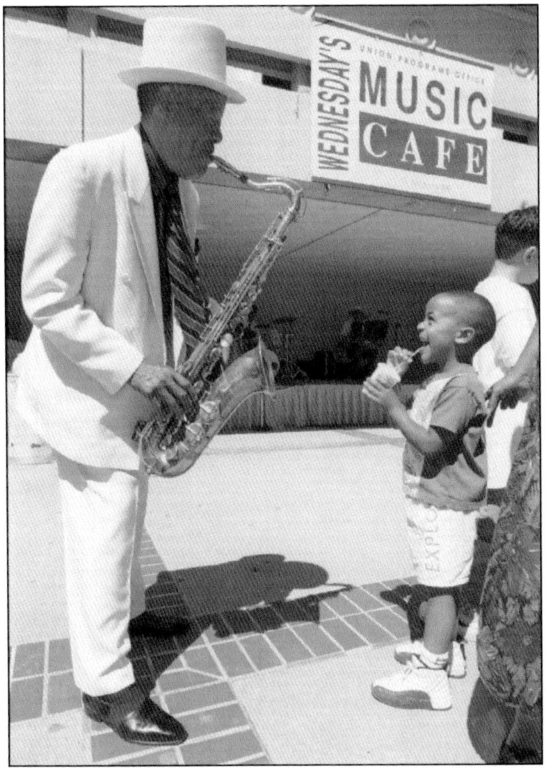

Legendary jazz and blues musician Art Lewis is playing for a young boy at the University of Texas at El Paso at the 1997 El Paso Juneteenth Celebration. Lewis learned his art by playing with other blues and jazz greats such as Albert Collins, Johnny "Clyde" Copeland, and T-Bone Walker. He shared his talents with anyone within listening range. (Courtesy of Dr. Maceo Crenshaw Dailey Jr.)

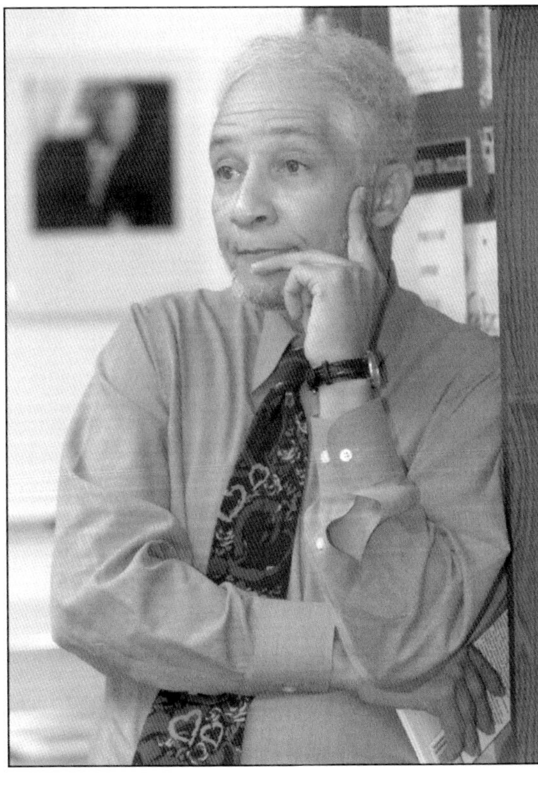

Dr. Maceo Crenshaw Dailey Jr. is the founder and director of the African American Studies Program at the University of Texas at El Paso. He has been instrumental in fostering research on the black community and in celebrations of African American history, namely Black History Month, Kwanzaa, Juneteenth, and Martin Luther King Jr. Day. He has served as president on local and statewide boards such as the McCall Neighborhood Center, Child Crisis Center, and Humanities Texas. He is a member of the Philosophical Society of Texas and coeditor of two books and author of another. He and his late wife, Sondra Banfield Dailey, established Sweet Earth Flying Press in 2004 with a mission to publish books by blacks and women. (Courtesy of Dr. Maceo Crenshaw Dailey Jr.)

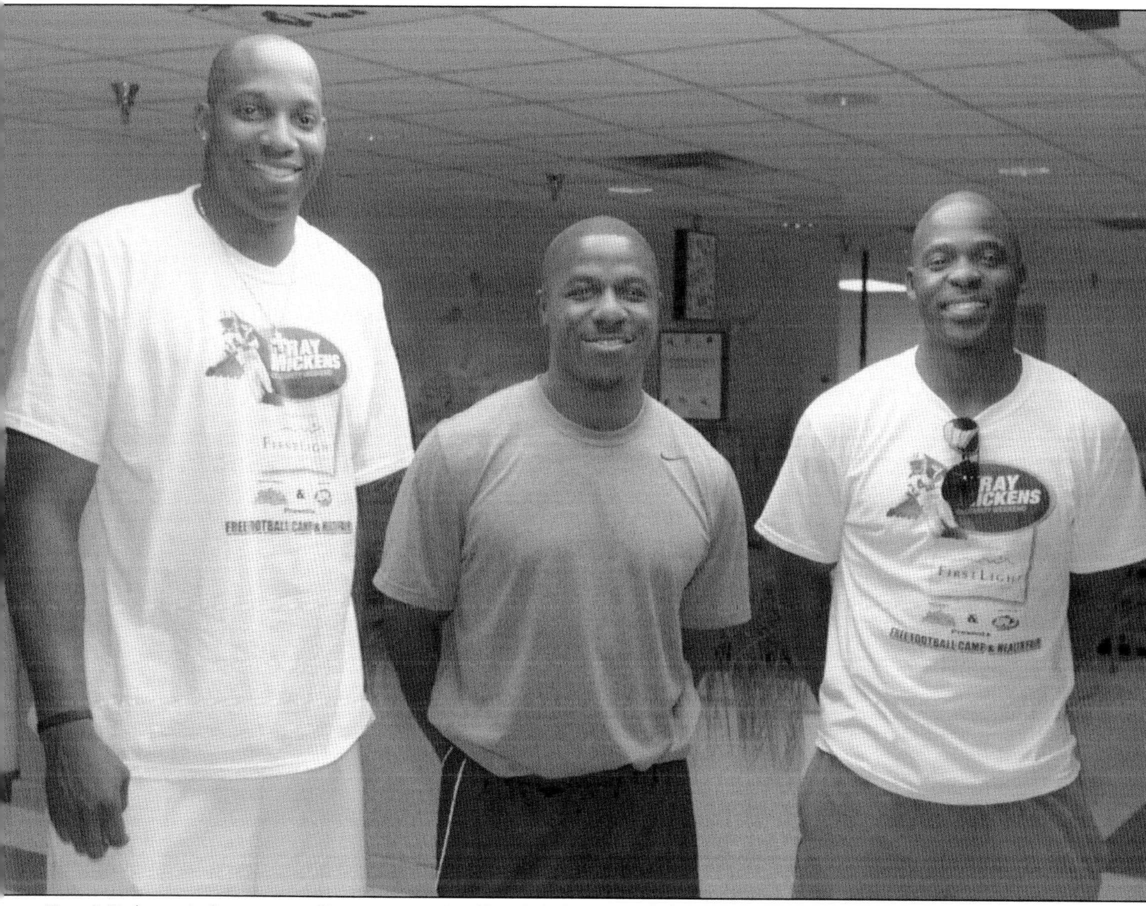

Ray Mickens is hosting colleagues at the Ray Mickens Celebrity Weekend, which features a free football camp for kids and a health fair. (Courtesy of *El Paso Times*.)

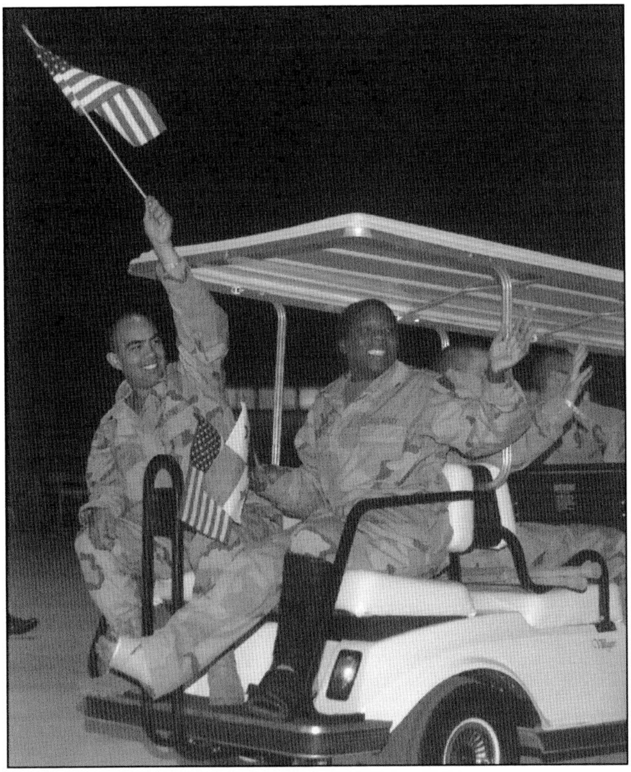

On March 23, 2003, Panama-born Shoshanna Johnson was taken prisoner when she and fellow soldiers of the 507th Maintenance Company from Fort Bliss were ambushed in Nasiriyah, Iraq, during Operation Iraqi Freedom. The first African American female prisoner of war endured 22 days of captivity before being rescued. She recounts her story in *I'm Still Standing: From Captive US Soldiers to Free Citizen—My Journey Home*. (Both, courtesy of *El Paso Times*.)

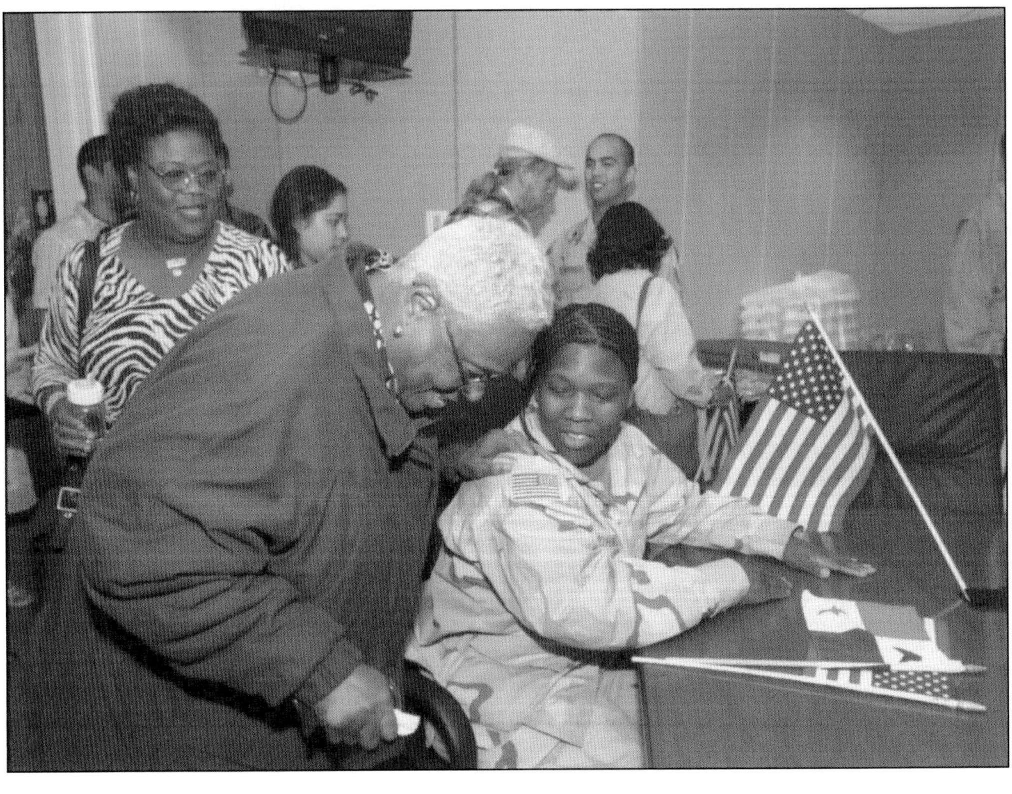

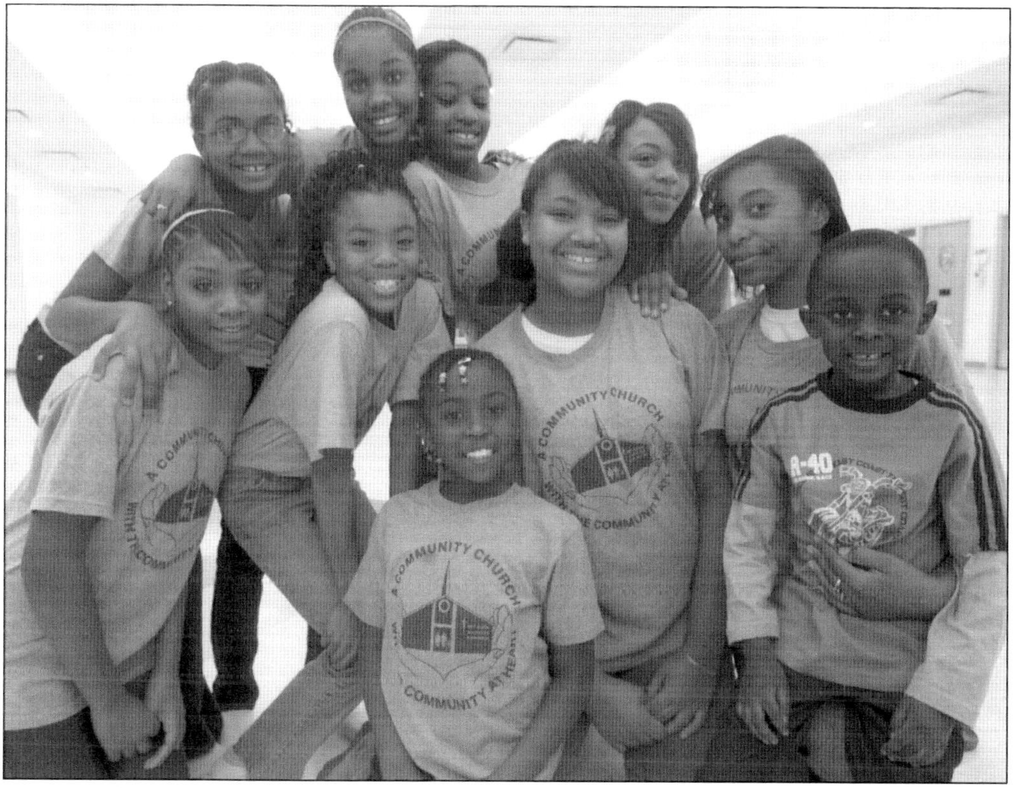

A group of youths are pictured at a community church gathering. (Courtesy of *El Paso Times*.)

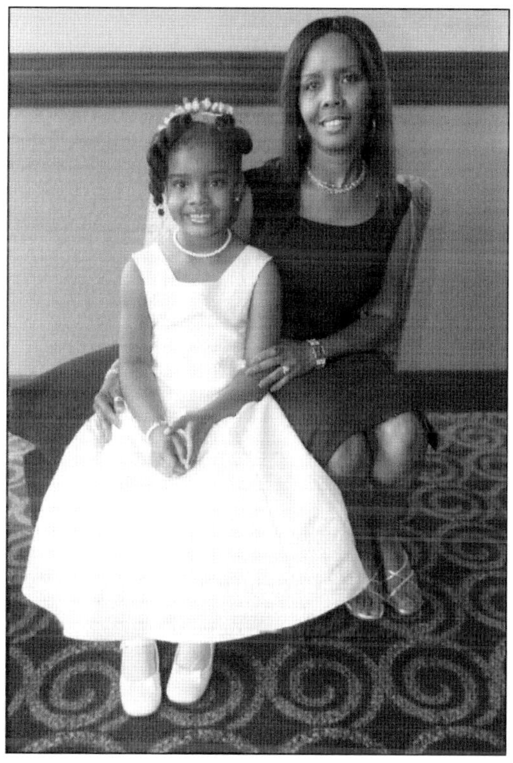

An unidentified mother and daughter are posing for the camera. (Courtesy of *El Paso Times*.)

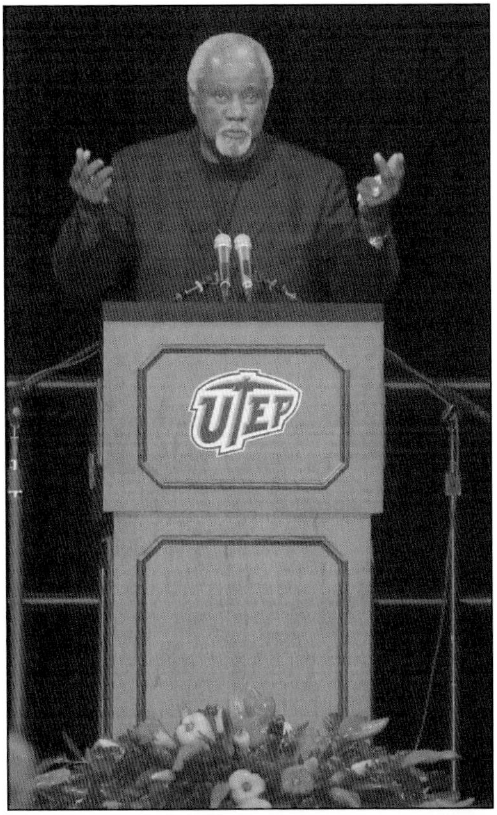

Coach Nolan Richardson addressed an assembly at the University of Texas at El Paso for Black History Month. (Courtesy of *El Paso Times*.)

Rev. Larry Williams gave a sermon at his Mount Zion Church on Martin Luther King Jr. Day. (Courtesy of *El Paso Times*.)

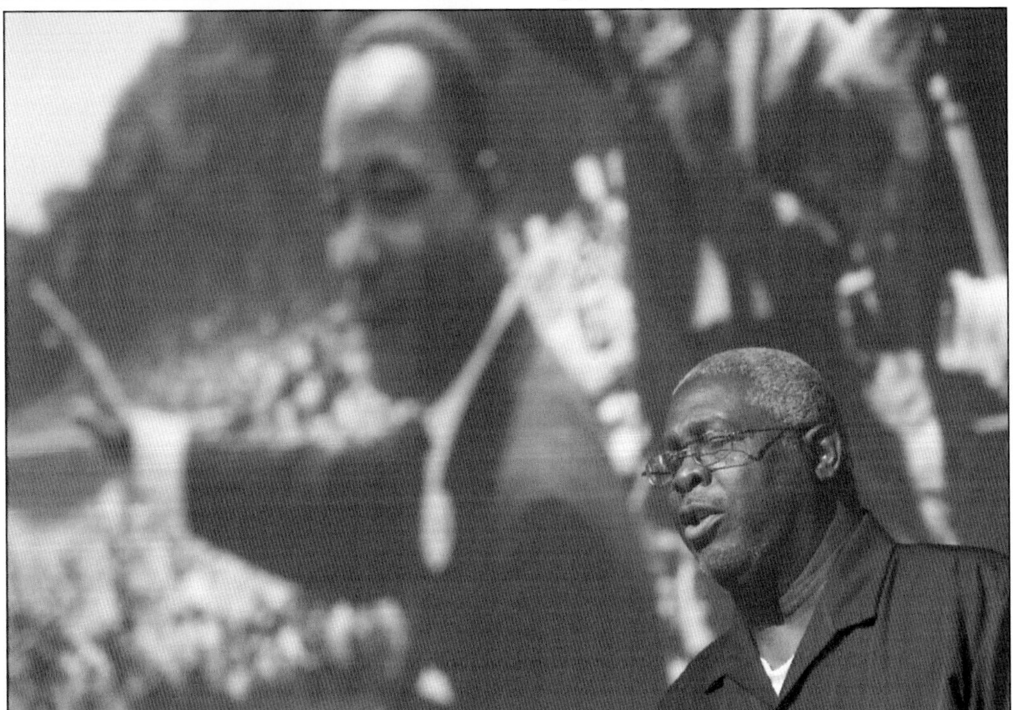

Alice Davis, grand marshall, dignitary, and former principal of North Loop Elementary School, is celebrating Black History Month. (Courtesy of *El Paso Times*.)

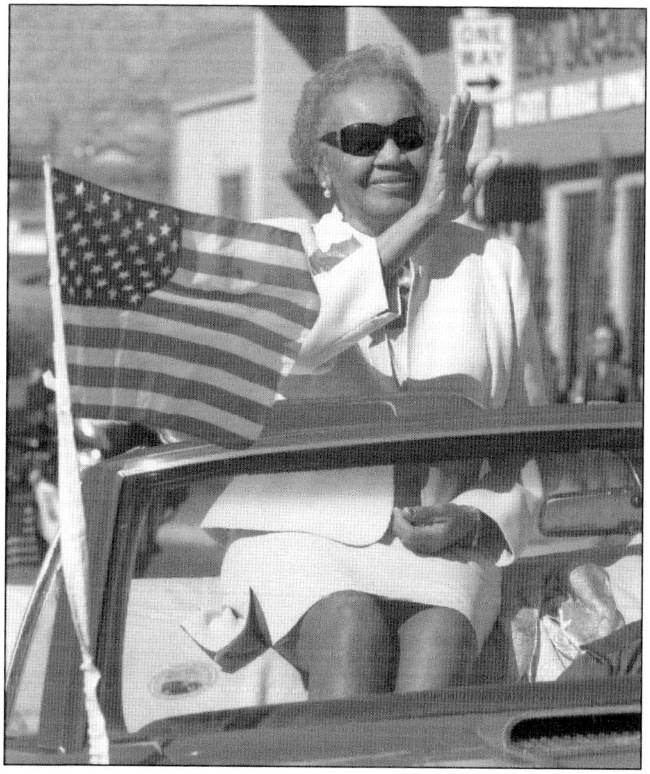

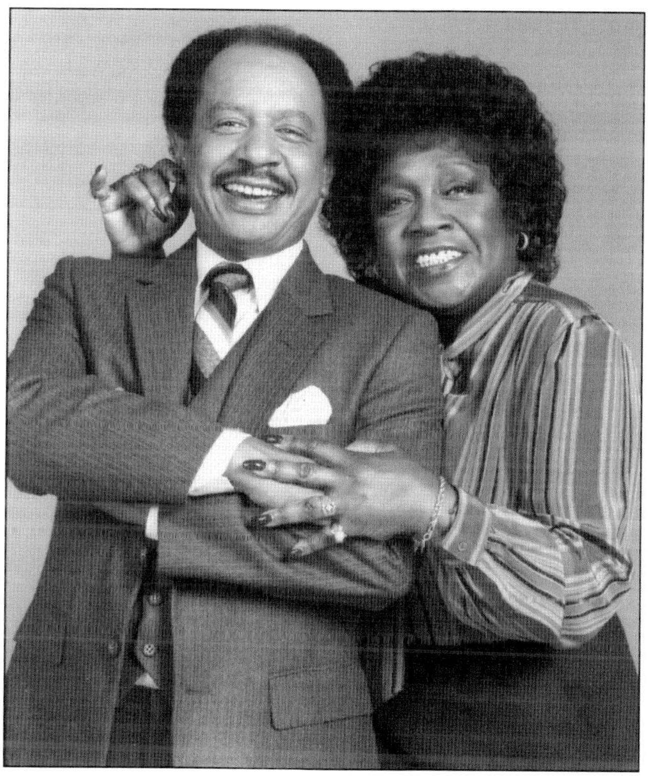

Actor Sherman Hemsley is best known for portraying the hotheaded George Jefferson in the hit 1970s television show *The Jeffersons*. After retiring from television, Sherman made El Paso his home and lived there until his death in 2012. He is pictured here with his popular costar Isabel Sanford, who portrayed his wife, Louis "Weezy" Jefferson. (Courtesy of Kathryn Smith-McGlynn.)

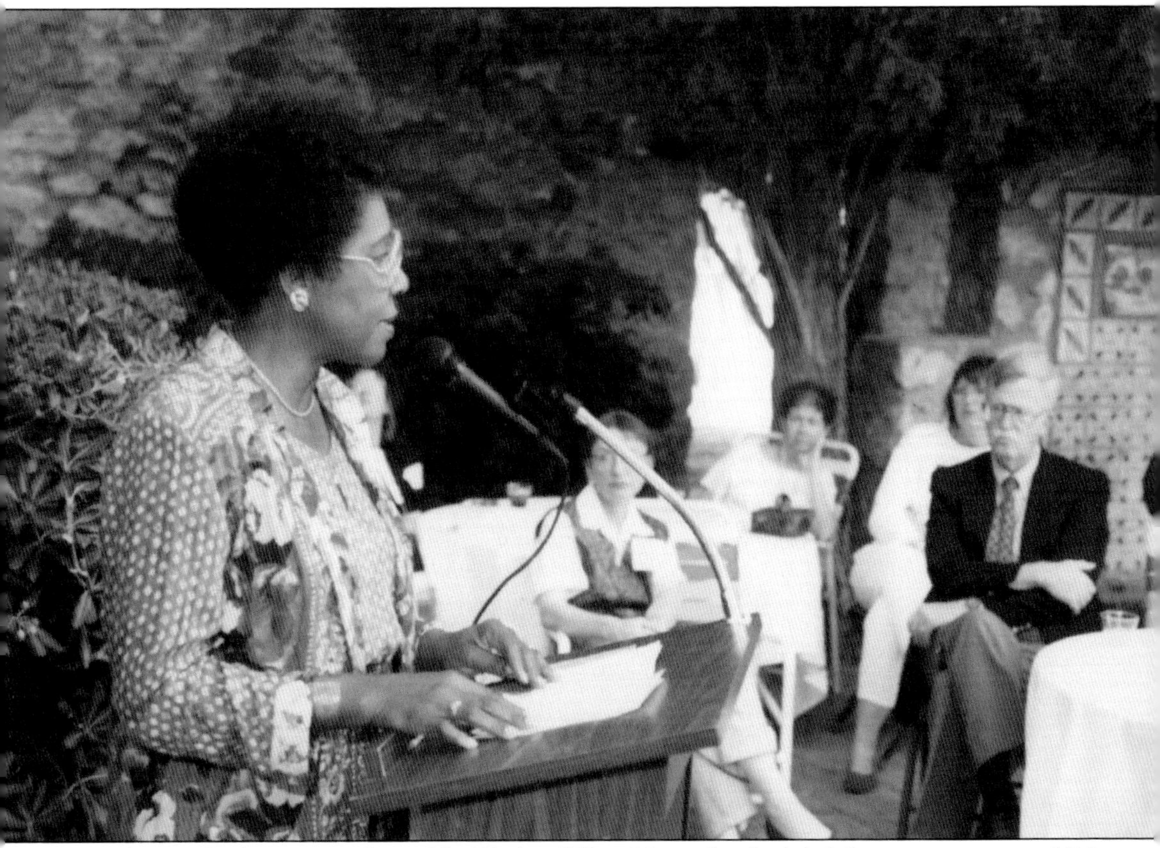

Rebecca Rhodes was president of the Thelma White Network, which led the campaign to establish the University of Texas at El Paso African American Studies Program and bring its first director to campus, Dr. Maceo Crenshaw Dailey Jr. The other objective of the Thelma White Network was to help African American students enter the university, feel comfortable, and achieve at the highest level possible. James Smash and Bonnie Mingo were two students who sought Rhodes's help to realize these objectives. (Courtesy of *El Paso Times*.)

Ouisa D. Davis was born in El Paso and raised both on the border and in Europe. Her mother, Dolores, was a jazz singer and the goddaughter of Ella Fitzgerald. An attorney, Ouisa Davis was the first El Paso black woman to serve as an associate municipal judge. She is pictured (left) with Sister Maureen Jerkowski at a Paso del Norte Civil Rights Project, which celebrated the legacy of civil rights struggles in the El Paso region and honored people working to protect and defend human rights. (Courtesy of *El Paso Times*.)

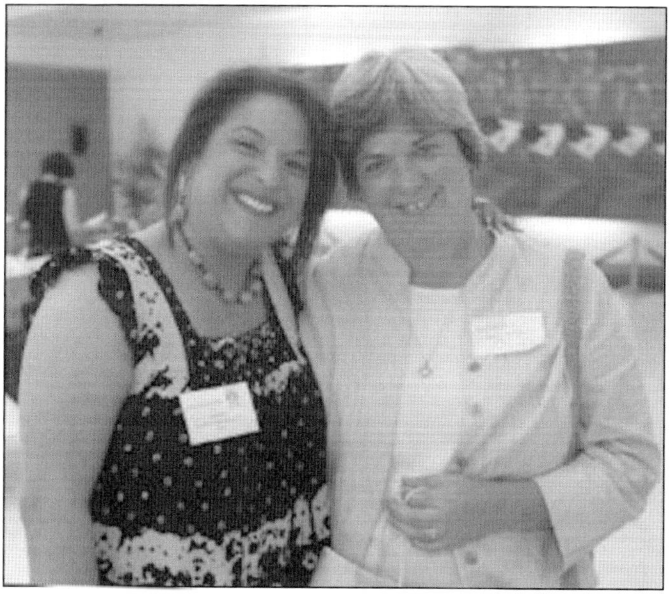

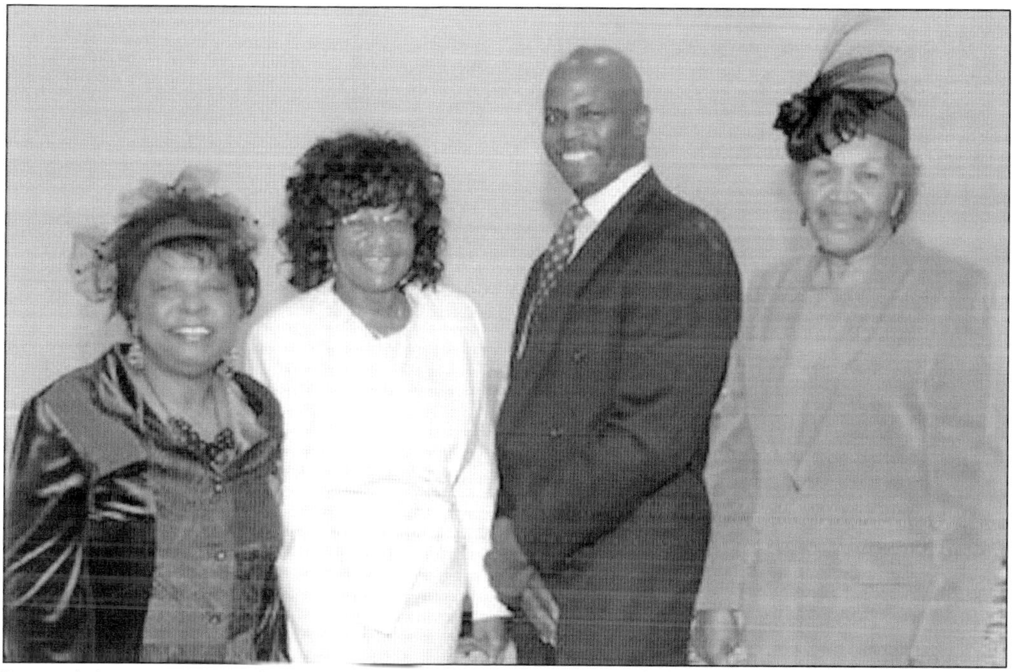

Retired Army major and teacher Jerome Tilghman cohosted the local television show *We Are Here* with Sue Pratt. He also ran for Congress in 2012 for El Paso District 16. He is pictured at the Phillis Wheatley Club's 27th annual Madhatters luncheon and fashion show with, from left to right, Earnestine Howard, Betty Mackey, and Alice Sellers. Phyllis Wheatley women's clubs were named after slave poet Phillis Wheatley. The club in El Paso was founded in 1933. (Courtesy of *El Paso Times*.)

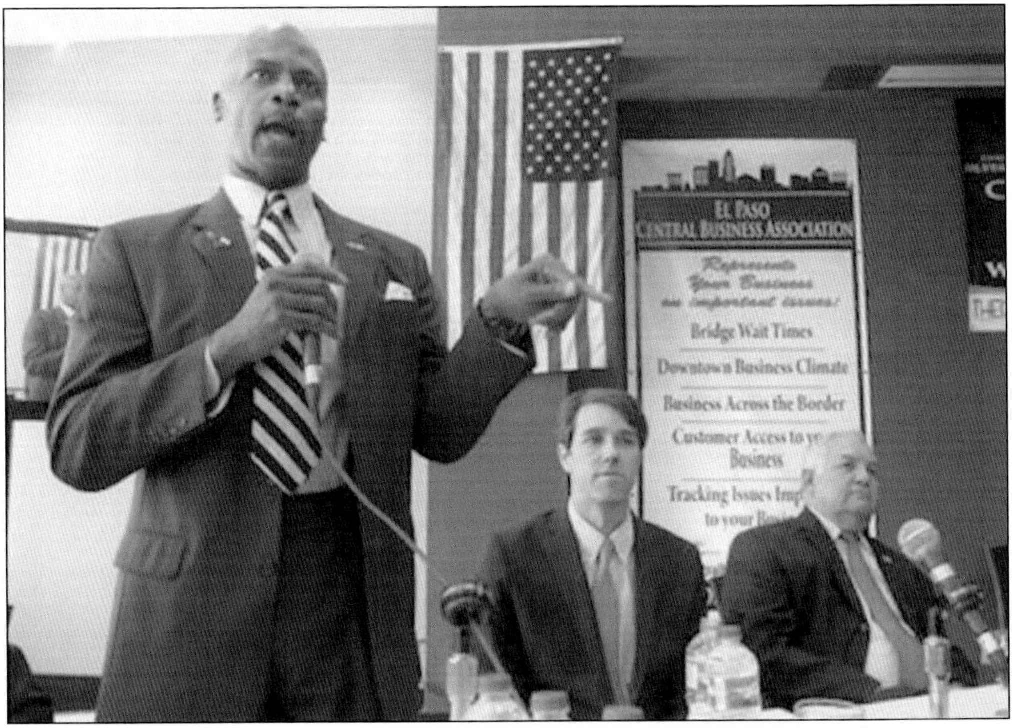

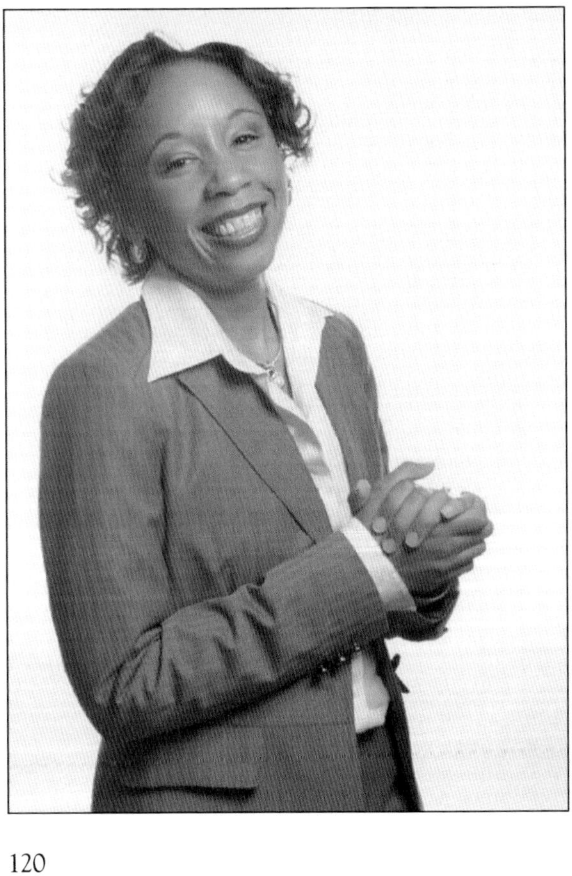

Jerome Tilghman is speaking at an El Paso Central Business Association political candidate forum. (Courtesy of *El Paso Times*.)

In 2011, Dionne Mack became the first African American director of library services for the City of El Paso. She is responsible for 13 libraries, a bookmobile, 170 employees, and an annual operating budget of about $8.4 million. Dionne is used to being a "first"—prior to coming to El Paso, she was the first African American woman to head a major public library system in New York state. (Courtesy of El Paso Public Library.)

As director of community and human development for the City of El Paso, William L. Lilly administered various programs for the city including the Community Development Block Grant, the Home Investment Partnership Program, the Emergency Solutions Grant, and the Homeless Housing and Services Program, as well as others. Lilly, who is originally from the East Coast, came to El Paso via Yuma, Arizona. He retired in 2014. (Courtesy of City of El Paso.)

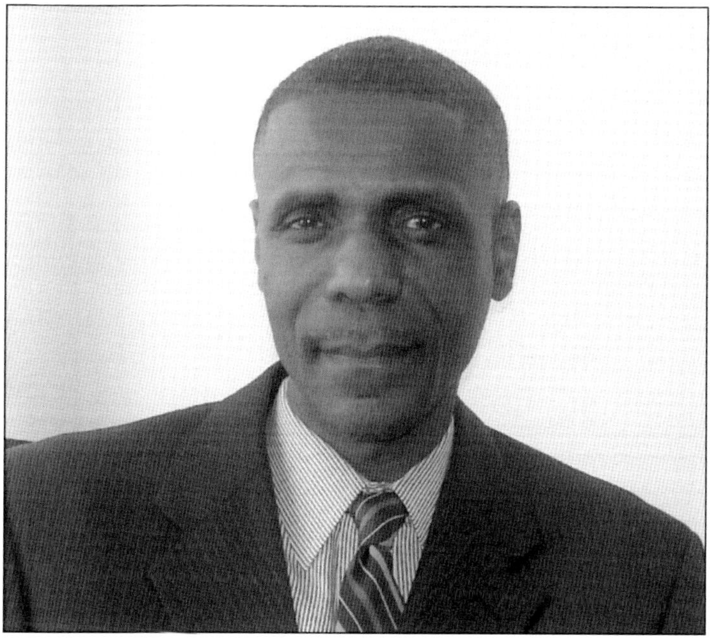

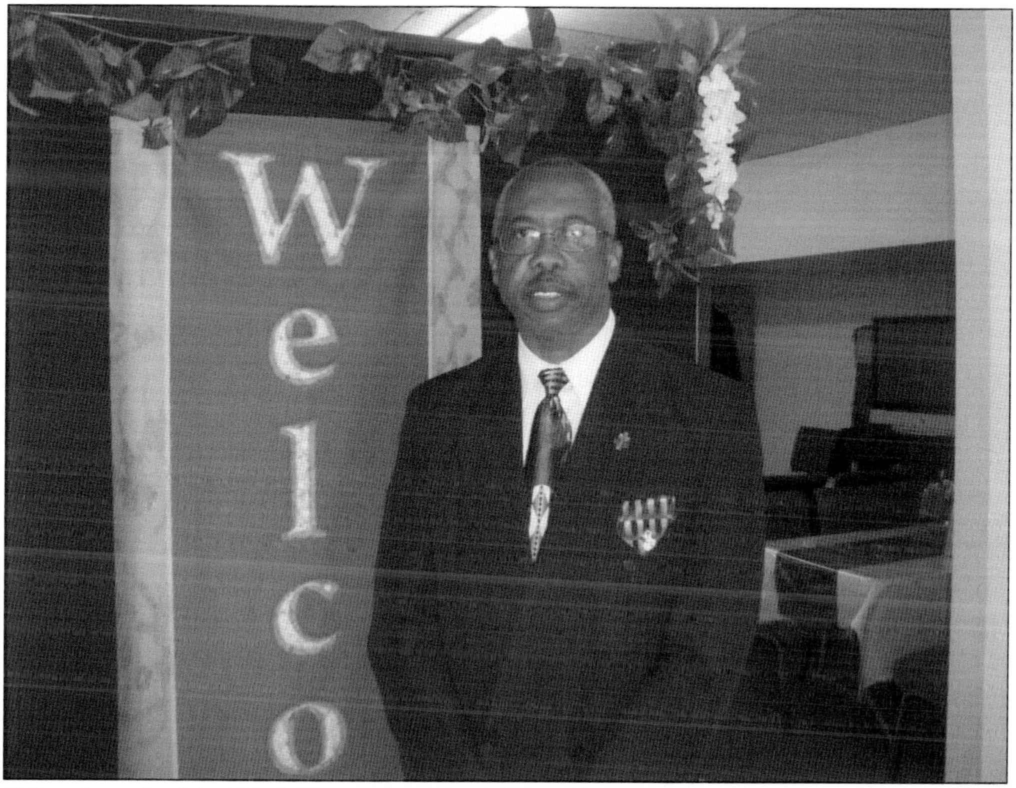

El Paso branch of the NAACP president Harold Howell is pictured here. Howell retired from the military with the rank of sergeant major. (Courtesy of El Paso Inc. and Harold Howell.)

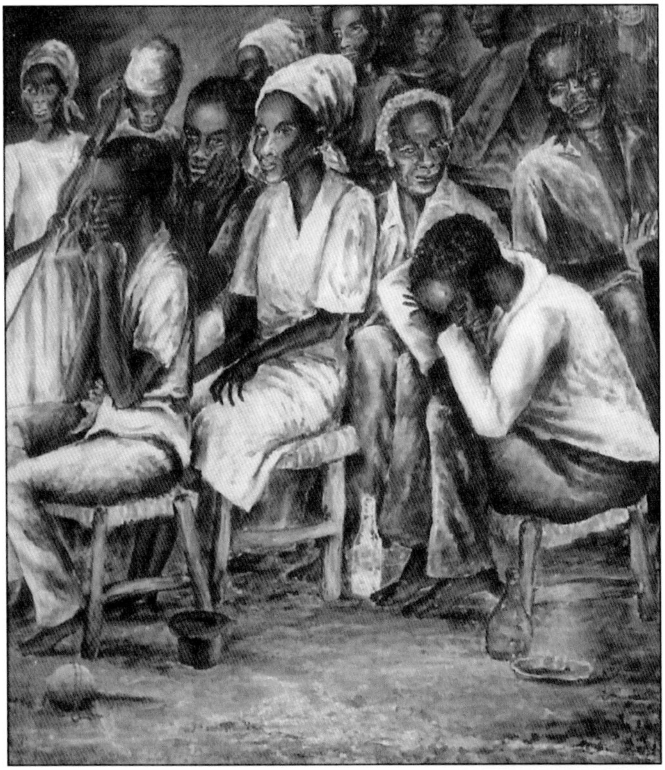

El Paso is home to many African American artists who add to the vibrancy and culture of the region through their work. These paintings are by artist James Millender. (Both, courtesy of Dr. Maceo Crenshaw Dailey Jr.)

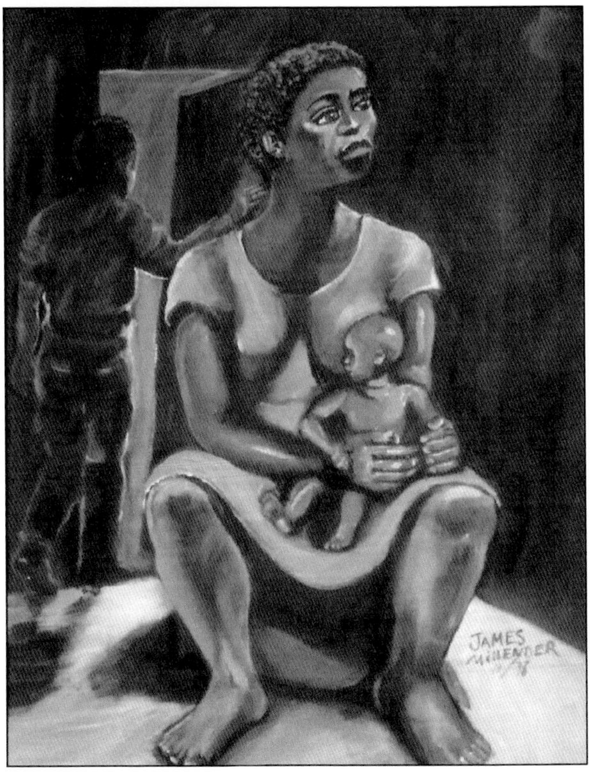

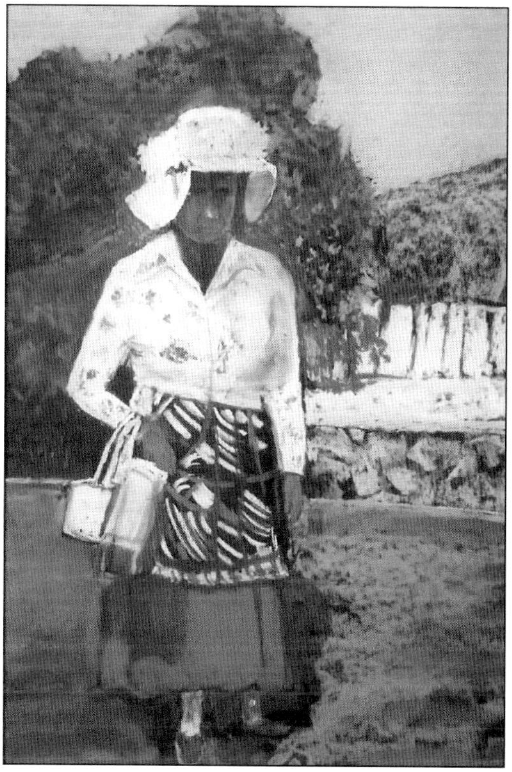

Pictured at right is artwork by a local African American artist. Below is a poster announcing an artist reception and exhibit in celebration of Martin Luther King Jr. Day and Black History Month. (Both, courtesy of Dr. Maceo Crenshaw Dailey Jr.)

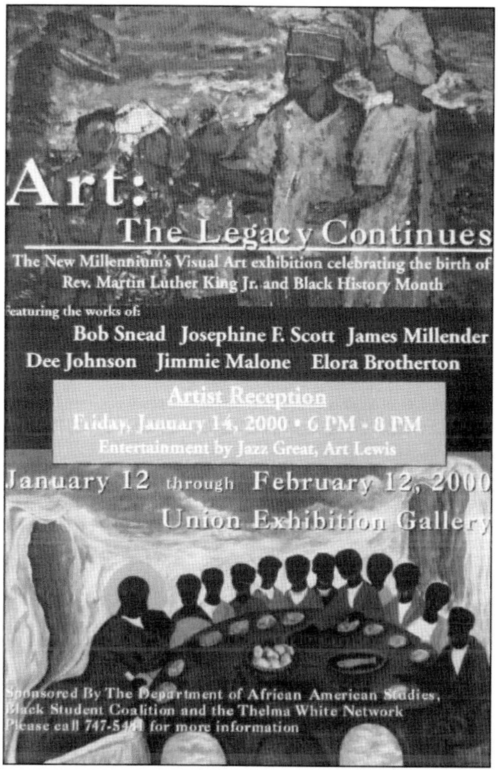

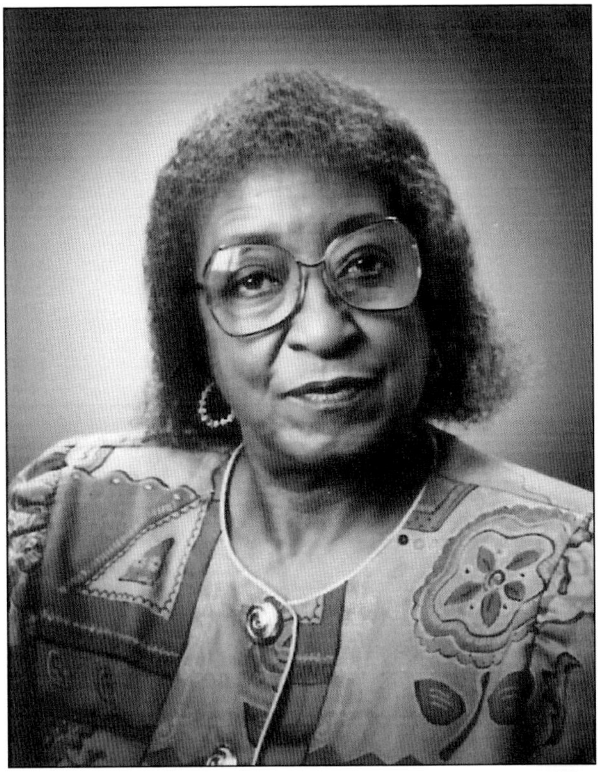

Viola Strait was Equal Employment Opportunity Commission officer at Fort Bliss. (Courtesy of Leona Washington Photograph Collection, Department of Special Collections and Archives, University of Texas at El Paso Library.)

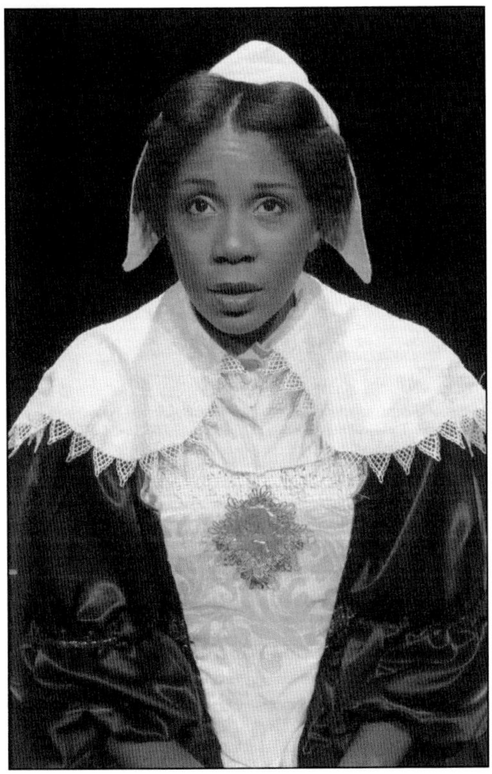

Kathryn Smith-McGlynn came to El Paso from New York City in 2008 with her husband, Sean McGlynn, and their son, Aidan. After noticing the lack of professional theater and moved by her mentor Dr. Maceo Crenshaw Dailey Jr.'s encouragement, she established El Paso's first professional Actors Equity company, Frontera Repertory Theatre Company. As cofounding artistic director and executive producer, Smith-McGlynn cultivates the region's creative capital. She is also a professor at the University of Texas at El Paso in the Department of Theater and Dance. She continues to perform on stage, television, and film. A stage director and writer as well, Smith-McGlynn has directed several plays and has written, directed, and starred in *Come Away with Me*, a one-woman show about the life of Harriet Tubman. In this photograph, she portrays Hester Prynne in the University of Texas at El Paso's production of *The Scarlet Letter.* (Courtesy of Adriana Dominguez, University of Texas at El Paso.)

A native El Pasoan and graduate of West Point Military Academy, Maj. Gen. Dana J.H. Pittard became the first African American post commander of Fort Bliss in 2012. A highly decorated officer, General Pittard is credited with several programs at Fort Bliss to reduce the suicide rate among soldiers. (Courtesy of *El Paso Times.*)

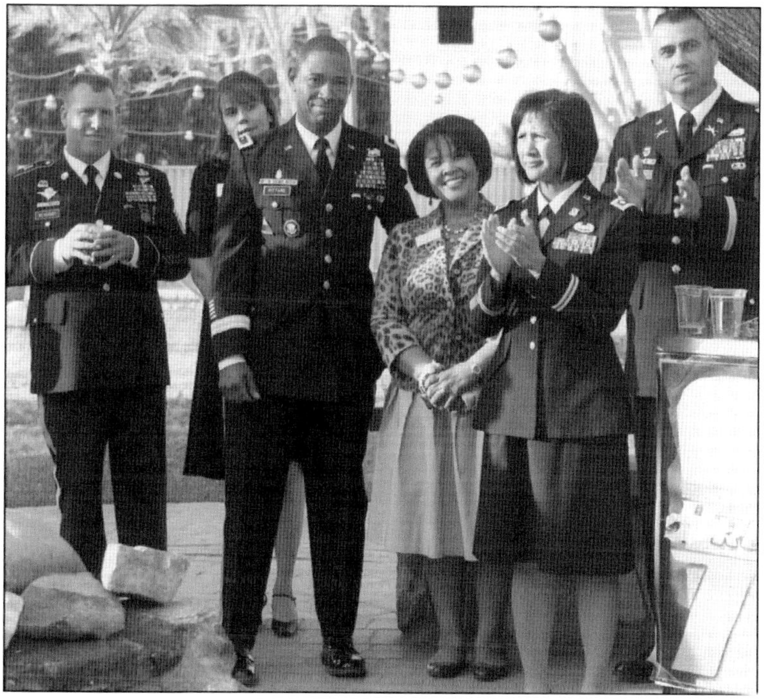

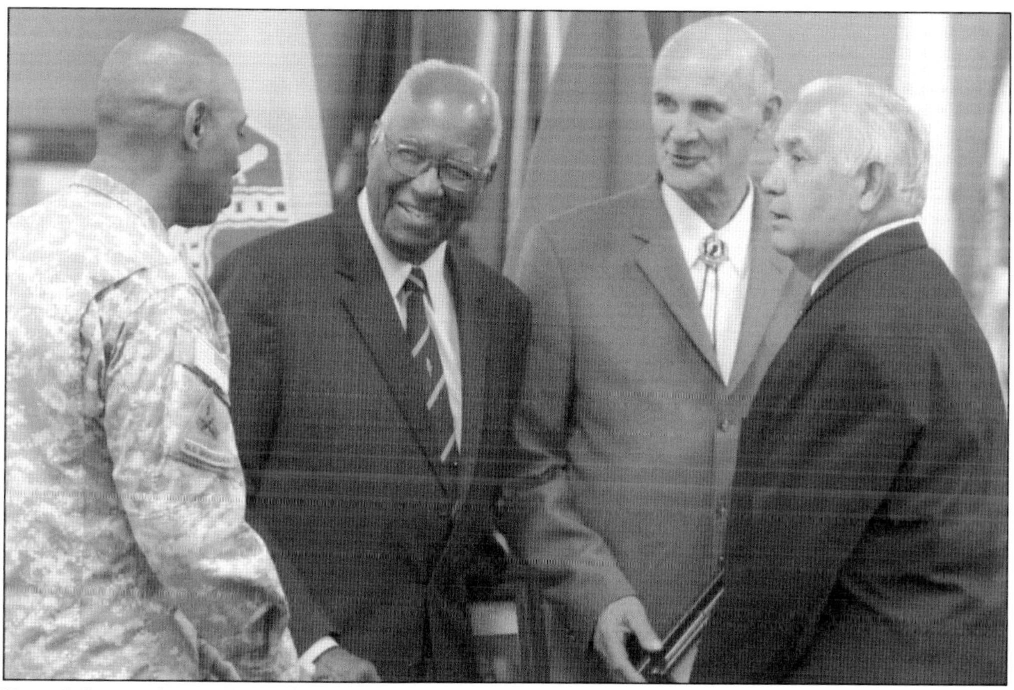

From left to right are Fort Bliss post commander Maj. Gen. Dana Pittard, Maj. Gen. Ed Greer, El Paso mayor John Cook, and El Paso congressman Silvestre Reyes. (Courtesy of *El Paso Times.*)

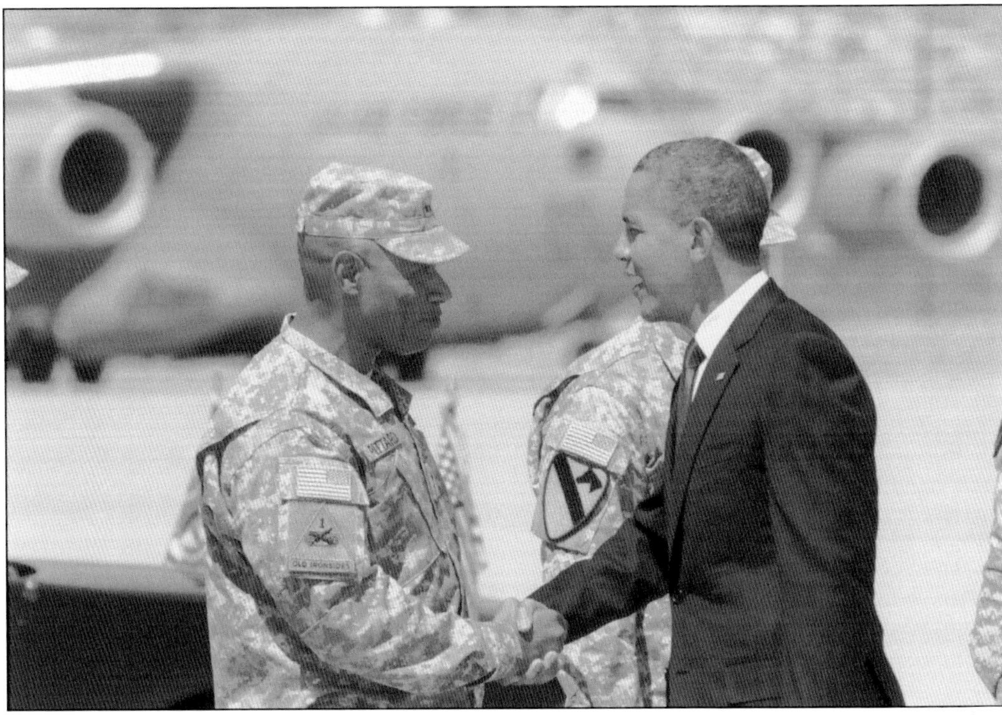

Maj. Gen. Dana Pittard and Pres. Barack Obama are seen at Fort Bliss where the president addressed the soldiers on May 10, 2011. (Courtesy of *El Paso Times*.)

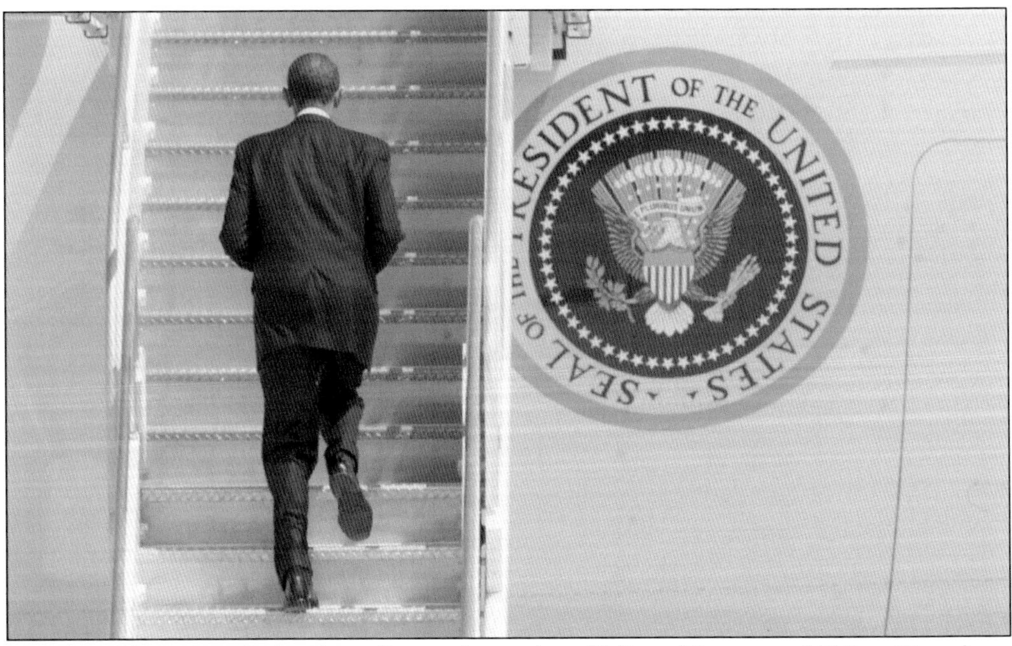

President Obama boards Air Force One to depart from El Paso. (Courtesy of *El Paso Times*.)

Bibliography

Barr, Alwyn. *Black Texans: A History of African Americans in Texas, 1528–1995*. Norman, OK: University of Oklahoma Press, 1996.

Bryson, Conrey. *Dr. Lawrence A. Nixon and the White Primary*. El Paso: University of Texas at El Paso, 1974.

Dailey, Maceo C. Jr. "Border Black: The El Paso Story." Brenner, Christine Thurlow, et al. *Dígame! Policy & Politics on the Texas Border*. Dubuque, Iowa: Kendall/Hunt Publishing Company, 2003.

Dailey, Maceo C. Jr. and Kristine Navarro, eds. *Whosoever My People Chance to Dwell: Oral Interviews with African American Women of El Paso*. Baltimore, MD: Black Classic Press, 2000.

Frost, H. Gordon. *The Gentlemen's Club: The Story of Prostitution in El Paso*. El Paso: Mangan Books, 1983.

Garcia, Mario T. *Desert Immigrants: The Mexicans of El Paso, 1880–1920*. New Haven, CT: Yale University Press, 1981.

Glasrud, Bruce A. and James M. Smallwood. *The African American Experience in Texas: An Anthology*. Lubbock, TX: Texas Tech University Press, 2007.

Glasrud, Bruce A. and Merline Pitre, eds. *Black Women in Texas History*. College Station, TX: Texas A&M University Press, 2008.

Haines, Cynthia Farah. *Showtime!: From Opera Houses to Picture Palaces in El Paso*. El Paso: Texas Western Press, 2006.

Horne, Gerald. *Black and Brown: African Americans and the Mexican Revolution, 1910–1920*. New York, NY: New York University Press, 2005.

Landon, Johnnie A. "The N.A.A.C.P. in El Paso, An Instrument for Political Involvement." El Paso, TX: master's thesis, 1972.

Mills, William Wallace. *Forty Years at El Paso, 1858–1898: Recollections of War, Politics, Adventure, Events, Narratives, and Sketches*. El Paso: W.W. Mills, 1901.

Porter, Eugene O. *Lord Beresford and Lady Flo*. El Paso: Texas Western Press, 1970.

Shabazz, Amilcar. *Advancing Democracy: African Americans and the Struggle for Access and Equity in Higher Education in Texas*. Chapel Hill, NC: The University of North Carolina Press, 2004.

Wiggins, Bernice Love. *Tuneful Tales*. Lubbock, TX: Texas Tech University Press, 2002.

Discover Thousands of Local History Books Featuring Millions of Vintage Images

Arcadia Publishing, the leading local history publisher in the United States, is committed to making history accessible and meaningful through publishing books that celebrate and preserve the heritage of America's people and places.

Find more books like this at
www.arcadiapublishing.com

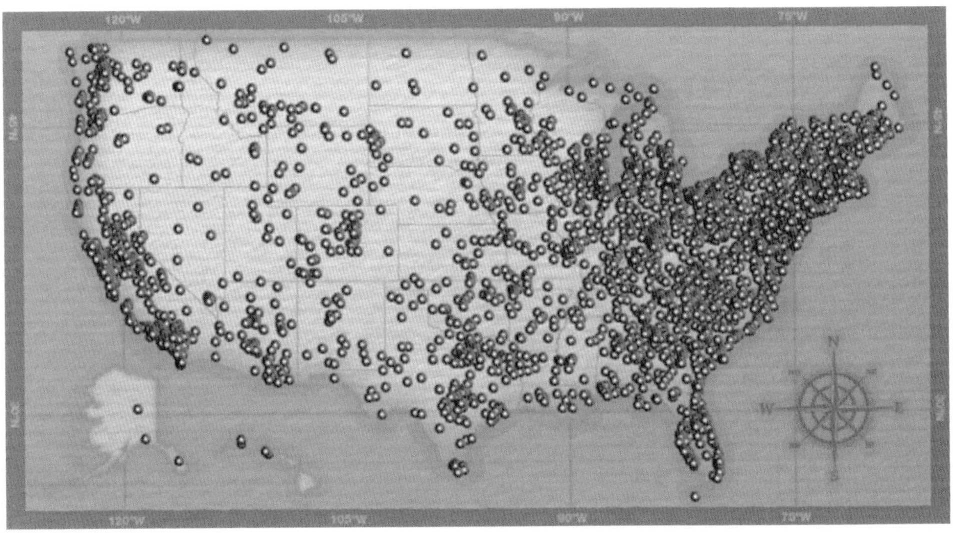

Search for your hometown history, your old stomping grounds, and even your favorite sports team.

Consistent with our mission to preserve history on a local level, this book was printed in South Carolina on American-made paper and manufactured entirely in the United States. Products carrying the accredited Forest Stewardship Council (FSC) label are printed on 100 percent FSC-certified paper.

MADE IN THE USA